# The Empty Stage

*A Memoir*

# The Empty Stage

*A Memoir*

Alan Roderick-Jones

PUBLISHED BY FIDELI PUBLISHING, INC.

The Empty Stage
IMDB# 2123454321

© Copyright/Alan Roderick-Jones Trust
Malibu, California 2019

All rights reserved. No part of this book may be used or reproduced by any means, graphic, electronic, or mechanical, including photocopying, recording, taping or by any information storage retrieval system without the written permission of the publisher except in the case of brief quotations embodied in critical articles and reviews.

ISBN: 978-1-948638-21-0 (soft cover)

Published by:
Fideli Publishing, Inc.
119 W Morgan St.
Martinsville, IN 46151
888-343-3542

www.FideliPublishing.com

PRINTED IN THE UNITED STATES OF AMERICA.

# Dedication

*To Rachel, my gift and partner in life.*

*Our daughter Ella and our son Rowan, whose creative forces have continually guided me from their birth.*

*To Reed Alana, Ella's daughter.*

*To Morgan my grandchildren's mother Jasper & Alice.*

*& those who know who you are who have been there in many a moment*

Editor: Robert Joseph Ahola.

The Desk of Rudyard Kypling

*Having been asked so many times to put on paper the thoughts that would recall my extraordinary journey of 79 years on Mother Earth, I strive to make them cogent and clear and blessed with some sense of perspective.*

*And so, we begin…*

# Table of Contents

| | | |
|---|---|---|
| One | In Every Nook and Cranny There Awaits a Surprise for You.... | 1 |
| Two | How Can You Ever Teach Or Preach That Which You Do Not Know? | 13 |
| Three | Times! They are a Changing! | 23 |
| Four | Awakening to Great Masters | 29 |
| Five | Flow Like the Wind Through Uncharted Lands | 37 |
| Six | Where Did You Get That Body? | 45 |
| Seven | Do Not Disturb Thyself By Thinking on the Whole of Thy Life | 51 |
| Eight | Adapt Oneself to Thy Lot in Life Even as it is Cast | 57 |
| Nine | Is it All Just an Illusion? | 61 |
| Ten | "Let Us Away Knights: This Fellow Will Arise No More" | 67 |
| Eleven | "Let's Get Out of Here!" | 75 |
| Twelve | Beware of the Villains | 83 |
| Thirteen | "What Are Your Intentions, Young Man?" | 89 |
| Fourteen | Perfection is the Key | 95 |
| Fifteen | Blow Up "Blows Up" the Production Code | 101 |
| Sixteen | The Tramp, the Countess, and a Chap Named Chaplin | 109 |
| Seventeen | "I Think You'll be Okay!" | 119 |
| Eighteen | A Uniformity of the Law in Nature | 125 |
| Nineteen | Alpha. Omega. Cinecittá. And Two Close Brushes with Death | 139 |
| Twenty | "The Lion" in Provence | 147 |
| Twenty-One | Where am I? | 157 |
| Twenty-Two | "Come and Sit with Me, Alan" | 163 |

| | | |
|---|---|---|
| Twenty-Three | Two Years to the Day! | 171 |
| Twenty-Four | Shifting Gears. Saving Graces. And a Bit of Déjà vu. | 181 |
| Twenty-Five | What is the Truth? | 191 |
| Twenty-Six | A Conscious Unfolding. | 199 |
| Twenty-Seven | Papillon and the "Rasta Man" | 205 |
| Twenty-Eight | Somewhere Over the Rainbow: I Am Okay | 209 |
| Twenty-Nine | "Elvis" is in the Building | 215 |
| Thirty | Our Miraculous Gift | 219 |
| Thirty-One | Under the Rainbow. Over the Moon. | 227 |
| Thirty-Two | Tehran. Tarzan. And a Leap of Faith. | 239 |
| Thirty-Three | Bo-Dacious! | 251 |
| Thirty-Four | A Blank Canvas Turns into a "Triumph" | 263 |
| Thirty-Five | The Parthenon and "Pirate Anne" | 271 |
| Thirty-Six | Let Go and Let It Flow | 277 |
| Thirty-Seven | A Vibration of Times Past | 293 |
| Thirty-Eight | Once in a Blue Moon | 303 |
| Thirty-Nine | The Irenic Principle | 317 |
| Forty | It is Never as One Expects | 321 |
| Forty-One | Legacy: Making a Difference | 331 |
| Forty-Two | The Last Hoorah! | 337 |
| Forty-Three | Let the Infinite Be Your Guide | 343 |
| Epilogue | Pieces of a "Paradise Regained" | 351 |
| | Acknowledgements | 353 |

# Prologue

It was as if it never happened and yet it did. There I was consciously looking at the Earth from some point far away in the cosmos. I felt a presence of Light to my left side, I then heard these words spoken to me from a deeply resonant voice: "Remember that you chose to come this time in order to experience the magnificence and perfection of Creation, knowing that: that which creates life, you are and that which is life, you are ... You are one."

Jolted by the awareness of the echoing voice and the vision of Earth before me, I instantly came back into my body, sitting at the base of a weathered old Big Sur pine tree that had chosen to grow on the edge of a high cliff overlooking the Pacific Ocean, and I began to weep.

A dear friend David Coyne who had been sitting close by caught a glimpse of my tears and asked: "Are you okay, Alan?"

I replied, "Give me a minute David. I've just had an amazing experience." As tears continued to flow, I picked up my sketchbook, opened it and began to write: *Hi! Darling Ella and Rowan, here is dad off his rocker again: but let me tell you what just happened...*

# One

## In Every Nook and Cranny There Awaits a Surprise for You.

**Where to even begin?** I ask the same question Charles Dickens once asked, so...let me drift back to 1944 in Wandsworth, London, Number 2 Oakberry Road. I was nearly four years old and my brother Phillip had just turned one.

My mother, Irene, had been evacuated to a farm located near the village of Flaunden in Hertfordshire. But for the weekend, she had taken us back to Wandsworth to be with our father, Frank Thomas Jones. Dad had been fighting the fires that sprang up all over London, offshoots from the German bombs that continued to strike London on a daily basis, creating such a devastation as England had never seen. Since he was deaf, Frank had been medically disqualified to don the uniform of the military. But this was his way of serving his community, and he did it with constant courage, never once flinching from the task at hand.

Memories of the war have always haunted me; they never quite leave me even now. I can still recall how my father had tried to explain the war to my four-year-old sensibilities. He had done so by taking a map on the small dining room wall, pointing out what was going on in France and why we were being bombed. Not certain though if it was at that moment or a bit later that he grabbed me by the hand, called to Mum and we all raced down into the small kitchen, up the narrow concrete stairs into the garden, diving into the earth-covered shelter as the sound of what I later learned was a German Dive Bomb passing overhead.

I do remember that terrifying unmatchable silence as Mum clutched baby brother Phillip firmly in her arms and dad pushed me under the cot—a silence shattered by a deafening explosion as the shelter shuddered from the impact. That was just as quickly followed by another silence—a safe silence like a sigh—where dad smiled, telling us that, "Luckily it did not come down on top of us. You can come out now, Alan."

At that age, I couldn't even begin to understand the word, "war," mentioned to me by my father, or what it meant. I only knew it terrified me. And it was something to be avoided. (It was only two years later at school, when the teachers tried to tell us the whys and wherefores of this global conflagration and the horror and pointless deaths of young men and women that I began to question my father, even granny.

Recalling that time we spent on the farm, I can still see images from my past as vividly as if they were in front of me now.

Our original Flaunden farm was close to an American Army Air Force base. I can still see—as if it were happening now—a white criss-cross net, as I am in my blue pram. Through a gap in the trees, I become an unwitting witness as two American B-24 Liberator bombers returning from a raid on Germany seemed to career off course and collide in mid-air, shattering into a thousand pieces through a plume of smoke and flame. (The utter disaster was lost on me then. But it stays with me even now, a moment frozen in time…something out of *Catch 22*, so real as to seem surreal.)

I can see my mother climb up a ladder in the cherry trees, bringing down a basket and showing its contents to me: giving me a little smack on the hand as I greedily grabbed for a handful.

I can still remember retreating with terror as a very large cockerel chased me through the orchard and jumped on my back, pecking at my head...and Mum running to catch up, which she finally did. Ah! And the colours of its feathers so clear to me now as I write! Then there was the large hog that had escaped from its pen, chasing me down and nosing me headfirst into the stinky cesspit. It is still there every time I pass a drain, that disgusting stench as Mum hosed me off, while everyone laughed at my utter humiliation. Then there were the immense goose eggs that Mum painted gold at Easter...and Dad and Mum churning down a country lane on a tandem bike with me in the side car, a car that suddenly detached and hurtled wildly out of control nearly into a ditch, saved at last by an old stone wall that broke the deadly momentum.

Another image flashes before me as I vividly recall the downside of World War II...that of two dustmen as they lifted a dead parachutist, parachute and all, into their dust cart, pulling the sides down and one of them saying, "Bloody odious German," while laughing loud...and my running back to Number 2.

"Mum! What does the word 'odious' mean?" I said it with a wide grin on my face.

"Where did you get that word from?" She curiously replied.

I also remember Christmas back on Oakberry Road, and that our Christmas stockings were large pillow cases that hung on the end of the bed. The season was strange, the memory strained and regrettably sad, as I was unable to understand, even then, why my parents had divorced. Even now, I'm still jarred with the recollection of an ambulance leaving, with Mum crying, and another as I held a kitchen knife in my hand and my father Frank with his hand raised, ready to hit me, striking down onto the knife as it pierced his palm.

Frank would often beat me with his hairbrush and a bamboo cane that he would hang on the mantel over the iron fire stove as if to remind us that "discipline" was never far away. Then there were the times when he would shut the door of the coal cellar behind me, leaving me armed with a poker in my hand, telling me that I had to "kill the rats" before he would let me out. The thought of rats all down below, waiting in packs just for me scared me so much that I would reflexively pee in my pants.

With the war finally over, Dad took us to Buckingham Palace where we saw all the soldiers on parade. When I asked him who those men were holding their swords, he replied, "They're the fearless brave Gurkhas from India."

My favorite memories were those when my mother's sister "Aunty Ned" took me to see a very long film called *Gone With The Wind*... and another called *Pinocchio,* which really frightened me, especially the part on Pleasure Island where they turned all the boys into donkeys!

Shortly after returning to London, Dad and Mum divorced. Father won the divorce, because he had managed to present evidence of "adultery" on the part of Irene. Apparently, Mum had been involved in an affair with an American colonel at the US Air Force Base, and had been forced to have an abortion. That was the allegation that sank her gaining custody of us. But what we did not know at the time was that Dad had also been on the loose evidenced by the fact I was soon introduced to a very pregnant Flemish nurse named Evelyn.

"This is your new mother," my father announced.

"Oh, no she isn't" I answered. "I only have one mother!" It was rather clear reasoning for a five-year-old, and I don't think my father ever challenged me on it again.

Dad's mother, my paternal grandmother, lived a mere 150 yards away from us on Wandsworth Bridge Road. She had looked after me when I had my tonsils out and my appendix removed. I never got to know my Grandpa Jones who, upon returning from the trenches in World War I, drove a horse drawn bus in London. Apparently, he had returned in body, but was not a complete human being, because (from what Grandma told me) he and so many soldiers like him had been poisoned nearly to death by the mustard and phosgene gasses used in the trenches in Flanders

Fields. Grandpa had complications from the gasses, as had so many others, and eventually succumbed to the toxemia that had riddled his system.

By the time I was seven, my father Frank's mother had died as well. I'm not exactly certain when it was that Dad showed me a gold ring that had a buckle on it. I remember that he seemed sad when he asked me "Do you know whose ring this is Alan?" I didn't really know what to say as he let me take the ring from his hand. "It was your Grandma's and she died today."

Later in my teens he finally told me the full story—that she, given to depression, had placed her head in the kitchen oven and committed suicide. Whether it had been my parents' divorce or was it the result of mental despair that menopause can create for some women of her age, is something I will never know for certain.

Now, as I drift back, I see those times that I would sleep over… and how she took the time and trouble to comfort me, knowing that I was missing my mother. She had two sons. My uncle Fred (who was the eldest) was married to Aunty Rene…who also lived on our road.

Recently, when I visited my half-sister Denise in Belgium after decades of not seeing her, she placed a weathered old tin biscuit box on the table without actually apprising me of its contents. To my surprise when I opened it I found it contained many photographs of my father, myself, Philip, Denise and Evelyn.

One I constantly pondered was of my father with a pregnant Evelyn, Fred and René. I realized at that moment that my uncle and aunt had conspired to help Frank in divorcing our mother. I had not seen Denise since she was 8 years-old, since it was about that time that Evelyn broke away from my father and returned to Belgium, leaving us motherless yet again, "step" or otherwise.

As memories jump from one to the other, I recall often walking to our local Peterborough school where our home-class teacher first thing in the morning would without fail pull up her skirt, remove a white handkerchief from her blue bloomers and blow her nose. She would have failed Political Correctness at all levels now. But it was a more innocent time, and the world was more accepting and grateful for what it had.

Being the naughty young boy that I was in those days, I often had a bunch of keys thrown at me by our art teacher, especially when I always tried to have seconds when it was Tapioca pudding, which we all called frog spawn. I also liked to walk around the park after lunch with schoolmates singing, "Oompah! Oompah! Stick it up your Jumper. Oompah! Oompah! Stick it up your jumper," lyrics from "I Am the Walrus," sung into worldwide renown by John Lennon— that originated with the little-known 1930s novelty song, "Umpa, Umpa" (Stick It Up Your Jumper) by The Two Leslies.

In the winter, the heavy fog from the London coal fires would be impossible to see through. And with a scarf around my face and my hand stretched out in front of me, I would find my way home through a maze of streets, at the ripe old age of seven.

Then there was the sandbox in the psychologist's office near Hyde Park corner that my parents had colluded to send me to, as they thought that I had tried to commit suicide. That misconception was purely due to my gobbling up the rat poison powder that brother Phillip had given me. (Obviously the dangers of life-and-death were lost on my brother and me, since both of us thought that that the rat poison was cocoa powder and something good to eat. And how that got translated into a death wish, I will never know.)

That fire of misconception was fanned again when, while playing Pirates on the five-foot-high wall that surrounded all the family gardens, I also engaged in an act of high-wire defiance. I had placed a noose around my neck from the washing line—wooden sword in hand—and running along the parapet, fell off the edge of it, virtually hanging myself. Fortunately, Mrs. Sutton, a neighbor putting out her wash, saw me and shouted for help. So there was another "attempted suicide" that was utterly unintended but nonetheless interpreted as an early kind of madness. So, there I was another time placing wooden bricks into the sand pit and fielding questions from an echelon of "concerned adults" about why I was trying to kill myself so often? That led me to a few more sessions at "the dark-haired lady's office," taken there by worried parents about "Alan's death wish" that never was.

Along the way and perhaps in an attempt to save their marriage, Evelyn had persuaded Dad to become a Catholic and subsequently had us baptized into the faith. Eventually, I took first communion and was only allowed to see Mum once a month. By that time, Mum was living with her mother, two of her sisters Esther and Doris, Doris's husband Hodge and son Michael at Westover Road in Wandsworth. As Phillip and I became older we were able see Mum more often and would sleep up in the third-floor bedrooms that had become our mother's temporary home. I loved to snuggle in those cold winter nights under the thick eiderdown and have the hot water bottle at my feet.

My mother's grandfather was a Russian Jew who had migrated from Russia and married an English protestant girl. "Granny," as I called her had inherited her father's looks. I never got to meet my mother's father as he unfortunately had died before I was born. After Granny died of complications from Rheumatoid arthritis, I remember sitting alone with Mum where granny lay in her bed, wondering why she was unable to speak and so cold, not yet understanding (because no one had explained to me) the importance of our breath. That same day I found myself upstairs in the tank room. Aunt Esther was there. We talked a little, and I noticed something wedged between the tank and the wall. I pulled it out to see a large printed photograph of a man who, now upon reflection, looked like Rasputin. Esther told me that it was in fact my great grandfather. I asked her if I could have it please. She said that I could. On returning to pick it up, I learned that she had destroyed it. Why? I am not certain, but even to this day, I'm still nagged by the thought: Could be that she denied her Jewish heritage?

Grandpa and Granny Ingram had eight children, six girls and two boys who lived in various regions of both London and England. At

Christmas, the family would gather together, and it was at the same time bizarre, comical and maddening in that it always ended in family fights with aunt Lily's husband uncle Chris (a Baptist minister) trying to calm everyone down. I loved the Christmas pudding especially when I found or bit into the silver six-penny coins that Granny had placed in it.

One morning I was in Granny's toilet and had pressed my fingers between my eyes, I saw the most blinding white light! Shocked, I pulled up my short pants and ran into the kitchen, shouting, "Granny! I can see light! I can see light."

"Did you wipe your bum, Alan?" She calmly asked, utterly unimpressed. "And pull up those pants," she said as she placed the smoked haddock on the plate. That radiant light was a revelation I was able again to recall in 1972—something I will unfold later…and in more detail.

Mum remarried and moved to a house on Comyn Road in Clapham Junction. Phillip and I along with Dad, Evelyn and Denise, moved to Eland Road just off Lavender Hill not even a mile away from Mum's home. (Maybe you remember the fun movie, "The Lavender Hill Mob" with Alex Guinness? That was the eponymous place.)

Aunt Esther with her barrister's ability to persuade was able to prevail upon Frank to allow us kids weekends in the junction with Mum and her new husband Jimmy. Jimmy turned out to be a generous soul who amazed me early on when he presented me with my first road bike, instilling in me a love of cycling that I still enjoy this day. (I now have two carbon fiber framed ones that I still ride everywhere I can, and it remains my favorite way of "getting around.") Sadly, they were destroyed along with everything else (everything!) in the November 2018 Malibu fires… another chapter.

During that same period Mum was working as a tailor in Kensington, and her boss Mr. Noel was tailor to Queen Mary, wife of King George V. Cleverly on her part, every time Mum would work on a suit for the Queen, she would knock-off a copy for herself. She was known locally as, "The Queen of Clapham Junction." With her flamboyant hats, handbags and shoes, she was such a stylish beautiful woman. And the memory that always comes back to me is Irene in her very 1940s dark blue slacks, light blue shirt and painted toenails—so very *a la mode* but, as I remember, never really happy. She did love her whiskey, cockles and mussels and never thought it wrong to leave her two sons outside the pub eating our packets of potato crisps while she got tipsy at the bar with her other boyfriend Harry—an impeccably dressed "Barrow boy toff," who also happened to be someone I really liked.

At this point in my life I was never entirely able to reconcile how the inner turmoil, heartache and loneliness of the divorce had rooted itself so deeply in my psyche…or how my personal objections to my stepmother Evelyn had seared such a wound on my soul. Was there ever, I wondered, going to be a release from that inner torment? I had always hoped, but there were times when hoping wasn't enough.

*(L) Grandmother with uncle Fred & Dad Frank. (R) Grandpa Jones. A World War I infantryman and hero, he eventually succumbed to the erosive toxemia from the deadly gasses of the Marne and Flanders Field.*

*Mum on the rocks at Devon.*

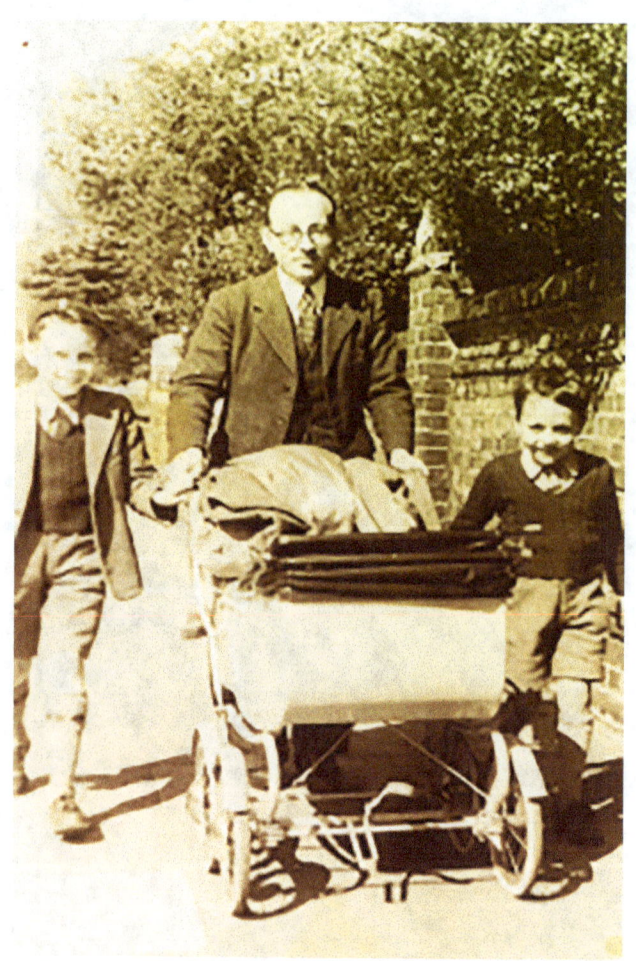

*(Me) Alan, (father) Frank and (brother) Phillip with Denise in the pram.*

# Two

## How Can You Ever Teach Or Preach That Which You Do Not Know?

**After I passed my exam** at the primary school, my Aunt Doris knew that, on the first day, I was a little scared to go to the new cap and gown grammar school called The Strand. So she had her son, my cousin Michael, take me. But before she did, she looked at me, crouching as she did so.

"You will always be okay, Alan, no matter what happens," Doris reassured me. "Success is there, waiting for you on the other side of the door!"

A *thurible*, is a ceremonial *censer* — a metal cup suspended by chains that is used to burn incense — that is used during Catholic mass. The incense is placed on hot charcoals inside the thurible's bowl-like container which has a lid with holes in it to allow the smoke to escape. It is swung during services and the smoke escaping through the holes in its lid is meant to symbolically represent prayers rising to God.

That Thurible became my three times a week early morning duty as an altar boy, serving mass in the Catholic church from age nine until I was twelve years old. There was a set pattern to the Thurible procession, and every altar-boy or acolyte had to know it: the Blessed Sacrament got three double swings, the celebrant of the Mass got one double swing and the congregation got three single swings.

One day below the church Oratory Father Patrick, one of the Jesuit priests, was close to our Boy Scout Den. I asked him if he knew God? He very deliberately paused to reflect and, after giving it much thought, answered in his Irish brogue: "No, young Alan, I do not know God, but I have a great faith and belief in God."

Out of my twelve-year-old mouth came these words: "If you do not know God, why are you preaching about something you do not know, father?" Silence followed. After that, he walked away from me, never more to broach the subject again.

I must have begun to question the Son of God at an early age, as well as God, the Father: Questions, I always hoped someone might answer.

*Who was this God who was always allowing humans to kill each other? Who was this God that permitted such monstrosities as War?* I often brought this up in the religious classes at The Strand, sitting at daily Catechism in some anteroom in the Church. The Jesuits, as teachers and priests, could never quite field my questions and could never seem to answer clearly anything I asked. And whenever I asked my Aunt Lily, she would always retreat to the Bible—the one that sat on the side table—scrambling for answers and seldom finding any that would suffice.

One early morning, ready to serve mass and placing the charcoal and incense in the Thurible, I looked up at a painting of Jesus—the one where he was wearing a white tunic and holding out a lamp. I really cherished that painting; it always spoke to me. (This was a Jesus I really liked.) As I followed the priest toward the altar, he turned and gave me the strangest look because I had just asked him why he hadn't chosen to wear a simple robe like Jesus. I do recall now that he and the other priests all wore silly hats, as if getting ready for some pantomime of *Aladdin and His Lamp*—another of the movies that Aunty Doris had taken us to see.

At The Strand I was more than inquisitive, constantly firing question after question about anything that I did not understand. Often being told on Friday that I was going to get the cane on Monday for any number of offenses for which I was usually guilty: one for throwing snowballs in the Fives Court; another for placing firework bangers in ripe pears and tossing them at the Prefects on Guy Fawkes Day. Arriving on Monday with the Sunday news stuck in the seat of my pants to class, I was prepared for any consequence of my actions. I would then be called out on the stroke of 11 a.m. into the corridor where our class teacher Mr. Taylor would grimly appear in his black cape ready to dispense his "justice." Cane in hand, removing his cap and ordering me to bend over, he would then lay his hard strokes six times across my butt. It didn't hurt that much, but I didn't dare let on. So, I finished any number of Monday mornings with just the appropriate measure of contrition.

One morning as we came into Assembly Hall on the "Battle of Britain Day" we beheld these words written on the blackboard: *'Never in the field of human conflict was so much owed by so many to so few.'* We all stood as a commander of the Royal Air Force (RAF) explained to us their meaning as spoken by Winston Churchill. This now famous reference was made in praise of the Royal Air Force crews who had fought the Battle of Britain, the pivotal air battle with the Luftwaffe when the Nazi invasion of our island seemed a *fait accompli*.

Pilots who fought in that air-battle were, from that day forward, known as "The Few," being specially commemorated every year on the 15th of September. Some believed that day and that battle turned the tide of WW II in Europe…and that all who followed from the Allied Armies would be indebted to these Noble Few.

Despite being the argumentative bugger that I was and a challenge to my teachers, I always finished each semester in the top five of my class.

Getting top marks in English, math, French and Latin, I truly enjoyed the challenge, and had in two years made a few close friends who meant a great deal to me. All the worse to find out that, at the end of the fourth term, my father Frank was pulling me out of school. And to my despair, and at my peril, I found myself asking him: "Why Dad why are you doing this? I love my school"

I argued and argued and yet my father removed me from the protestant Strand School to send me to Clapham College, a Catholic school that was also under the supervision of the Jesuits. It was where my brother Phillip was going, so it all made sense to Dad. Still, being so untimely ripped from my shining days at the Strand left a mark on my "academics" that never did quite heal.

Why and what happened to my scholarly left-brain consciousness, I suppose was the passive-aggressive result of my silent rebellion. Everything at Clapham was simply beyond the periphery of my vision—other than art, geography and history. So egregious were my rebellions and so evident the drop-off in my grades that the school Headmaster Father Peter finally called me into the office to ask me why had I failed my exams? I had no answer for him. (I think that Dad was with me that day.) But everyone knew that I had just stopped trying.

While at Clapham, some good things took hold for me. I ran the mile and cross-country races for the school, the longer the distance the better, events at which I excelled though never quite enough to be a champion. We would arrive by coach at lower Wimbledon Common for soccer and the annual long-distance cross-country race. Bursting out of the pack at the end, I never won but never gave up trying. Every year, exhausted in that last agonizing mile, I would strain to catch tall lean lanky Tom, who left us all "eating his dust." Coming in second never pleased me but I learned from it all—that accomplishment and humility are two sides of the same coin.

I also remember enjoying the girls as they cheered me on at soccer, invariably causing us to show off, which was kind of a mating thing.

Other than that, it was just a game. Girls were another matter. But that would come, as all things do, in time.

Home life with my stepmother was never an easy thing. And I never quite adjusted to the shocks to my young system. The change of schools, missing my friends, a loss of all points of reference—these all combined to add to my confusion.

Cycling on Fridays to Boy Scout Camp came to be my escape. As soon as I got back from afternoon class, I would immediately fill my backpack and bike 25 miles from my house to a small village called Down, near Biggin Hill Airport. I was always a little apprehensive especially as it grew dark just as I rode along the shadowy lane past Darwin's creepy house. Arriving at camp was like reaching safe-haven after being pursued by ghosts. And I'd let it all loose in a single breath as I disembarked from the bike, signed-in and went to pitch my tent at a campsite that was allotted to us, and it was like a second home—safe, secure and part of a group with a shared sense of direction.

The competition amongst the boys in the scout patrols, mine being the Pewits, was to see how many merit badges we could be awarded at the end of every summer camp. Astronomy, cooking, camping, lifesaving, kayaking and many more—all these were levels of achievement and literally "badges of honor."

I enjoyed being by myself in the winter, especially when it had snowed. On Fridays I would take the train, hike along the dark country lanes to the camp, and set up just before all daylight was lost. I'd make a cabin my home for the weekend, light the stove and even though there was so much smoke that poured back into the room, I always loved the smell of the wood fires burning. The mornings often came with a hard freeze where the ice broke off the water supply. And I would always clean up areas of the camp for the chief warden, only to arrive later at Eland Road, reeking of campfire smoke.

Spring with the carpet of bluebells in the woods was a season when our scout troop would all go for long weekends to Biggin Hill. Sunday morning, taking communion in a small local church, walking, eating a juicy breakfast, back to camp through the strawberry fields—these were a few of my "favorite things," in a Proustian stream of remembrance.

Dad became a Scout Master, and I had the honor of receiving the highest achievement in the Scouts, my Queen Scout award. We were in Jersey for our summer camp that was located very close to a Catholic Monastery. In the mornings we were awakened by the dulcet harmonies of all the monks chanting in unison. It continued as we lit the fires, made the tea in the "Billy-cans" and stirred the oatmeal-porridge made tastier by the coolness of the morning.

One morning walking along the cliffs, we came across a spate of German Bunkers—their gun turrets still haunting the shoreline. And upon exploring them we were able to go down at least two more levels into the battlements themselves. Germany, I found out much later through a British TV Series, actually occupied Jersey during the Second World War—a little known fact with an eerie sense of proximity.*

Upon returning from that particular trip, my father and I were stunned to find that my stepmother Evelyn had left without warning, taking Denise. The closets were empty, and we were abandoned, a man and two boys on their own. But there is a resilience in youth that often defies description. In a short time, Phillip and I became permanent dish and bottle washers, cleaned house, shopped and cooked meals, taking on the wifely duties with a kind of manly acceptance. Housekeeping and house repairs came to be performed by rote. And, believe me or not, I spent one school holiday with a paintbrush in hand as I painted the front of the house from top and bottom.

---

*I have to note as another point of reference about that stage of the war that my wife Rachel's grandfather was Lieutenant General Sir Alexander Hood, war-time Director General of the British Army Medical service who very pointedly told (Prime Minister) Winston Churchill that he had to delay the D-Day invasion. Otherwise it would be another Gallipoli—a massive mistake that would take its toll in thousands of casualties. He insisted upon this, as they were not sufficiently prepared medically to deal with casualties. Fortunately, Sir Winston listened to his advice and delayed the invasion.

It was also about that time that I met an American scout named Kirkpatrick McDonald at the 5th Annual Scout World Jamboree in 1957. The Jamboree was at Sutton Park, Birmingham, and it was a massive event. We were both seventeen and seemed to share a similar sense of life. We got on well, and before we parted Kirk said, "Let's stay friends. And let's keep in touch." We did. We wrote to each other off and on and only would I find out later just how important that friendship would be and that there are very few accidents in this journey of life. (Because in 1960 I flew out to San Francisco, and we are still friends to this day.)

It was also about that time, that my father had decided to give my young life a better sense of direction: "What do you want to do with your life Alan? You could join the Civil Service, like me, earn one thousand pounds a year and have a pension." That followed Dad's line of suggestions, regaling me with his view of the future over a morning's breakfast. As you can imagine, this young teenager getting ready to leave school said "No" to his father—a father he was disagreeing with in so very many ways. Dad at that point in my life was something less than a role model. He was in truth a man I had some issues with—especially the various women that now occupied the lower bedroom, as our family help and his lovers seemed to interchange.

One thing I had no issue with about my dad were his cigars. They were Cuban cheroots. I could occasionally pinch one or two and slip off to the cinema (where they allowed smoking in the loges).

There, in the back row of a local movie house, puffing on one of my dad's cigars, I sat and watched James Dean in *Rebel Without a Cause*. Filmed in a new widescreen format called Cinemascope and directed by Nicholas Ray, it was both a social commentary and a stark refutation of previous films depicting troubled teenagers as one-dimensional delinquents. A groundbreaking attempt to portray the moral decay of American youth, it turned out to be a landmark film. Along with Dean were young Natalie Wood and Sal Mineo, two promising gifted actors on tragic trajectories of their own.

Dean had already made impact on me as both tragic hero and role model in his breakthrough first film role as Cal in *East of Eden,* and I still consider *Eden* to be one of the most stunningly conceived films of its time, especially the cinematography by Ted D. McCord. In 1990, *Rebel Without a Cause* was added to the Library of Congress's *National Film Registry,* which deemed it to be a filmic work that was, "culturally, historically, and aesthetically significant." It was in fact a mirror of our time.

At London Central Hall I sat down in this large imposing room along with thirty to forty other male and female teenagers. The morning light cut across my desk, the clock came to 10 a.m., the bell sounded, I wrote my name at the top of the paper, glanced through the pages of the exam sheets, sat and wrote no more. I wanted to go to art school. So, all this academic nonsense seemed of no value to me. I didn't fill out a single answer. I didn't see the need.

So! How did my father respond to my not taking the exam? He threatened to throw me out of the house to fend for myself, even at that age. I can still remember that he was fuming while holding his cigar in one hand and Drambuie in the other, and I felt that if he still had that old cane he used to carry, he would have struck me with it. It was then that I reminded him that it was he who had taught me how to draw. "Remember dad? It was you who showed me the way!"

Shortly after that life-changing revolution, I decided to set my course of action. So, I put a portfolio together and applied to a number of art colleges in London. I was accepted with a scholarship to Chelsea School of Art. (The scholarship would give me just enough money for my paints and it was only a bike ride away.) In the summer holidays I found a job in the cake department of Joe Lyons. At Joe Lyons the rules were set: you were not allowed to take any cakes out of the factory: but I would sneak out one or two and let Mum have them.

It was there for the first time in my life that I experienced a few advances from some of the middle-aged women. They could be cheeky on occasion, openly teasing and very descriptive with their sexual innuendos. With the money that I earned I brought myself a guitar, saved the rest for that special day in the future when I would be able to fly to California to visit Kirk, my friend from the 1957 Jamboree.

David White and I, along with two other Clapham College friends, formed a skiffle group. Lonnie Donegan was a very successful singer-composer at that time. We tended to play his songs along with other American black musicians who were being recognized by people like Brian Jones of the Rolling Stones. We went to a club in Soho, only playing there once. At other times, we stood on corners and outside pubs with an upturned hat on the ground in front of us, singing our hearts out and hoping to catch on. As I recall we were not that good, but you couldn't convince us at the time. (Enthusiasm trumps all else when you think you're on a mission.)

*In East of Eden (above), James Dean (as Cal) surprised both Director Elia Kazan and co-star Raymond Massey by spontaneously hugging his father then running from the room, a hipshot moment of genius that "made the scene." Later, for his role in the film, Dean received the first posthumous Oscar nomination for Best Actor.*

*I placed the above photo and the one on the following page here as the films really hit my inner core re my relationship with my father.*

*In* Rebel Without a Cause, *James Dean defined a generation.*

## Three

## Times!
## They are a Changing!

**It's spring, 2018,** and I'm in the car driving back from Oxnard. Having just enjoyed a Mexican lunch of Mahi-mahi and Chili Rellenos, I'm listening to a song by John Martyn "Searching Back Through the Friends I Have Known, Just Now," and I am laced by a chain of recollections.

So clearly there in front of me in a flashback stood handsome blond stalwart Don Underwood, a local friend who came to hang out with me at my house one day in 1957. He mentioned that the previous Friday he had gone dancing at Wandsworth Town Hall.

"So many gorgeous chicks!" he said.

"You mean girls." I responded.

"Yes, so many. Come with me tomorrow. You'll see. Maybe you will find a girl. I know you will."

I didn't have to think too long. *A girlfriend,* I thought to myself. *That would be cool.*

So, the next day Friday I met Don at the top of my road. Dressed for an evening on the town, we walked down to Clapham Junction and took the 37 Bus to Wandsworth Town Hall, and that's where it all began. My eyes opened wide and would never close again.

The Mods, with their short jackets and pointy-toed shoes, short slicked down hair, were Perry Como fans. The Rockers with their leather jackets, Levis and Brylcreem™ slicked back greasy hair were fans of Elvis, Buddy Holly and the Big Bopper, just to mention a few. The Teddy boys—with their Edwardian long jackets, waistcoats, slim-Jim trousers, hair waved and slicked back—had long sideburns. I still do not know what sounds they listened to: but one of their well-known dances was a slow shuffle known as "The Creep." These were all the trends and styles, and let's not forget the Trads—*Beatniks* as they called themselves—with their sloppy various coloured sweaters and long hair. Eel Pie Island on the river Thames was their perennial hangout. They listened to Acker Bilk, Trad Jazz and a young band that later came to be known as the Rolling Stones. "The Stones" played there and very often favored a strong, crude Cider to drink.

The Town Hall that Don and I walked into on Friday night was vibrating to the riotous sounds coming lately off the English and American charts. Don had been right about one thing: There were so many beautiful girls. Girl after girl walking by very intentionally, many glancing my way at that moment…or convincing me they did. To say I was nervous would be right on the nail. I had never danced. And I was somewhat terrified that I'd have to.

Don introduced me to a group of lads standing to the right of the stage, and I still remember them well: Dicky Dobson, Gary Warren, Butch, David Smith, Tonya Blackmore, Pamela Smith, Peter Mines, and John Burnett, a jazz lover—all looked so together with their James Dean style coloured jerkins and perfectly washed out jeans, a popular new brand that I later discovered (at Gary's) were called Levi's… It seemed they all had pointy-toed shoes, some with buckles and what seemed to be high heels. Gary saw my inquisitive glance and picked it up with an offer:

"They're Giorgio's and Fred's! We have them made especially for us...If you like I'll take you to get yourself a pair."

I looked across the dance floor and soon enough became aware that I'd caught the eye of a rather attractive girl. I didn't stare. It was a casual glance, but I think she stared at me because suddenly this guy came running toward me and smashed me in the face.

"You screwing my bird, John?" He snarled angrily.

Well that triggered my new pal David—maybe at five foot three on his tiptoes—who came immediately to my defense, head-butted and pummeled my attacker to the floor, managing to bite clean through his lip somewhere on the way down. There was blood everywhere, and they were both escorted out of the hall. And all I could think of then was that if there ever existed a physical incarnation of Mighty Mouse, it was David. So diminutive in size but with the heart of a lion: what might be called "a stand-up guy," in every sense of the word.

As for me, I stood there shaking, probably from head to toe. That's when a girl named Pamela came over to me and asked me if I would like to dance.

"Dance?" (The other side of my terror.) "I'm not certain I know how!"

Pamela was as much at ease as I was uncertain, and it didn't take long with her guidance for me to learn the dubious art of swing dancing. Pamela was my first girlfriend, and together we discovered the innocent wonders of teenage sex. We became very close and uncovered those feelings we call love that flood up from the loins and into our hearts and souls, to fill those silent places within ourselves.

Gary's house was on a line of streets that paralleled Wandsworth Common, which was also close to Wandsworth Prison and just around the corner from my aunt's. It became the hang out for all of us. We listened to John Coltrane, Dave Brubeck, Miles Davis, Mose Allison, Gerry Mulligan, Charles Mingus, Thelonious Monk, and the soft tones of Chet Baker. We played poker into the wee small hours of the morning. Our girlfriends at the time would come over later. Then we took off on our Vespa scooters…maybe to the Flamingo in Soho or some other club.

To keep up with the others I exchanged my old Lambretta for a Vespa and would pick up Pam. Pam and Gary's girlfriend young Tonya were virtually inseparable and remained "best friends forever." And wouldn't you know it, when Rachel and I moved to Malibu in 1978 who should I bump into but Tonya, who was now married to one of the Wexlers, a successful Hollywood film family. She told me that she and Pam had stayed in contact with each other over all those years.

Back in the day, we would go to the Flamingo and the Marquee in Soho. At the Flamingo, young unknown musicians such as George Fame, Steve Winwood, Van Morrison, Eric Clapton and Joe Cocker would be singing, jamming or working on new material along with "comers" such as Long John Baldry and Chris Farlowe.

This club was where many of the black American servicemen would come on Friday and Saturday nights. They had an amazing grace and style in the way they danced, a clever technique that I tried in vain to copy as best as I could. These great young soldiers, sailors and Air Force men would bring us our Levis jeans. After paying the going rate, we would take the jeans back to Gary's, wash them, hang them on the line and place lengths of wood in the cuffs so that when they dried they would become bell-bottoms. And more than occasionally we would bleach them white.

Dressed in bell-bottoms and the small Giorgio pointed toed shoes we were the height of fashion, or so we thought. But fashions change, and so did we, moving with light-speed to the next big thing. Life is relentless in pursuit of itself, a lesson soon to be learned.

*The "Vespa Lads," Butch and Garry, in a leisure moment in 1958.*

# Four

## Awakening to Great Masters

**Here I was on my first day**, walking up the entrance steps to Chelsea Polytechnic, not remembering exactly where the art school was.

"Can I help you, young man?" came the query from a soft-spoken man. There was a cherubic friendly face (I wish I could remember his name) who was one of the doormen at the college. He reminded me that the art school was on the top floor. And I ended up in the years that followed making the climb five thousand times or more.

I spent four creative visionary years at Chelsea, learning how to draw, sketch, paint with oils, watercolors, sculpture, lithography and just a dash of fabric design. My eyes were opened to a world of ancient and modern art from all centuries past. Going to so many galleries and art exhibitions, I really began to identify the works of so many of the masters. So, studying art in all its facets became a personal mission for me. When I studied and perused the drawings of the icons of Renaissance art, prodigious artists such as Leonardo da Vinci, Michelangelo, Raphael and Titian appeared to me as true gods of the visual universe. Even now can I only remotely capture the splendors of their forms.

Reading books on various artists, my favorite turned out to be that of Vincent Van Gogh and his letters to his brother Theo. Those became my artist's bible. I still have a copy of that book. And I continue to be taken by the eloquence of Vincent's writing and his singular passion for life. He viewed the world with a different lens, and we've all inherited that on every canvas of everything that ever caught his eye.

"*On the positive awareness that art is something greater and higher than our own skill or knowledge or learning. That art is something which, though produced by human hands, is not wrought by hands alone, but wells up from a deeper source inside a man's soul.*" These words, Vincent's words, still touch me even now!

Upon reading those passages he had written to his artist friend Anton Van Rappard, I recalibrated my thinking. And from that day forward my approach to my art began to change completely.

Illustrative of the cachet that this school provided, we enjoyed the best of both worlds—of meetings with remarkable men (and women). We had teachers who all had become recognized for their work, including Prunella Clough, Edward Middleditch, Henry Moore and Elizabeth Frink, famous even then for their sculptural genius.

During this period, I was drawn to and more than that—absolutely smitten with—the young women in all the four years who were with me every day. There were maybe seven male and twelve female students in my class. Some of the girls from wealthy families were using the college for what seemed to be a finishing school. Obviously, it was hard not to be emotionally drawn to at least four of them during those years of discovery, and in doing so I was told much later, that my London accent had become affected with its H's…if you get my gist.

Fabian Peake, with his hairstyle, bore a resemblance to James Dean. Even in his mannerisms, *The Rebel Without a Cause* was evident: But it turned out that he did have his cause, and a lovely one at that. Having, over time, become a successful painter and writer, Fabian married one of the art school girls, Phyllida Barlow who had become a famous sculptor in her own right.

We had many things in common, Fabian and I, our Zippo lighters being one of them. We would light up our *Gitanes Maïs* cigarettes as we painted. The "Maïs" had no saltpeter in them and would constantly go out, hang on our lips, yet again another badge of how "cool" we had been at the time. I had the chance to meet Fabian's father only once at his home in Chelsea, the wonderful artist and writer Mervyn Peake who had illustrated and written many books, one being the illustrated *Gormenghast Trilogy*, a classic even today. It was a sad moment when Fabian introduced me to him, for he was drawing with a large black marker pen, and even at that time was shaking virtually out of control, suffering through some advanced stages of what I later came to realize was Parkinson's disease.

Other names flash by in recollection from those years at Chelsea. Barry Gizzard, Geoff Norfolk, Michael Moon, Francesca Tangye, Susan Sweet, Zuleika Dobson, Arlene and many more drift in and out—some who went on to notable careers, others who faded, lost in the maze of memory never to be heard from again.

During that time, rowing took on a particular significance in my life, forever affecting my sense of teamwork and the power of the group dynamic. I became a member of the rowing crew that was part of the Chelsea Polytechnic, Chiswick Boathouse. It was where I would find myself with the crew and coxswain three times a week during the college terms. We would train in the water tank with the blades that had holes in them. Saturdays and Sundays on the river Thames, no matter what

*A Classic Collegiate Crew Rowing Poster (for Eights)…*

the weather, we underwent our acid test, and the training was both rigid and rewarding.

Our coach was an Olympic oarsman who taught us how to breathe in tandem like a Roman Galley. After years of training, this constant discipline finally paid off. When our eight breaths became as one, the blades hit the water with such a power that we were able to pass another crew within six strokes, thus winning the University Eights in my last year at Chelsea.

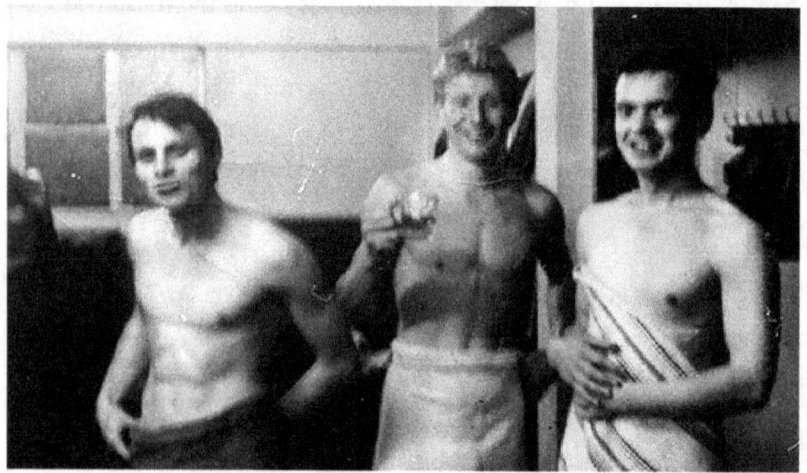

*A celebratory post Regatta shower in the Chiswick Boathouse, 1960*

I worked again at Joe Lyons in my summer holidays, eventually saving enough British pounds sterling to purchase a flight to New York the following year. Pam was still my girl in those early years, and all the gang became even tighter. Trips to Brighton, Hastings and Angmering on our Vespas became a weekend ritual, and we enjoyed a special chemistry that came to enrich us over time.

I was still living at home with my father and my brother—by necessity, not by choice. I was never happy there and plotted my exit path. In the meantime, I found myself spending far more time with my mother and often staying in the top bedroom at my Aunt Esther's.

Across from the college on the now trendy Kings Road was a small record store where I would go to listen to and purchase the recordings that became quite my collection of black soulful blues songs of penitentiary music. These were the same sounds that originally brought together Brian Jones, Keith Richards and Mick Jagger of the Rolling Stones. The Stones, still an unknown quantity at the time, would come and jam about once a month for the Saturday Dance night at Chelsea.

Lucy Bartlett, a college girlfriend, had invited me to her home in St. Johns Wood. I was surprised when she introduced me to her mother, a TV personality I recognized from BBC and ITV. Later that night, driving home in the rain I was broadsided by a car that had run a red light and smashed me to the ground. The driver panicked and drove away, making it a "hit-and-run," and the guilty party was never found.

I had slid head first along the wet tarmac with a familiar sense of the imminent disfigurement that would prove to affect my appearance and my health from that day forward. My face was a mess: my front teeth were all gone, and I found my blood splattered everywhere. Through it all, I still managed to drive, and made it to my Mum's house, more or less in one piece. When Mum opened the front door and saw my swollen face, dumbstruck and more than gravely concerned, she immediately called for an ambulance that took me to a local hospital. While I was still laid out in bed at Mum's, Pam came to visit me. Unable to kiss her with my toothless face, we somehow made gentle, caressing love. A couple of weeks later I walked out of a dentist's office with a new set of front teeth, false but rather nicely done.

At this point in the late 1950s and early 1960s art films in black and white had become the rage with London art students and entertainment cognoscenti. Jean Paul Belmondo, Alain Delon, Jean Moreau, Marcello Mastroianni. Sophia Loren, Anna Magnani, and Toshiro Mifune were just a few of the actors whose faces, forms and distinct acting styles graced the silver screen.

I made a special effort to see the work of some directors who had already proven to be modern masters of the French, Italian and Japanese films that caught our imagination. Jean Luc Godard, Federico Fellini, Akira Kurosawa, François Truffaut—all had unmistakable styles, each with its own signature and sense of irony. Two films by Fellini, *La Strada* and *La Dolce Vita* and two by Kurosawa, *The Seven Samurai* and *The Throne of Blood* were among those that made such an impression on me.

They were prodigious directors, extravagant in style, rich in potent imagery and daring in their grasp of content. They influenced me into becoming an introspective dreamer, walking out of the theatres completely immersed in another world; theirs. Who would have guessed that these works were like fires to ignite my passion at the time to pursue my lifetime profession in the world of film design?

*A scene from* Seven Samurai *by Akira Kurosawa*

La Strada *by Fellini*

# Five

## Flow Like the Wind Through Uncharted Lands

"America! Here I come!" I sing the song now as then, because at some level I was convinced it was always meant to be. It was the summer of 1960, and upon returning it would be my last year at Chelsea. Kirk and I had laid out the whole summer in the USA, making our plans through letters sent back and forth, and the itinerary was set for me to arrive in New York. From there a friend of Kirk's, "A Yaley," was going to meet me, and we were scheduled drive across country, sharing petrol and expenses all the way to Hillsborough, California.

Well, an iPhone and a little texting would have proved quite helpful then because…whoever was going to meet me, missed me, never even showed up. On top of that misconnection, no one had warned me about the "dog days" of summer in New York City. The sun and August heat off the tall steel buildings turned Manhattan into an oven. And I definitely wasn't wearing the right clothes. Staying in the steam bath of a summer in New York was too much even for a day. So I made some inquiries, and the next thing I knew I was on a Greyhound bus heading west.

Even now I have to look at the map to remind myself of the route the Greyhound took to arrive at Salt Lake City. Cleveland, Chicago, Omaha, and later Cheyenne, Wyoming—I was touring America whether I wanted to or not. Having never travelled this far, it was just such an adventure. Bus-riding along the wide four, and sometimes six lane highways with cars that I had never seen before, I felt in some ways like a brother from another planet.

Here I was from the land of Rovers, Vespas, Jaguars and maybe a Bentley or two, gawking at the gaudy display that Detroit had brought to Western Civilization. Before my trip, I'd never seen any of these flashy offspring of Detroit's finest designers except in the magazines *Life* and *Post* or maybe Mum's *Readers Digest*. Cadillac El Dorados, Fords, Mercurys, Chevy Impalas, Pontiac Bonnevilles—these cars were finished with such bright, blatant, wonderfully garish colors, mind-boggling headlights and wings with large red tail lights set into them. They were like gaudy spaceships from another planet—hideous and beautiful at the same time. And big long trucks would roar past the likes of which I had never seen before. Then when we came alongside a train it seemed to take a lifetime to pass it, pulled by two yellow engines. Then, when I started counting the railroad cars themselves, I marveled to find them loaded with cows, automobiles, tractors, anything you could imagine—such a "variety pack" of American life that I gave up counting after reaching the number 54.

I opened my window and let the wind wash my face. (Where was I, after all?) So many questions that I asked the people that were around me. People of all ages—a baby crying, a mother breastfeeding right next to me, fields in all directions with no sign posts, a lone stop where a very young woman got off at stark crossroad—all so stark and surreal and so much a slice of "American Gothic." The sight of this young woman standing there against that blank canvas of the stark American plains caused me to flash to Cary Grant in *North by North West*, wondering which way he is going to go. The lady was lucky when a man waved at her from a great looking red opened back Ford pickup truck. It took my mind off myself and seemed to comfort me at the same time...at least enough for me to nod off until we'd arrived in the West.

Then a tap on my shoulder from the old man behind me: "Time to wake up boy. We've arrived!" It was our first stop...in Chicago.

As I stepped down from the bus that had parked outside the Greyhound station, there was a certain smell, this smell that still awakens so many memories, as aromas definitely have the ability to do. It is the scent of city life that you get in America. I'm unable to place my finger on it, but somehow the nose always knows: The old buildings, the diesel from the trucks, the ocean of petrol exhausts, people's old clothes, the donut shops and bad American coffee—all these things formed that sensuous soup that I've always loved to savor. And each locale has its own special flavor everywhere you go!

As the bus driver pulled out my bag, he pointed me in the direction of the closest hotel, confidently confiding to me that it was one he often stayed at. I could see the hotel sign in front of me, an easy walk. It was a large five-story old brick corner building. Upon entering, I was immediately struck by this bizarre mélange of smoke and distinctly American aromas. It was dark inside, and the large stained windows with their half open shutters cast the evening light across well-worn wooden floorboards. My initial impression was how very *film noir* it all seemed, and I felt somehow as if I had just walked into an old Humphrey Bogart movie. Men of various ages were sitting, sleeping, playing chess, reading newspapers and magazines, making them seem like fixtures as permanent as the chairs and couches in the lobby. Off to the side, in a corner bar, a pair were sitting on stools, already lost in the swill of early afternoon cocktails.

The only woman in the entire lobby sat behind a large reception desk, with well-worn wood and an ashtray filled with half-doused cigarette butts. Behind her were all the room numbers with hooks for the keys and open boxes for mail. It resembled a film clip out of *The Maltese Falcon*. So, this was America?

"Can I help you, young man?" the woman, asked in a low-pitched smoker's voice.

Back on the bus, we continued west on to mountains and pines. Impression after impression flew past my window, until we arrived in Cheyenne, Wyoming. There I had my first close encounter with a genuine American motorcycle officer, AKA "the Law," astride his Harley Davidson that had two belts slung across his hips with a holstered pistol on each. And on either side of the front wheel there were two leather scabbards with rifle-butts sticking out of them. Here I was in the Saturday morning pictures watching the serial, "The Range Rider," West of Cheyenne with Jock Mahoney who I expected to suddenly ride into town. Where was the local bakery, the long loaf, the fish and chip shop for the chips that we stuffed into the loaf, eating as we walked home over Wandsworth Bridge?

Another day and another night…then on to Salt Lake City. Never having known the history of the Mormon religion, this city was a learning curve for me. The old cabin and the first encampment park, the monumental Mormon Tabernacle—a place of worship that I was not allowed to enter try though I may—this was a truly alien world, disconcertingly cultish. And though everyone was terribly "nice," I wanted to get out of town.

By that time, I'd had just about enough of the Greyhound bus and its strange network of stops, so I decided that I would hitch. I got a local ride to the highway. An open car came by with two young men, they stopped and offered me a lift, but my every instinct said "No!" Upon looking into the car I couldn't help but notice that the rear seats were cluttered to the windows with empty cans and rubbish. They also looked as if they were about a week and a half past their last bath. They were a little too friendly, and so I declined. (Call it instinct, if you will.) And in about a half-an hour, this big Mack Truck with the Bulldog emblem came screeching to a halt.

This was one of those trucks, the first of its kind, with a sleeping cabin behind the driver. A man with a tan and a Texas twang leaned out and asked me where I was going and on hearing my voice and mentioning San Mateo, said with a gunslinger's drawl:

"Hey man! Talk like that and you can keep us awake. Where are you from, anyway?"

"England! London!" I replied, which seemed to be enough.

"We'll drop you off in San Mateo. We're going to San Francisco. Tell us all about England! We'd really like to know." They seemed genuinely interested. And we got to share ideas. I sat in the middle of both these great guys, and I was on my way to Kirk! What luck! What damnably wonderful luck! Perhaps things were about to turn.

The long haul through the Western countryside opened my eyes even further. America was such a vast landscape with so very many facets. Finally, in need of a lunch, we pulled into a truck stop. It was my first classic American Diner, banded in shiny metal, looking like someone had wrapped a caboose in aluminum foil. Inside it, were your red leather booths with jukebox coin slots on the wall side of each table, fully occupied stools at the counter, and a lady in her white cap and buttoned-up peppermint striped work dress.

When I asked her if I could have a glass of hot milk, she replied with a look of dismay that it was unusual to drink hot milk.

"Well," I said, "my mother never breast fed me." I think all the other truck drivers in the entire restaurant burst out laughing, and she finally walked away, shaking her head in disbelief…and trying not to be amused.

Now through the high Sierra Nevada Mountain Range and the Donner Pass, I'm struck by the ghosts of the history and a kind of psychokinetic imprints that still seem to haunt the region. On April 16, 1846, nine covered wagons left Springfield, Illinois on the 2,500-mile journey to California through the Donner Pass, in what would become one of the greatest tragedies in the history of Westward migration.

The Donner Party tragedy was an infamous chapter in American frontier history: two-thirds of the men in the original group perished, while two-thirds of the women and children lived. Forty-one individuals died while forty-six survived. According to their chronicles, five had died before reaching the mountains, thirty-five perished either at the mountain camps in the freezing weather or trying to cross the mountains, and one died just after reaching the valley. Despite three failed rescue attempts in the winter of 1847, 64% of the party were either killed, starved or froze to death. And there were even allegations of cannibalism…though never proved.

(Once I had settled into 190 Bridge Road, Hillsborough, I did find out from Kirk's father, Graham, a chronicle that revealed the entire story of Donner Pass: *Back to the Trail.)*

No snow, no freezing weather but such a visually stunning high mountain road that our "Bull Dog" Mack dug in and hauled us up and through The Sierra Nevada Mountains. The distinct aroma of the pine trees wafted through the truck windows. And upon returning in 1978 to California this high mountain song to the senses became my petition to Creation: *Please may we have a home among the pines?*

After two terrific adventurous days, the Texans dropped me off in San Mateo outside a train station. I enquired as to where I could leave my bags. According to my Brit logic, if anyone could tell me where to find Bridge Road it was certain to be the postman. So I left them in a locker at the local post office.

At last, having located Bridge Road and feeling like Ulysses in *The Odyssey,* I walked alongside a tall thick hedge, peeping through the branches and eventually spied an expansive garden and a pool! The acreage was vast, and I felt as if I'd found an English country mansion. But what it turned out to be was much better; it was a second home.

Eureka! At last, there it was: the most imposing house, covered in Ivy so thick that it smothered the bricks beneath it. And there I stood at the gates, looking down the driveway—long and curved but ending in line of sight. It was a study in opulence, the kind that was reassuring—letting you feel just impressed enough without making you feel ill at ease.

The garage was huge, and just outside it sat a light blue Corvette, and a long white winged Chevy Impala with a red stripe inset on its fender and doors. And there was Kirk hosing it down, a California "dude" giving a little love to his latest toy. Another person unknown to me at the time was one of Kirk's friends who was plucking out a mellow strain on a banjo. Kirk looked up and saw me and, in a wave of his hand, pointed to the Banjo player.

"Alan you're here! What happened to you? That's Sherman, my friend from Yale. He missed you." Before I had the chance to answer him, I felt this presence behind me, turned to see the most stunning woman with an inquisitive look on her face.

"This must be Alan. How long are you staying?" she queried, in a warm voice.

At that point, I hadn't even given a second thought to my visit. "All Summer!" I answered her, entirely out of reflex. (If I had harbored any alternate thoughts about my stay, they were straightened out by the sight of her!)

"Oh goodness really? He is great Kirk! I love him already! I will have to find him a job…and maybe a haircut?" Kirk's mother Phyllis placed her arm around me "Come! You must be starving…Where's your bag?" I told her that it was at the post office. And from that moment on, the rest of the day and my stay unfolded like a magical mystery tour.

*A Classic 1961 Chevrolet Impala: My ride for the summer of '61.*

# Six

# Where Did You Get That Body?

**I soon discovered** that Graham and Phyllis MacDonald were a couple proficient in producing XY-chromosome offspring. They had five sons: Kirk the oldest, then Chris, Larry…and Hunter and Graham the twins. Phyllis was such a force of Nature—vivacious, alert and alive, words that even now I find hard to describe her. She had been an actress on Broadway, headhunted and charmed off to a film career in Hollywood. After starring in a film with Harold Lloyd, Phyllis eventually gave it all up when she met tall handsome Graham, finally bearing him five sons and becoming a devoted mother to their boys.

Coming from my small London home and being shown around, reminded me of the feelings I'd had when I went to St. John's Wood at Lucy's home. This obviously meant a certain wealth, and it prompted me to wonder if there was an opportunity for a London lad like me? No worries, for when I dived into the pool all those thoughts were washed away. I became part of their family, painted a bedroom, went to the post office and received a temporary Green Card. (How easy was that in 1960? And my, how things have changed!)

The McDonalds were an authentic Scottish Clan and took their heritage seriously. In fact, their Den was a designer's homage to the red MacDonald tartan—replete with curtains, upholstered chairs and a drape or two—the lounge and rec room where they introduced me to my first taste of Bourbon.

One evening I was taken to my first baseball game at San Francisco's Candlestick Park. Upon entering the stadium, I felt as if I had just stepped into a painting. The stands encircling the vivid green grass with the mound and the player's dugouts…and just beyond the outfield I could see the Pacific Ocean. That night, I saw Willie Mays hit two home runs. And years later when I came to realize just how much of a baseball icon "Say Hey" Willy was, I brought my son Rowan two Willy Mays baseball cards. Remembering that, I can only hope he still has them tucked away?

Back with the McDonald clan, I soon found out that brother Chris had just gotten me a job digging ditches (a good summer work for a young jock). And on the first day I was three feet down in the ditch, digging away with a work ethic that I was certain would ingratiate me to my bosses…when the foreman came over and made it a point of scowling down at me.

"Slow down Alan! We have plenty of time! You're working too hard!" I had forgotten how strong the rowing for the University had made me, so apparently I had been showing everyone up.

After work and on the weekends, we would drive home through the Peach farms, invariably stopping to buy bags full of peaches and head home biting into what seemed at the time the most luscious fruit on earth. Much of the time, we spent swimming and visiting some of Kirk's female friends, many of whom had a good bit of money and that California vibe.

"Where did you get that body?" The heading was a remark that Gibe Folger said to me, a comment I have never forgotten.

I had just been swimming in Abigail "Gibe" Folger's home pool. And as I pulled myself out of the water I heard Gibe say, "Alan where did you get that body?" And upon hearing the comment I turned to Kirk, rather naïvely asking, "What does she mean?"

"Your body Alan, look at all your defined muscles! It's beautiful!" Gibe said, as she placed her hand on my six-pack stomach. I was so naïve. I had no idea that I looked the way I did from crewing, especially to the young women around the pool. And Gibe had been the self-appointed one to make something of an issue of it, and a compliment to boot.

Years later, to my utter dismay, I came to find out that Abigail Folger, "Gibe," had been gruesomely murdered, along with Sharon Tate and five others in the *Helter Skelter* serial killings orchestrated by Charles Manson and carried out by his groupies, an event that haunts me to this day, as it has done to so many.

San Francisco was home to Richard Guggenheim. Richard was a newfound friend I spent a few days with at his family ranch in Napa Valley. The Guggenheims were a well-known family across the United States—rich and apparently all related in one way or another. At Richard's family ranch I rode my first horse ever across a patch of dry grassy fields already ripe for the harvest.

Kirk took me camping up to Mount Lassen. And upon our return I said my goodbye to the McDonald clan. It was a bittersweet moment. I couldn't thank Phyllis enough for treating me like "family," and for all the love and show of utter humanity.

Fortunately, the friendship between us continued over the years. And I saw both Phyllis and Graham again in London and much later many times in Hillsborough in their new home on Fern Hill Drive. She always called me her "sixth son." She even met my son Rowan when we took him up for his first day at Cal Berkeley. I often would drive to see her and take her out for a lunch. She would love to sit and hear stories of my work in film. Her studio was a clutter of sketches, unfinished paintings and multifarious pots filled with paintbrushes of every size and shape. Sadly, she left us in 2007, but still her memory lingers—one of vibrant life and infinite joy.

I waved my goodbyes. And the three of us—Richard, Kirk and I—left in the Chevy Impala on a cross-country trek, heading this time for Boston and the schools of the Ivy League. Kirk dropped Richard and me off at Harvard where Richard was studying. I spent four days there on its storied campus (the "American Oxford") found my way to the Boat House for the "Harvard Crew," where they allowed me to train in the tank, so I could get back into shape for good old Chelsea Poly.

In a few days, I joined Kirk at Yale. I met and listened to The Yale Whiffenpoofs, their famous collegiate *a cappella* group—the one that kind of started it all. The Whiffenpoofs were established at Yale in 1909, and as such remain the oldest such group in the United States. Little did we realize at the time that by the year 2000 collegiate *a cappella* groups would become the modern rage…spawning TV shows, international competitions and film series like *Pitch Perfect, Pitch Perfect 2, et al.* that would still be the talk of cover music, even as of this writing.

One afternoon, during my forays into the Ivy League, Kirk McDonald hit me with the spontaneous announcement that we were off to Vassar College for "a mixer." Vassar was an all-girl's school at the time, just as Yale was all-male. (Gender-blended Universities didn't take hold until the 1970s.) Meryl Steep had been a Vassar grad. So had Anne Hathaway. So had Jane Fonda and a lady named Jacqueline Kennedy Onassis. Vassar put out the crème de la crème of the American feminine mystique. (Perhaps not surprisingly, my daughter Ella went on to attend Vassar and, upon discovering the "Old Stables," was given permission to clean them up and thus created the college's riding team.)

All I knew at the time was that it was a great fun evening. I did not even have to light my own Disque Bleu (French) cigarette, for suddenly a Zippo flipped open in front of me. Holding it, a lovely blonde Vassar co-ed was gazing at me in wonder. Captivated by my "British accent" and my exotic non-American vibe, she seemed to find me a creature out of time—a rakish Cockney from Mars (or something). Anyway, the cliché about American women finding "European men" attractive is true in every sense. So, there I had a newfound friend (and girlfriend) for a brief time who also came to London for my 21st Birthday.

Next stop was Montreal. I flew to stay with my Uncle Cyril and Aunty Lily who had moved there when Cyril was offered a Baptist Ministry. My only memory from being there was "a stream of consciousness" I had about this delicious cereal that I had every morning and that (to this day) I am still unable to find. It had these great tasting honey chunks with something called "crunchy granola."

By September I had returned to school and found myself back to Eland Road where my fantasy had come crashing down to that dull numbing lassitude I always felt at home. I was disheartened (but not surprised) by my father's utter indifference, not really caring to hear anything about my American journey. It was perhaps the final blow, not a quarrel or a rout. It was just time to get on with my life. It was time for me to move out.

*Vassar College in Poughkeepsie, New York. In 1958 it was an all female University. My connection with it has been wonderfully synchronistic.*

# Seven

## Do Not Disturb Thyself
## By Thinking on the Whole of Thy Life

**Leaving my father's house** on Eland Road, I rented an upstairs front room in Gary's mother's home that I moved into shortly after my return. The windows overlooked the changing seasons out on Wandsworth Common. Finally, back at college after my wild American Summer, I immersed myself in what turned out to be a memorable year—rowing, life drawing, painting, prepping for my final exams and relishing the labyrinth of solitude at times.

There may have been a reason why I somehow became a partial recluse. Although I still held onto a silent passion for one of the girls in the class that came in just after mine, I chose to embrace a monastic approach to my art…for reasons I'll never be able to entirely explain.

It may have been the fact in the Museum of Modern Art in New York, I had become aware of four canvases, a solid white square, a solid green triangle and a solid black square. After seeing these hanging on the wall as an epitome of artistic expression, I felt like giving it all up. And I very well might have, had it not been for fact that the Bay Area Figurative

Art I had seen in San Francisco had made such an impression on me that I would take on any discipline to follow in that tradition. It had become one of the most salient postwar developments on the West Coast. On my return from the US, I had also made the wrong decision in separating from Pamela at that time. (Hindsight is always 20/20, and I was at a loss for discretion.)

After reading a *Sunday Times* article I became conscious of the fact that while I was travelling in America I was completely unaware of the bigotry in the Deep South. We had never in school been taught anything about the intense racial divide that existed there. I began to question the human values of the racial animus that had recently begun to show its ugly face in London, especially in gentrifying areas like Brixton and Notting Hill. The more I read of the lynchings, the black-only washrooms, partitioned drinking fountains, and bus and train seating restrictions, the more I developed an intense dislike of any nation that sponsored such segregation. This kind of irrational hatred without foundation bothered me for months…if not for years. And even today it still does in so very many ways.

There was great old art store called L. Cornelissen & Son on Great Russell Street that, for artists and designers, has always proved to be a cornucopia of discovery. Down the road from the British Museum it was, in terms of atmosphere, something straight out of Dickens' *Old Curiosity Shop*. In business since 1855 it came alive with character and magnificent creative spirits, with its shelves stacked with bottles of pigments and assorted packets of traditional artist's materials—something it still does to this day. My good friend Fabian Peake and I would often pay this store a visit, coming out with our selection of large tubes of oils and brushes, and experiencing something more…a small piece of art history that always managed in some small way to urge us along our way.

Our band had still managed to hold together, and we continued to develop our on-stage skills around Soho, all the while managing to book other gigs in local clubs in town. In the mornings I still went to help

Harry with his greengrocer's barrow—a day job that gave me a few extra pounds for art supplies as my focus was really on my art and the exams that were on the distant horizon.

Meanwhile, I undertook trips to the North, to the North of England and Scotland. On one such journey, I slipped into the bedroom of the Clan MacDonald of Lochalsh. Kirk and Richard had arrived just in time to take me on a golfing vacation to play upon some of the most famous fairways in the world—at St. Andrews, Carnoustie and Troon and other sacred venues. Kirk had arranged for us to visit the Clan MacDonald castle. And when I went to bed the first evening, imagine my surprise to find my tired body encased in blue silk sheets—bedclothes that I was told had caressed many a prince and princess. The guest list at the castle had included Princess Margaret and Lord Snowden (Anthony Armstrong-Jones). I caught sight of them both around St Andrews while I was there.

(And more recently had been treated to my first golf lesson in Palm Springs, a very Zen experience.) It must have paid off, because when I later played nine holes with Rick and Bruce, Rachel's brothers, in Aldeburgh Suffolk, their golf balls went spinning left and right and mine shot straight down the middle. After a few holes of observing my canny, well-directed shots down the fairway, Bruce exclaimed: "Are you sure this is your first game?"

My final year at Chelsea, Danny Denishveskya, a year ahead of me, had already left school. One day purely out of the blue, he called me and asked if I would like to visit him on a film location where he was working with his father on a film called: *The Loneliness of the Long-Distance Runner*. Adapted from the bestselling book, it promised to be a cult film. And still I hadn't the slightest idea about what I was going to experience that day.

As it was, I took the train and found myself a short time later on my first film location in the midst of a long day's shoot. Danny introduced me to his father and a promising young actor named Tom Courtenay.

Later, he invited me to Shepperton Studios where I met an art-director named Ted Clements, along with the film's stars, Steve McQueen, Robert Wagner and a starlet named Shirley Anne Field. Danny gave me a pretty complete breakdown of the crew, all its functions and who did what for whom. The lighting, the set design, the sound set up and the cameras—all the intricacies of filmmaking suddenly caught my fancy, although I have to admit that, at that time least, it never occurred to me that there would ever be a future for me there.

Those last summer months I was still rowing for the college, and somehow, we managed to win the Henley Regatta – Wyfold Fours and the University Eights. That was the very last time I would sit in a slim wooden scull. But what a way to go out—on top?! Victory is sweet, and memories persist.

Nudes in life classes as I painted and sketched became a part of the atmosphere in my final year. Light as it fell across the naked human body, be it male or female came to be my focus in these life classes. I would just draw the light as it fell on the objects themselves, and one learns that creating forms and figures often comes with what one leaves out. There before me on the paper or canvas was light creating form. The exam came and went. I did pass and probably expected to apply to the Royal College of Art as did my friends Fabian Peake, Michael Moon and Patrick Caulfield (who had left the previous year)—and who, in the meantime, had become an extremely successful draftsman and artists, in ways that almost escaped notice. In the final days of May and June I said goodbye to my friends, not realizing that I would see so few of them ever again. One doesn't always plan these things. Life takes on a force of its own. And, whether I was prepared or not, life had far more in store for me than I ever might have imagined.

*L. Cornelissen & Son, London: arguably the most renowned artist's supply store in the world…My inspiration to "carry on."*

# Eight

## Adapt Oneself to Thy Lot in Life Even as it is Cast

**The guitar was in its case,** and I was waiting for the car to pick me up when there was a knock on the door. A postman handed me a telegram to formally inform me that our scheduled gig for that night in Croydon had been cancelled at the last minute. I was disappointed but fatalistic. By that time in my life, I had experienced so many surprises that virtually nothing surprised me. As it turned out on that fortuitous evening, this became the moment when my perceptions of what the future would hold changed forever.

Sure enough, on the following Monday a letter arrived from Ted Clements, the Art director I had met during my visit to Shepperton studios. The query was clear and to the point: *Would I like to come down that week to the studio?* They were looking for an intern to work with them on a film called *The Victors*. This gust of opportunity out-of-the-blue threw me for a loop, completely stunned me and pleased me all at once. Somehow due to this bizarre request I would be working on a film, in a role that I had never even considered before then.

Here I was about to apply for the Royal College of Art, and I was suddenly being hit with a total change of direction. Did one's fate change course in such parallax ways as this? Question asked and answered. So much unexpected had happened to me that I now expected to be surprised. As it was, question after question poured across my mind, leading to the surprising conclusion: why not give it a shot? Not that my change of direction wouldn't come without a challenge.

Sunday, before my fated meeting, the call went out that we were going to ride to Brighton. There we were, the girls and the guys all hanging out on the beach, when suddenly a wave smashed into my face like a fist and sent my false teeth flying, disappearing into the sea without a trace. The hunt was on! Everyone waded in, laughing their heads off groping in the sand for Alan's teeth. "We have to find them, must find them! I have my first interview on Thursday!" I shouted this while on my knees, searching in the sand, and finally riding back to London toothless.

To say I was apprehensive wondering what this day would reveal, especially given my missing teeth, would be an understatement. Upon arriving at the Studio Gates, I found my name on their list. Granted access, I was directed to *The Victors'* Art Department. It seemed as if the walk took forever as I wended my way through prop buildings and stages. Finally catching the eye of a woman sitting in a chair who looked decidedly familiar, I smiled and she smiled back and even waved a little. That was when I realized I was smiling at the superstar Susan Hayward. And for some strange reason I couldn't explain, it seemed to settle me down. Then there it was: a long open area with a stage to the left of me and a reservoir to my right, two Nissen huts to the left in front of a gargantuan building. Soon enough I came to know it well as The Silent Stage, a place that was to be familiar and transformative all at once.

As I approached it, a tall slim man was walking towards me. It was Ted Clements. "Welcome Alan!" he said, taking my hand with a firm shake while escorting me towards a small wooden hut.

As I stepped inside, I saw two drawing boards, a sketch on the walls and, on the side of one of the boards, what seemed to be a montage of scribbled notes pinned to it. I was introduced to Geoffrey Drake who noticed me looking at the notes. " They are all yesterday's notes to myself for today," he said. "Come and sit down." And he pointed to an old bent wood chair.

The interview went well, and he told me that I would receive five pounds a week and, if I made models of the sets that they were building, I would receive an extra one-pound for each model. At the time, I had no idea what he meant by "models" but pretended that I did. Knowledge would come later, and experience came along with it.

All I knew at the moment was that I had the job. I would start next Monday and would have to be ready to start work at 7 a.m.

"Seven, sir?" I said in surprise. (I was a night creature, after all.)

"Yes, Alan every day we expect to start at seven. All the film crew does as well. I look forward to having you on my team! See you Monday!"

I had to learn how to juggle my time and make it to a job far away without the benefit of a car or an easy travel schedule. In a short time, I figured it all out. First, I had to find out the train schedules, set the alarm for 5:45 a.m., leave without waking Mrs. Warren and Gary, walk across the common to Clapham Junction station, and take the train and hopefully get there on time.

I did it, even though I fell asleep, which became my morning Monday to Friday regular habit. Until a set decorator, Peter James, picked me up just a short walk across the common.

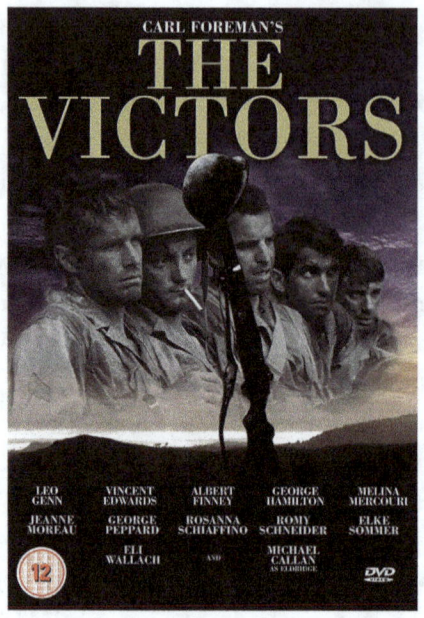

# Nine

## Is it All Just an Illusion?

**It was the autumn of 1961.** "Good morning, sir," were the words that came out of my mouth as Geoffrey came out of his office, approaching me with a kind but business-like expression.

"Alan, good morning! You made it. Good! Now I am going to take you for a coffee. Let's get you oriented, and call me Geoff."

We walked towards The Silent Stage and went inside. And upon entering this giant environment, my jaw just dropped. I wasn't prepared for what came next. There in front of me was the most surprising and awesome new reality that I had experienced up to that point in my life: a set like no other—a striking Italian Street, perfect in every detail, filling the interior of this stage as if part of another world.

The square was populated by English extras dressed in American army uniforms. There were jeeps, trucks and women dressed like Italian villagers, leaning out of the windows, washing and hanging laundry… and scruffy children running through the walled-up cobbled streets of the road.

As I turned around, standing there before me only a few feet away was the legendary actor Eli Wallach on the same set with a beautiful dark-haired Italian ingénue named Rosanna Schiaffino. (Also, on that same soundstage, I would soon come across a coterie of Hollywood's hot young lions, including George Hamilton, George Peppard, Peter Fonda, James Mitchum and Vince Edwards who rounded out the cast. To say the least, I was a little star struck, and have probably never lost that sense of wonder.)

After a short time, Geoff introduced me to the director Carl Foreman as his new P.A., and then the Director of photography, Christopher Challis.

After the introductions, Geoff stepped back and pointed to an area approximately ten feet away from the camera. "Alan," he announced, "I want you to come here every day for the first week and stand approximately this far away from wherever the camera will be, because this is where it all happens. From time to time during the day, I'll come and see how you are doing."

Such an outstanding start to my career to have a mentor like Geoff, who knew exactly what I would learn by those five days spent on set and the irresistible hook that it would create. I did make enquiries whilst on stage about my director, eventually discovering that *The Victors* was his anti-McCarthy Era film.

A brilliant writer who was a victim of the "Red Scare" era of 1948-54, Carl Foreman had been blacklisted in Hollywood for his alleged Communist sympathies.

Ushered in by the House Un-American Activities Committee, investigating the purported Communist party infiltration of the notorious "Hollywood Ten," the HUAC investigations soon fanned out over the six years to take down hundreds of actors, producers, directors and screenwriters, including Foreman, who was one of the last and most notable to fall.

Rather than succumb to what was an outrageous attempt to ruin his career, Carl Foreman expatriated to England in 1951 and made his home in London, where he wrote and was now directing his first feature. The Hollywood establishment later reinstated Foreman in October 1997, along with other writers, directors, actors and producers. Unfortunately, since he had died in 1984, his "redemption" was posthumous. Still, he never really stopped working in all those years.

(Carl Foreman was best known for his work on *The Guns of Navarone* [1961], *High Noon* [1952] and *The Bridge on the River Kwai* [1957]. I also understand that he was an uncredited screenwriter for his work in *On The Waterfront.)*

I also remember that it was on that first day that Geoff took me over to meet the Art Department in the Nissen hut. I cannot imagine the look on my face when I saw what was going on in there. The first person I met was Wally Smith a brilliant draftsman— then John Bodimeade with a beautiful illustration in front of him. I saw Ted who had written the letter—a brilliant draftsman largely responsible for showing me how to take care of myself. Also among the group was Maurice Fowler, the film's Art Director and Martin Atkinson who had a peculiar ability to audibly slurp his tea. Individually and as a group, they had formed a formidable team…and to these young eyes at least, rather intimidating.*

How, on looking at all their work, was I ever going to get to their level? These were major industry players, and I was a fly on the wall. The last film that Wally had just worked on was *Lawrence Of Arabia*, a fact he mentioned as casually as having a cup of tea. Over lunch, Wally suggested that I should buy myself a drawing board, purchase a set square, some HB pencils and take a print of one of his drawings—a plan and elevation of the bombed out French Street. He then later gave me a roll of tracing paper to lay over his drawing, a technique he suggested that would help

---

* At a later date over coffee, Wally sat with me and clued me in on an indelible part of the creative process by telling me something I'll never forget. "Alan," he said, " It is much easier to trust someone who has self-doubt, because that doubt is like a reflection of the truth. Anyone who is cocksure or deals in his own absolutes should not be trusted. And a healthy mind often holds opposing thoughts at the same time." Obviously I am not certain that I completely understood him at that moment. But later, during the course of the year, those words often came back to me.

me learn how to draft by tracing it. Following such good advice to the letter that is exactly how I learned the craft. And yet not even then did I realize that this was just the beginning.

At first, they gave me full size details to draw up and also showed me how make the models of the sets—sets that were so realistic from the front…and yet when you approached them from the rear you quickly saw that it was all an illusion.

Earlier I mentioned the male cast members for *the Victors*. But this was a large ensemble piece, and it was replete with some of the most luminous *femmes fatales* on the silver screens of Europe. Melina Mercouri, Jeanne Moreau, Romy Schneider, Elke Sommer and Senta Berger—were some of the hottest actresses of their time. And, of course, one could not forget an eager young Albert Finney…who was indirectly responsible for truncating my not-so-promising career as an actor.

Earlier during the shooting, Carl, on an impulse, had asked Geoff if I could play the English soldier that George Hamilton kills. "No" was his reply "I want him to carry on in my art department." And guess who ended up playing that part? A newcomer named Albert Finney!

During the shoot, the crew were working one night on the back lot, and Geoff had asked me to come to see the large model of London that was going to burn that night—a recreation that depicted London during the Blitz. It was the most freezing weather that England had experienced for many a year. When it came time to put the burning model out all the fire hoses were frozen and the model was completely destroyed.

Another night after the shoot it was so foggy one could barely see even a few feet away. I had been forewarned to make certain I put on extra warm clothes; and even those were not enough. So… there I was standing at the gate waiting for a bus…and freezing. Suddenly a Rolls Royce Shadow appeared out of the fog, the rear window rolled down and George Hamilton poked his head out and said, "If you are going to London, jump in, Alan."

*George Hamilton, George Peppard, Vince Edwards et al. on the set of* The Victors.

As we slowly made our way through the thick fog, George opened the door to see if we were close to the side of the road and we accidently scooped up a man on his bike. You can just imagine all the laughter that came from that incident.

I have often maintained that time flies when your life is running on adrenalin. Before I knew it, I had only one week left on *The Victors*, and it seemed as if I had only just begun.

We always went to the refectory for morning tea around 9 a.m. I was standing in line when I overheard someone behind me saying to another person that they were looking for a junior in the art department on *Becket*—the legendary impenetrable Art Department on *Becket!*

Motivated to seize the initiative, I quickly quit the line and ran across the studio to the Old House to the Art Department Offices. I met Maurice Carter the Art Director who shortly introduced me to the Production Designer John Bryan. On the spot, I got the job as a junior—one level up from a P.A. In a point of irony, I later came to find out that the two people behind me were the brothers Ackland-Snow.

On my first day in the Old House I actually met Brian Ackland-Snow who was drawing up an exterior for Coventry Cathedral. He acknowledged me with a silent glance that caused me to wonder why? Soon enough, I would come to find out. The brothers Ackland-Snow, Brian and Terry went on to production design many films, Brian receiving an Oscar for A *Room with a View* and Terry who worked on many productions, including *Aliens,* and the 1989 version of *Batman*… and who continues to run a school of film design at Pinewood Studios.

# Ten

## "Let Us Away Knights: This Fellow Will Arise No More"

"Will no one rid me of this turbulent priest?" Sometimes quoted as "troublesome or meddlesome priest" this condemnation is an utterance attributed to Henry II of England, which led to the assassination of Thomas Becket, the Archbishop of Canterbury, in 1170. While it was not expressed as an order, it caused four knights to travel from Normandy to Canterbury, where they cut Becket to the floor inside the Cathedral itself (an absolute "no-no" in the era of Sanctuary).

This of course was immortalized in the film *Becket,* directed by Peter Glenville and starring Richard Burton in the title role, Peter O'Toole as Henry II and John Gielgud as Louis VII, the King of France. Written by Edward Anhalt, a gentleman I would meet much later (1984) at his home in Beverly Hills, it turned out to be one of the most critically acclaimed films of 1965. As a result it was nominated for 12 Academy Awards that year, including one for Richard Burton and Peter O'Toole as Best Actor, John Gielgud for Best Supporting and Peter Glenville for Best

Director. Ultimately only one Oscar was awarded—to Edward Anhalt for Best Adapted screenplay.

As I recall the very detailed set construction for The Silent Stage exterior had steps that led up to the construction of the 1126 Canterbury Cathedral facade. On walking through the tall ornate paneled double doors, there before me was the massive interior of Coventry. Rows of soaring columns that supported arches that took your eye in perspective to the ancient altar. Walls to the left and right of us graced us with lofty windows that permitted just enough the light to bring depth and tone to this set. This was the illusion that I was now beginning to understand that I had at my very fingertips, something that with a pencil in my hand surrounded by books of architectural reference I could recreate any time I wished. There was one gift that the Set Decorator Robert Cartwright gave me: *Meyer's Handbook of Ornament* which he told me was the Art Department bible of reference for all architectural details you will ever require.

Richard Burton and Elizabeth Taylor had just finished principal photography on *Cleopatra*. And it was obvious to everyone that they were madly in love. Elizabeth would pay many a visit to the *Becket* sets, and Richard's dressing room was right above the office I was sharing with the set decorators. So we all knew her comings and goings.

They would often have lunch in Richard's room and it would be hard to describe especially if we happened to take a short lunch, unwittingly returning to the audible chorus that resonated above us. There were many times when Elizabeth would rankle the housekeeper by dancing in her high heels on the 14th Century oak table that stood in the center of the upper hall.

It became a social custom that a large group of us would go to the King's Head Pub in Shepperton Village for lunch, and the liquid lunches would occasionally get raucous.

On one such occasion I had hitched a ride with Ted Clements who after one drink decided that he would challenge Richard and Peter to a drinking competition. O'Toole and Burton were both in costume but didn't hesitate to take the man up on his offer. And so the drinking began. When it came time to go back to the studio, no one could seem to find Ted who had apparently disappeared, leaving me without a ride. Richard Burton saw my problem and asked me to sit with him and Peter who suggested, "having a wee jar." (And for anyone who's been with the Irish or Welsh, there is no such thing as "just one.")

When it came for their 3 p.m. call-time, I found myself utterly smashed and being hoisted up and escorted to the limo by Richard. He opened the back door, sat me down and crawled past me as Peter got in the other side.

The limo came to a halt as Richard said: "Right here," about fifty yards from the front of Coventry Cathedral set. Peter opened my door, took me by one arm and Richard held me by the other. What a threesome walking towards the stage! And here I was, "the meat," in the midst of a strolling celebrity sandwich. Who should come out of the stage? John Bryan the production designer who happened to be my boss. They both let go and I dropped to the ground.

"We are totally responsible John for Alan's demise. We have to go and work now." Peter announced this, taking full responsibility for my condition, and having himself had a lid full. After this rather embarrassing moment (for me), O'Toole and Burton, both drunk as lords, went in and nailed the dialogue, professionals to the core.

I on the other hand was tucked up in a bed by the housekeeper of the Old House, and John was still looking for Ted—a lost afternoon that my nascent career managed somehow to survive.

Just a note on their *Hamlet:* or should I say, dueling Hamlets? This infamous production challenge got its impetus due to a lighthearted agreement between Richard Burton and Peter O'Toole while they were filming *Becket.*

After one afternoon's shoot, O'Toole decreed that, after the principal photography on *Becket,* they should each undertake concomitant onstage productions of Shakespeare's *Hamlet*—one each, staged under the direction of John Gielgud and Laurence Olivier in either London or New York City, with a coin toss deciding who would be assigned which director and which city: O'Toole won London and Olivier in the toss, with Burton being assigned Gielgud and New York. The theatre crowd, one day in New York, were very upset because Peter as a guest actor was drunk, he said if you think I am drunk? Wait till you see Hamlet." On walked Burton, totally sizzled, but never missing a line.

The production was critically acclaimed and a financial smash, achieving the longest run for that particular play in Broadway history at 137 performances. Such are the caprices of famous men and the magic they can create, coming from a whim and finishing in legend.

"Let us away, Knights; this fellow will arise no more." These were words supposedly said by a clerk who had entered the Cathedral with the Knights from Normandy. Several contemporary accounts of what happened next exist; of particular note is that of Edward Grim, who was wounded in the attack. This is part of the account from Edward Grim:

"The wicked knight leapt suddenly upon him, cutting off the top of the crown, which the unction of sacred chrism had dedicated to God. Next, he received a second blow on the head, but still he stood firm and immovable. At the third blow he fell on his knees and elbows, offering himself a living sacrifice, and saying in a low voice, 'For the name of Jesus and the protection of the Church, I am ready to embrace death.' But the third knight inflicted a terrible wound as he lay prostrate. By this stroke, the crown was separated from his head in such a way that the blood dyed the floor of the cathedral. The same clerk who had entered with the knights placed his foot on the neck of the holy Becket and scattered the brains and blood about the pavements, crying to the others, 'Let us away, knights; this fellow will arise no more.'"

Rather a gory description, but not uncommon for the times. Apparently, the nobles of the middle ages had a strong stomach for such things.

In the lower corridor of the Old House one would often pass actors who were working with Stanley Kubrick on his film *Dr. Strangelove*. Sterling Hayden, Peter Sellers and George C Scott often haunted the halls… along with Kubrick himself.

Ken Adam was the Production Designer for Kubrick and created the iconic set, "The War Room." I was able to walk through on the day they were pre-lighting just prior to their locking down the set. And I stood impressed by the angular design and do remember being introduced to him. Ken was knighted some years later, becoming Sir Ken Adam, which I assume was mainly for all his work on the original James Bond 007 films that established a certain seminal layout for those original sets. He was also responsible for the large James Bond Stage at Pinewood studios and so many more films that he had production-designed.

*A classic poster for Becket, nominated for 12 Oscars in 1965, including two for Best Actor.*

*Elizabeth Taylor visits Burton on the set of Becket*

*O'Toole as Henry II and Burton as Becket share an early conspiratorial moment.*

*Exterior of Canterbury Cathedral
outside the Silent Stage at Shepperton Studios.*

*Interior of the Canterbury Cathedral Set on the Silent Stage at Shepperton Studios.*

# Eleven

## "Let's Get Out of Here!"

**It was November 22, 1963** at 12:30 p.m., and John F. Kennedy, the 35th President of the United States, had just been assassinated. Everyone remembers where he or she was on that day, if not that very hour.

I had been off sequestered working on a project, when I got the news to check out a broadcast on BBC 1. And there it was: the deathly milestone and a loss of innocence for us all. I was pierced to the heart with compassion for this young American president for whom I had garnered so much respect. He was a young man of vision, hope, dignity and class and had raised the bar for us all.

In the next few days, I had gotten a call from Geoffrey Drake asking me if I would be free to join his Art Department on a film called *Lord Jim*. They would again be shooting at Shepperton studios and I would be his Art Set Assistant. I told him that I would be finished on *Becket* in two weeks and would love to work with him again. "That would be perfect, Alan," he replied.

It was a film based on the book. The novel, *Lord Jim,* is an iconic work of fiction by Joseph Conrad, thought by some to be virtually impossible to consolidate into a film. An early and primary event in the story is the abandonment of a passenger ship The Patna left in distress by its crew, including a young British seaman named Jim. He is publicly censured for this action, and the novel follows his later attempts at coming to terms with himself and his past.

Richard Brooks was the director. He was nominated for eight Oscars in his career, and is best known for *Blackboard Jungle, Cat on a Hot Tin Roof, Elmer Gantry* and Truman Capote's *In Cold Blood,* as well as having acquired reputation for being a great screenwriter, having written twenty-two of the screenplays he had directed, Richard Brooks may accurately be defined as one of the legends of film. *Lord Jim* was certainly no exception. It kicked off with such an amazing cast. Peter O'Toole would again be playing the title role with a supporting cast that included James Mason, Curt Jurgens, Eli Wallach, Jack Hawkins, Paul Lucas, Daliah Lavi and Akim Tamiroff—just a few actors that I knew from their past work, and whom I had come to know early-on in the first few years of my career.

The art department for *Lord Jim* had two Art Directors: Ernest Archer and William Hutchinson. Eddie Fowlie who was David Lean's Prop Master, John Graysmark, and Alan Tompkins all had been in the art department on *Lawrence of Arabia* and were carryovers to this.

On The Silent Stage we were building a great three-quarter to full-size steamer ship that replicated The Patna. Once completed, the tip tanks were placed along its side, along with wave machines and huge propellers for the wind. Then, as the stage was built to contain water, it was summarily flooded, all combining to recreate a perfect storm at sea!

Outside of the stage Geoff introduced me to Freddie Young who was already a famous Director of Photography (DP) having won an Oscar for his work with David Lean on *Lawrence of Arabia*. Freddie had a light meter hanging around his neck. I pointed to it and asked him what it was for. He turned to Ernie Day, his camera operator and said, "I think we have a good one here Ernie!" They both smiled and walked into the stage to meet Richard Brooks.

Ernie, as we called him "Mr. Archer," persuaded Geoff that I was ready to draw up the full-size model of The Patna. This was my first real challenge on the drawing board. I had many photographs and all the drawings of the set. When I was finished, so I thought, I realized that I had not drawn up any of the ship's lamps. This model that was twenty-eight feet long looked just like the ship that was on stage, and the day it was taken from the construction shop happened to be the same day that all the Asian extras arrived.

The extras were all attired in white tunics and led to the stage by the Second Assistant Director Michael Stevenson. Michael is still a dear friend and always worked as a Second AD, and as such was very close to David Lean, so much so that he was with him on the day he passed. In fact, Michael was such a prominent figure that he was mentioned by Terence stamp in his memoir, *The Ocean Fell into the Drop* for his lifelong work as a 2nd Unit Director and friend.

All the art department were on stage when the first day of shooting commenced. The extras were standing on the deck and had not been given any advance notice about what would be happening. Richard, our director, wanted them to be totally surprised…and they were!

I have to note that the first day of shooting turned out to be one of the coldest days that England had experienced in nearly eighty years. The Reservoir that ran parallel to the studio was frozen. When the first call for "action" was made, the wave machines began to churn into motion, then four huge propellers mounted on scaffold for the wind, began to turn. The rockers under the boat created the stationary forward and side roll.

"Turn over! Camera roll! Tip tanks! Action!" The first AD cried out.

One by one the six tip tanks let loose their thousands of gallons onto the deck and the Extras went flying in all directions as wave after wave smashed into them. Now they knew why they were there. The director looked at his watch. "Lunch!! Help them down, get them dry and give them a Brandy!" He walked away and turned back, "On second thought, give them a Coke."

Angkor Wat was the location where the crew would be heading to in a week. A famed Hindu Temple in Cambodia, it was a classic site on 16 hectares erected to the God Vishnu. It was the "perfect venue" that had somewhat fallen into decay.

Bill Hutchinson, along with Geoff, was already there getting the various other sets and locations ready. On various stages around the studios, sets were being prepared for the crew's return. The facade and interior of a village hall in a fictional country called Patusan were conformed to duplicate the setting in Joseph Conrad's book. As I walked onto the stage where the painters were putting the finishing touches to the Ruins of an Angkor Wat Temple, I was impressed by the relentless carving that Nature does on us all, the overgrowth and huge tree roots made better by good set design. Painters, I later discovered, can truly make or break a set.

The Patna had now been removed from the silent stage. And Geoff, before he left for Angkor Wat, let the set decorator, Vernon Dixon, take me on as an assistant to help with whatever he required me to do.

On the vast open stage, we were now going to recreate a jungle with banks on either side of a river, as well as a convincingly perilous ferry crossing. The jungle plants were outside, waiting to be moved in. And the scenic artist, Roby Ronertson, began to paint the 30-foot-high by 300-foot-long backdrop that had to be ready inside of five days. That took the work of Roby and his assistant, painting with countless rollers, working day and night until he had his jungle…and there it was: on time!

No words can really express my admiration for our industry's scenic artists who, in today's world of Green Screen and computer technology, have virtually disappeared.

Back in the early years of film, it was a different story. Set artists were all that. And I clearly remember standing one day and watching Ferdinand Bellan as he painted a hundred-foot back drop that his assistant had marked out in squares. Ferdinand had arrived with his sketch that included the squares and began to paint from the bottom left of the backing.

When I returned there was an unrivalled Charge of the Light Brigade. Horses were his métier that they were going to shoot to provide the palette for the credits of Tony Richardson's overlooked masterpiece, *The Charge Of the Light Brigade*. As part of his illustrious portfolio, Ferdi Bellan has also been associated with the following productions as co-designer: *The Third Man, Anne Boleyn, Sumarun, Madam du Barry, Thief of Baghdad, Four Feathers, Cleopatra, Becket* and *The Agony and The Ecstasy*, to name just a few.

By the time we were in production, the political conflict in Vietnam had become a nightmare, which made some of the shooting downright dangerous.

"Let's get out of here!" were Richard Brooks' words, upon noting the selected locations.

Peter (O'Toole) was on the Ferry as it made its way across the jungle river. "Cut! Get your arses down!!" Those were the peremptory commands coming from the Director, shouting to the extras wading in the freezing water. He asked the prop man Eddie to hand him the rifle that he was using to clear the pigeons off the roof. Rifle in hand, Richard himself fired directly over the extras' heads and they disappeared under the surface. "More Smoke and stay low! Action!" he shouted.

One day, upon completing the scheduled locations, Geoff asked me: "Alan do you have your script?" I replied that I had left it at home. "Well, Richard wanted to know who this man with two surnames was that had one of his scripts. A limo will take you home and bring it straight back to his office."

On returning I knocked on Richard's door and went in. He was having lunch, he immediately recognized me, took a set of keys and keychain from his pocket unlocked a metal chest, dropped the script in and locked it back up. "I've been ripped off so many times, with so many shows I've done! I will not take any more chances, thank you, young man!" Another lesson learned that came into play at a later date. Then he took his pipe from the ashtray, lit it, picked up his script and walked back towards the stage with me, chatting as we went.

*Peter O'Toole on the set of Lord Jim.*

*Richard Brooks with Daliah Lavi going over the next shot.*

*Peter O'Toole and Richard Brooks confer over a scene in Lord Jim.*

# Twelve

## Beware of the Villains

**The Krays, Ronnie and Reggie,** were twin brothers, infamous London East Enders, nightclub owners and notorious crime figures who flourished from 1960–1968. On top of that, they were ruthless killers and somewhat proud of the fact. And I was about to have an encounter with them that I would not soon forget.

When I first met Michael Stevenson on the set of Lord Jim, he was the 2$^{nd}$ AD. John (Tiger) Stevenson, Michael's father, was a heavyweight who would fight anyone in the East End of London and had two boxing matches with the Krays' father, another great Boxer.

At the time, Michael and I were both very clothes conscious and would often go window-shopping in the city to check out the styles. He asked me if I would like to come with him on Saturday to a party in the East End. I had my doubts, but he managed to reassure me. "Don't worry it will be okay. I know most of them. They won't bother us."

So! There we were having a drink chatting with a few of the faces I recognized from being extras on various sets when suddenly glasses went flying across the room and chains were being brandished. Someone from one of the gangs began smashing faces. Michael grabbed me, and we both quickly dived under the kitchen table. There we were hiding beneath the tablecloth as bodies flew all around us like a kind of a brawl in a B-western. (Bullet dodged, or so I thought.)

Another kind of reality struck on Monday evening when I popped into the Potters, my local pub, to meet Peter Mines, Gavin Hodge and Bob Richards. By this time, I had left the apartment in Wandsworth and was now living in a small flat on Kings Road. Standing at the bar, glass in hand and ordering my friends drinks there was a sudden silence and everyone around me disappeared. A fist smashed into my face as my glass went flying and crashed across the room. "You! Come with us! You're the one who sounded his H's. You know Charlie Price. We want him. Come with us!"

I have to admit I went into shock. I was shaking from head to toe as two very burly men frog marched me out of the pub and into the back of a large black car. Ronnie Kray, head of the Krays was sitting there as if waiting for me while twin-brother Reggie got in beside me, both impeccably dressed in their tailored suits. Seemingly on cue, another young burly enforcer sitting in front seat turned and punched me in the nose.

Blood (my blood!) went everywhere across the back to the car, while Reggie noted matter-of-factly, "If you get that on my tweeds you'll get another."

They then drove me around Fulham and Chelsea, frog marched me through countless bars looking for Charlie, all to no avail.

After what seemed like an endless night's search, they drove along the Kings Road, finally turning into a side street in a way that made my blood run cold.

Reggie hauled me out of the back, the man in the front got out and pulled a hammer from his pocket, moving toward me with malicious intent and ready to move on command.

That was enough! My adrenalin at last propelled me into flight. I instantly broke away and took off, and for some unexplained reason, they let me go. I only had to run around the block into Kings Road and my apartment was right there opposite the Old Age Pensioners' Home.

The only thing I could remember was a phone number. So I dialed. "Hallow! I can only remember this number! Who are you?"

"Alan it's your Mum," came the answer, so calm and matter of fact. "Take some hot milk with a little brandy and you will be right as rain in the morning."

Both physically wrecked and more than a little bit traumatized at the time, I didn't go to the Studios for at least three days. And, finally, on the third day there came a knock at the door.

I went down the stairs opened it to find the same pair of rough young men in black suits who had originally seized me at the bar. Nowhere to go (they'd found me after all) I stood in the stairway expecting the worst, but to my surprise they had actually come to apologize.

"It was all a mistake!" One said (The one who had smashed in my nose). "We're here, gov, on behalf of the Brothers Kray who want to apologize for smashing you up."

I was shaking and could barely understand their heavy Cockney accents. Still I managed to hold composure, just long enough to thank them and, still in shock while watching them leave, calmly closed the front door and collapsed at the bottom of the stairs.

After I returned to the studios, Michael had obviously told the extras in the Churchill studio pub at Shepperton Studios that I really had nothing to do with Charlie Price. He could not apologize enough, and Charlie went into hiding.

One of the best British films of the 1960s was *Séance on a Wet Afternoon*. I was very lucky to have worked on this film with Ray Simm the art director and Bryan Forbes' extraordinary direction with riveting tracking shots, evocative cinematography, great set pieces, John Barry's haunting soundtrack, a serpentine plot, and amazing acting from the two leads, Kim Stanley (as Myra Savage) and Richard Attenborough. (Richard also produced the film.) Everything about Brian Forbes.' *Séance on a Wet*

*Afternoon* was expressly understated and deliberately gothic. The story, although unusual, is told in a linear way so that whatever plot twists did come avoided all the cheap tricks that defined so many of the suspense films of the sixties.

I drew up the house that we ended up building entirely on stage at Pinewood. Brian had talked to Ray about not floating the ceilings in order to have a realistic feeling for the actors while they were shooting. So, all walls and ceilings were fixed. The environment was closed, and one could actually feel and sense the claustrophobic verisimilitude—something many critics praised once the film was released.

We also were on location around London; so the atmosphere was explicit.

And the film was so well received one critic was moved to write: "This is an almost forgotten masterpiece by British director Bryan Forbes, in which everything is unique. The soundtrack is macabre and chilling, the story and setting eerily authentic (the atmosphere of the old house is comparable to the one in Robert Wise's *The Haunting)* the cinematography is great, and the editing is almost perfect."

The greatest bonus for the film was Kim Stanley's acting in the role of Myra Savage. Perfection would be the right word to describe it. As she was already regarded as "America's finest actress," Kim, in her stunning electric performance, proved how deeply method actors can dive into their character. She should have received an Oscar and did win a New York Film Critics award for her performance. Peter James was our Set Decorator who worked with me later on *The Lion in Winter* and in Sri Lanka on *Tarzan*.

*Kim Stanley and Richard Attenborough in a scene from* Séance on a Wet Afternoon.

# Thirteen

## "What Are Your Intentions, Young Man?"

Prior to going on my first location to Ireland, I worked on a small black and white film called *Invasion*. In a way bad films become a blur. I only vaguely remember helping to design an almost comically crude Alien spacecraft, and that was about it. Had it not been for the fact that the Art Director was Scott MacGregor, I would have forgotten it entirely. But there are other moments and times that are indelible to the last detail.

In the late 1960s Arethusa (on the Kings Road) was one of the hottest new clubs in London and—in that heyday of private clubs—became so exclusive it was for members only. My dear friend Peter Young and I had arranged to meet there one Friday night.

Along with Annabel's and the Clermont Club, in 1966 Arethusa was the place to be seen. And whoever happened to be in town would always try to book a Saturday or Sunday lunch there. Whether it was Richard Burton with Elizabeth Taylor, Rhonda Fleming, Ava Gardner, Steve

McQueen, or Rod Steiger (and definitely Michael Cain!) it became the bar célébre for all the shiniest people.

Terence Stamp and many a young actress or model, Mick Jaeger of the Rolling Stones and occasionally The Beatles (although they preferred Tramps, and another trendy club called The Ad-lib) would gather there and share the two star Michelin menu and the deliberately pricey wine list.

At Arethusa one Friday night I found myself in "The Gents," standing at the wash basin next to John Lennon, and acknowledging each other with a nod. Kind of felt unusual to be so offhanded with a legend, but this seemed to be a night to be rubbing up against some very VIPs. Coming out of the restroom, I turned to go back to my booth only to find right next to me a man who had to have the largest thighs I'd ever seen. As he was pointed out to me, I looked up from the thighs to recognize NFL gridiron star Jim Brown. Brown in fact had quit the League in his prime to pursue a career in Hollywood…and ended up co-starring in a breakthrough filmic juggernaut of male bonding called *The Dirty Dozen*. We shared a drink. And later the film and the man drifted on into legend.

Peter always blamed me for getting him into the world of cinema as a set decorator, although he has since won two Oscars: one for the first (Jack Nicolson/Michael Keaton) version of *Batman,* and the other for *Sleepy Hollow* (both directed by Tim Burton). During one of our infamous lunches, Peter arrived with Tony Woollard who mentioned that he was off to Ireland to art direct a film and had been told about my previous work. Suddenly in an aha! moment, Tony dropped the suggestion: Would I like to join him there, since he had it in his budget to take on an assistant?

By this point in my nascent career, I had saved a little money and had brought myself a small white 1500 Fiat. Taking my new cherry auto on the trip, I booked passage on the ferry to Ireland and proceeded to drive from Dublin to County Clare across the verdant countryside—taking in the ancient towers, narrow lanes and endless stone walls that seemed to frame all the small fields on the Emerald isle. Enjoying a meandering journey, I finally arrived at the small seaside town of Lahinch, where Tony was waiting for me.

*Time Lost and Time Remembered (We Were Happy Here)* was the title of the film…which ended up being simply *We Were Happy Here*. I was having a draft of Guinness with Tony when he introduced me to the director Desmond Davis. Desmond began to describe to both of us how he was going to direct his film when Manny Wynn, the Director of Photography arrived. And after a rambling conversation, I finally came to realize that they were all saying this would be my first film that no sets were going to be built—it would be all locations and dressing. Sarah Miles, Cyril Cusack and Julian Glover were the cast, and they were due arrive inside of a week.

The location scout had come back with choices, and our locations were finally selected, and we began to shoot in this quaint old harbor village. When the tide went out, the seaweed that was trapped there spat out a noxious aroma. We didn't hang there too long and moved on to another location where the tide was rolling in and just that wafting scent of the ocean that seemed to feed one's soul. At our next location, we came across congeries of cottages inhabited by the local fishermen that had thick thatched roofs, no running water and no heating other than reeking peat fires. Somehow, they had survived for hundreds of years living exactly like this. But tens of thousands, due to a 20-year scourge of famines, had fled to America in what amounted to the infamous Irish Diaspora of the mid 19th Century.

Soda bread and fresh caught fish formed the staples of my diet for most of the film. One afternoon the prop man asked me if I had asked the young lad to clean my car?

"You better go look and see what he is doing," he said laughing. And there was this young boy who I thought could use a few coin was scrubbing the hood of the Fiat with a Brillo pad.

The shoot was so different from what I had previously experienced and not the long hours of the studio. One Sunday, we decided along with Sarah Miles to hire a boat for a fishing excursion. We had these long lines with eight to ten hooks on them, we must have passed through a large shoal in the depths of the dark green Atlantic for as we started to pull the lines in there was a Mackerel attached to each hook. We had a packed lunch and dozed off for a while. On waking up, I noticed that all the fish had disappeared and there was Sarah leaning over the edge throwing the last two back into the sea.

"Sarah what you doing?" I asked, going over to her. She replied, "It just wasn't fair!" And she wanted them all to go home. Having given "catch and release" a whole new meaning, we all returned fishless to the docks. And as we walked along the harbor wall we just laughed and joked with Sarah that maybe next time she would let us save a few for our evening's supper.

Cyril Cusack was an Irish actor of some renown at that time. He had two young daughters who lived in Ireland. Sinead was the youngest and quite a beauty. And I suppose we had that mystic connection that words cannot explain. The eye-contact was a lock, and everybody noticed, not the least of whom was father, Cyril.

At that point during the shoot, a few of us had taken up residence in this old Georgian House, and on the last day of filming there was a decision to have the party in our Manor. We had booked two Céilí bands—one upstairs and one below. All the locals were invited. And there was dancing everywhere, as the Céilí music will invariably cause you to tap those feet.

Seizing the opportunity, Sinead and I went upstairs to see the other band, where we found a chair and she sat on my lap and we kissed for the first time. Well…who walked in through the door but Cyril, looking stern as a judge?

"What are your intentions young man?" he sternly queried, wearing a slight scowl, as he walked straight towards us. I looked at him and replied that "you should ask Sinead sir" as Sinead oblivious of her father continued to kiss me and I moved her head to the side, we both laughed and carried on kissing. As Cyril walked away, he turned "You two be careful" he said, smiling as he nodded his head at us both!

We met a few times later; but our relationship ended in innocent ways. A couple of years later, Sinead married actor Jeremy Irons, and pursued her own successful career as an actress on stage and in film.

*Cyril Cusack and Sarah Miles in*
I Was Happy Here, *1966*

# Fourteen

## Perfection is the Key

**Ted Haworth and Peter Murton,** two of the most accomplished Production Designers in the industry, were my mentors in film design and excellent teachers to boot. When I met them, they were working together on a musical titled *Half a Sixpence*, starring English pop star Tommy Steele. Ted had come over from Hollywood and brought some extraordinary credits with him. *Some Like It Hot, Sayonara, Strangers on a Train, The Longest Day* and *The Body Snatchers*—were just a few of the many films where he had been the production designer. For his part, Peter was my art director and one of the best advisors I ever had.

There we were again on The Silent Stage at Shepperton. Ted introduced us to the first coloured Trans light. In fact, it was a black and white 30-foot-high by 180-foot-long photographic backdrop that wrapped around the stage. Ted had the scenic painters colour it from the back, and the director of photography placed floor light panels around the base and up lit it. Peter, I know, was a little concerned that it would look real, because the seam of the photographs had to somehow disappear when they adhered to each other. It did and it didn't: but Ted was showing us English guys that he was ahead of the game.

What I really learned from both of them was the thorough way that they would approach every aspect of the design. Perfection was always their objective and excellence their result, as they were both such highly gifted sketch artists that their impact on me was indelible and eternal. Our friendship through the years continued, and we always kept in touch.

After working with Ted and Peter, I was soon off to Pinewood Studios to work on one of the "Carry On" series, *Carry On Cowboy*, the seventh in a list of classic comic films. In the meantime, I had been making new friends, moving apartments and really enjoying London life.

It was the late 1960s. Life as we knew it was in a constant state of flux. Hairdressers were stars. Vidal Sassoon had his Salon just off Hyde Park. On the top floor was the men's Salon, and sometimes on Saturday mornings we went there for our haircuts. Tony Hicks of the Hollies was dating a model friend of ours named Jane Lumb. In the '60s at least, the upper class was mixing with the middle and lower classes, and accents seemed not to matter anymore. It was suddenly a creative cauldron of talents, unlimited and Large. Limitations were a thing of the past. Nothing was off limits.

Jane was one of a new group of local friends that joined our merry band at another Kings Road restaurant called Casserole. Along with Robert Melbourne, Mim Scala, Adrian Hunter, Jamie Stewart Granger, Ingrid Bolting. Jose Fonseca, John Gaydon, Esmond Cooper-Key and actor Ian Quarrie (an unrepentant ladies' man and a close friend of Roman Polanski)—all these luminaries and could be found dining virtually every day at Casserole. Polanski was in pre-production for *Rosemary's Baby* around this time. Everyone seemed to be there. Apple crumble was the favorite desert, and it always sold out fast.

John Gilbert who later became a family friend was the son of Louis Gilbert who had directed three earlier James Bond films, including *You Only Live Twice* and *The Spy Who Loved Me*. John also had been the music producer for the successful rock group Genesis (that starred Phil Collins and Peter Gabriel) and was an associate producer on Michael Caine's breakout film, *Alfie,* a box office smash of 1967 that his father produced and directed. So, it was quite a scene in Chelsea then. Not forgetting Bob Richards, Gavin Hodge and Peter Mines…Did I forget anyone?

Yes! I did! I forgot to mention my old friend Sebastian Sed. Sebastian had created the industry famous Sed Cards. He had a mews house and invited me to share it with him, which I did. He was very successful, and the majority of the top models in England and Europe had their photographs taken and their specs printed on the back of his legendary Sed Cards, several variations of which are still used today. At the same time, there was also Eugene who had great taste in music, turning me on to Marvin Gaye and Kenny Lynch, a pop star at this time with a hit, "Up on the Roof," also appearing in various TV programs.

The "Carry On" series I was working on was one of the most successful ongoing series in the history of British Film. Beginning with *Carry On Doctor* and following with *Carry On Nurse,* the series saw the successful release of 32 more films and at least a dozen TV specials that played out over a 34-year period from 1958 to 1992. The cast of the "Carry On" series was something of a repertory affair, using a body of the same actors in each sequel. Sydney James, Jim Dale, Kenneth Williams and Bernard Bresslaw, Edina Rona—these were a few of the regulars, missing only Dirk Bogard who agreed to appear in the *Carry On Doctor* sequels while giving the others a miss.

Bert Davey, the Art Director, entrusted me with the great job of drawing up the Western Street for the *Carry On Cowboy* set.

"Make it look old, Alan… as if it's been around for many a year." He made his request as he placed a few books on my desk. I made certain that I saw *High Noon* based on Carl Foreman's screenplay, and gleaned from it the feeling for the façades and walkways.

Being on stage in the Saloon and other sets during the shoot, it was hard for me not to burst out laughing, listening to all these comics ad-lib their lines, always turning them into jokes to the frustration of the two producers with their eyes on the clock. It was very much like herding cats. But what a great bunch of cats! And you could have made another movie just from the outtakes.

My next gig turned out to be several months on a project with a hot new British Rock Group, The Dave Clark Five. Dave Clark and his group were an English pop rock band formed in Tottenham, London in 1957 who had, by the early 1960s come to rival groups like the Beatles and Rolling Stones in popularity. In fact, their single, "Glad All Over," had just knocked the Beatles' "I Want to Hold Your Hand" off the top of the UK Singles Chart in January 1964. *Catch Us If You Can* (or *Having A Wild Weekend*) was the title of the new project that Tony Woollard called me in on. It was going to be another film done all on location, starting in London… in what amounted to an early music to film spectacular like *Help!* Or *A Hard Day's Night,* films later done starring the Beatles.

"Come and meet me at this old church in Tottenham!" Tony sounded excited. "I think we can use it as a hangout for the bands!" So, the next day I met Tony, along with Ian Whitaker our set decorator. Manny Wynn was again with us as the film's DP and had also come along. And when I finally met up with them, I could understand why Tony had been so animated about this particular venue. It was perfect!

The director John Boorman showed up later with a crew, and so it all began: our somewhat hysterical few months' adventure with The Dave Clark Five. There were many locations that included travelling across the bay to Burgh Island off the coast of Devon, the Roman Baths in Bath, the Salisbury Plain, Kew Gardens, Smithfield Market, Syon House and the opening sequence in the Tabard Gardens Estate, London—these were a part of our nonstop schedule, each location more challenging than the other.

The actress Barbara Ferris was David Clark's love interest, and the cast chemistry could be a bit dodgy. But Ian and I had fun dressing out the empty church. This was John Boorman's first film as a director, but within the next years he went on to direct *Point Blank, Hell in the Pacific, Deliverance, Zardoz, Excalibur, The Emerald Forest, Hope and Glory, The*

*General, The Tailor of Panama* and *Queen and Country,* seeming able to work nonstop. Over his career, he has directed 22 films and received five Academy Award nominations, twice for Best Director—one for *Deliverance,* and the other for *Hope and Glory.* During what could have, in the wrong hands, been a disjointed mess, John proved to be so together, cool and laid back that *Catch Us If You Can* became a successful production, and I gained great respect for him, something I continue to have to this day.

What I have always so appreciated in these past 57 years of being part of any creative team are the variety of locations around the world that I have been honored to see. From the early predawn violet light to the golden hues of dusk, I have been blessed to behold a thousand different faces on planet earth—locations so far and wide; each one unique. I think that my favorite though is waking early in the deserts, where there is just such an overwhelming earth fragrance that on taking a few focused deep breaths my entire being felt compelled to say, "Thank you," to mother Earth.

*Sydney James and Joan Simms in* Carry on Cowboy.

# Fifteen

## *Blow Up* "Blows Up" the Production Code

*Blow Up!* The film is a snapshot of the 1960s, pun intended. The plot itself is a Chinese box dropped into a day in the life of a glamorous fashion photographer, Thomas (played by David Hemmings) and inspired by the adventures of real-life "Swinging London" photographer, David Bailey and other contemporaries such as Terence Donovan and David Montgomery.

The American release of this counterculture film with its explicit sexual content (by contemporary standards) was in direct defiance of the still rather strict Hollywood Production Code. Its subsequent critical and box-office acclaim proved to be one of the turning points that led to the final abandonment of the code in 1968 in favor of the MPA film rating system. In 2012, *Blow Up* was ranked Number 144 in the Sight & Sound critics' poll of the world's greatest films.

Michael Seymour, when I met him at Pinewood Studios, was the assistant Art Director working on *2001/A Space Odyssey*. He mentioned that he needed a little help on a small film that was going to shoot in

London with an Italian director Michelangelo Antonioni and produced by Carlo Ponti. He had not worked with the Art Director Asheton Gorton before. But he thought it would be great if I could come and join them just for a short while—to draw the interior that would be David Hemmings' studio apartment in the film. They had found a London location, a loft, and Asheton wanted to make major changes to create more verisimilitude. I was onboard.

To do so I had to tread a fine line, as I had promised Ray Simm that I would definitely be with him on his next project, a film called *The Wrong Box* that would start filming in six weeks time. Michael was happy now that he was able to let me get on with the job. I met Roger King who was also credited as an assistant art director. And the cast of players was luminous—a Who's Who of hot young up and coming actors at the time. Led by Hemmings and Vanessa Redgrave, the film also had Sarah Miles, John Castle, Jane Birkin and Verushka von Lendorff (the world's hottest model in the late 1960s) and even Jeff Beck, who played himself.

The year was 1966. And it turned out to be a turning point in the social revolution that was going on everywhere in Western Civilization. From the outset, the year was incendiary—with images of freedom protests, atom bombs, flower power, and on a distant continent there was an American nation divided by a war that nobody wanted. It was a time when all innocence was lost, and a generation rose up to express itself in a changing of the guard. In England, the rock and roll generation with countless new off-the-chart bands with tremendous talent and infinite repertoires continued to perpetuate the "British Invasion" of the US. And it worked…in spades.

Ernest Archer, who was one of the three art directors working on Stanley Kubrick's *2001 (A Space Odyssey)* called to see if I was free to come and spend a few weeks making models for some of their sets.

I mentioned that I was waiting for Ray who had booked me for his next project, *The Wrong Box*. When I went over to meet with Ernie, I stepped onto a soundstage where they were already constructing this phenomenal rotating interior of a Space Station. John Graysmark was standing with Harry Lange and Gus Walker, overlooking the set. (I had met John on the set of *Lord Jim:* but not Harry prior to that day. As it turned out, Harry and I would end up sharing offices in 1976 working on *Star Wars* at Elstree.)

Gus Walker, the construction manager was conferring over the details of how to place a camera within the circular inner floor so as to follow the hero when he had to circumnavigate the set as it rotated.

The personnel for Kubrick's Art Department alone numbered in the dozens: at least forty-seven people, eleven of whom were brilliant draftsmen. For my contribution, I found myself cutting cardboard, making a model of the Black Monolith set. I had painted a scenic backdrop of the stars to go around the model. Stanley Kubrick came over to look at it and asked me why it wasn't a photographic backdrop. I replied that I would get it fixed for him, finished the model and never saw him again. Within a few days I was back at Pinewood with Ray on *The Wrong Box*.

Directed by Bryan Forbes and Art directed by Ray Simm, *The Wrong Box* was a 19$^{th}$ Century period piece. And for my part it required some very focused work—hours on the drawing board with Ray peering over my shoulder, agonizing over every detail. The hardest job was drawing the train engine for a crash that would be a defining moment in the film. Somehow, it was easier to detail the Victorian and Georgian interiors with their ornate doors, staircases and moldings than it was the train itself, which was being constructed on the back lot at Pinewood Studios.

Imagine how I must have felt walking onto various sets and there were the glitterati of British film. John Mills, Ralph Richardson, Michael Caine, Peter Cook, Dudley Moore, Tony Hancock, Norman Rossington, Nanette Newman (Bryan Forbes' wife) and the utterly hilarious, always drunk, Wilfred Lawson—formed the core of this glorious ensemble of extremely gifted people…rounded off by Peter Sellers whose brief appearance was memorable enough.

And yet, in his way, it was Wilfred Lawson who captured the hearts of the crew, keeping us all in silent fits (and sniggers) in every scene he did with Caine. Wilfred was holding a tray and delivered his dialogue in such a slurred way, walking slowly towards Michael: "Mr. Michael, Mr. Michael!" I was the way he said it, drunk or not drunk, that it made it so hard not to laugh. Then again, I came to realize that that this was exactly why Bryan hired him for the part. His delivery even of those few lines was a classic.

All of the smaller roles were also strongly cast with several of the best comic actors England had to offer in that decade that turned out to be a heyday of British comedy. Some sections of the film were funnier than others, while others were unfortunately labored and dull. It is that sort of story, that sort of comedy. But it adds up to a lively lark. Peter Sellers only had two scenes in the entire film, but those two scenes, for the time that he was on, were two of the finest things Peter ever did.

During the shooting of *The Wrong Box,* we had a set that was Peter's doctor's office. It was surrounded by nets as a protective measure, as there were so many cats in the set, an opportunity to steal a scene not to be lost on Peter.

In a masterstroke of improvisation Peter, in costume and sitting at his desk, asked me somewhat offhandedly if I could find him a kitten. I did and, kitten in hand, shortly returned to the set, turned it over to him and then watched as he opened a drawer in the desk, placed the kitten inside and carefully closed it.

On the next call for "action," Michael Caine comes into the office intent upon persuading Peter to write him a prescription. Peter in turn takes a pen and places it in the inkwell, signs the paper, opens the drawer, takes out the kitten, uses it to blot the signature, then places the furry little guy back into the drawer and closes it. Bryan had no idea that Peter was going to do this, though it was so typical of Peter Sellers that he was always improvising, making the most of his comic genius in every frame of the film.

*Peter Sellers displays his improvisational genius, in* The Wrong Box.

The Wrong Box *Director Bryan Forbes also directed* Séance on a Wet Afternoon.

Around this time, I met Robert Montgomery and David Puttnam who was (later) made a Baron and a CBE for all his work in film, receiving the Best Picture Oscar for producing *Chariots of Fire,* and producing other film classics such as *The Mission* and *The Killing Fields.* Roby had left David's agency and was now acting as his own an agent for many successful fashion and portrait photographers. His brother David was a great portrait photographer, also celebrated for his work in fashion. Roby and his wife Sally became very close family friends, and we still see each other at their home in Kent.

He knew the work I had been doing in film design and wanted to know if I would be interested in designing sets for his clients' commercials and magazine stills. This was "bread and butter" work I continued to do for many years, meeting some of the best photographers in this field. Julian Cotterall had all his Folding Studio Field cameras built for him, and the film was developed by an assistant in the basement of his Kensington Home.

David, though, surprised me as the only cameras he used for his personal work were Woolworth's plastic ones. Roby, to his dismay, would have to rent all the cameras he used on his shoots and of course he had the clients pay for them. I worked on a kitchen spot with Clive Arrowsmith shooting the stills. I had mentioned to the clients that maybe we should not dress the kitchen as usual, as the cabinets were "the hero."

So, when they walked in there was only one orchid in a tall glass vase on the countertop. The sight of it in the midst of the stark surroundings was a classic. And they loved it so much it became their symbol for advertising for many a year, an offhanded bit of set decoration that turned out to be immortal.

One of the perks of Pinewood Studios turned out to be their terrific, ample bar, where Maurice Carter and Jack Maxsted would often spend their lunch. I had worked with them both on Becket and they were in the preproduction stages of designing *The Quiller Memorandum*, a spy thriller.

"Will you come and join us?" asked Jack, and I did. Brian Ackland-Snow and I were the draftsmen, Ferdinand Bellan was the scenic artist. Maurice, the art director, and Jack associate art director. The film was to be directed by Michael Anderson and written by Harold Pinter. It was another great cast, including George Segal, Senta Berger, Alec Guinness and Max Von Sydow with about a dozen locations in Germany that I scouted out with Jack.

Maurice had designed some wonderfully complex sets that were built on various stages at Pinewood where the construction crews were so accomplished with their decades of experience. The quality showed in the finished sets and models that they built. They were also responsible for all six of the Sean Connery Bond films designed by Ken Adam—*Dr. No, From Russia with Love, Goldfinger, Thunderball, You Only Live Twice* and *Diamonds are Forever*. Remembering the two phenomenal sets, the Rocket Volcano chamber and The Submarine docking bay, I was always impressed by the sheer size of those enormous sets, all built impeccably by first-rate craftsman.

In 1980, I did meet Ken again on stage at the MGM Studios on Washington Blvd, remembering as I walked onto the enormous Art Deco set for *Pennies From Heaven*. Ken had associate produced that one. Phillip Harrison was the Production designer with Ken's influence as the Visual Consultant.

There were many days that I would find myself walking behind Edward G Robinson, sitting having breakfast with Karl Malden, happening onto Alec Guinness dressed as Charles I, or watching the multi-talented Richard Harris laughing as he tap-danced while rehearsing his role as Oliver Cromwell. Judy Garland in the Pinewood Bar, Dirk Bogarde buying a beer in the Shepperton Churchill Pub—these scenes and so many others became the precious coin of my recollection, and were taken into account during those special moments of reflection and gratitude.

*The images from* Blow Up *that caused such a flap in 1966 would barely get a PG-13 today.*

# Sixteen

## The Tramp, the Countess, and a Chap Named Chaplin

Acknowledging the persistence of memory (or perhaps the persistence of cannabis) I recall that when I was ten years old I would go with my fishing rod on the 37 Bus to Richmond. When I got there, I would buy a quarter pound of Hemp seed from the tack shop. After that, I would go directly down to Richmond Bridge, walk along the bank past the boathouses set up my fishing post, throw in the Hemp and wait for the fish to bite. (Obviously the fish knew something we did not...that weed can be good for you☺)

Fast forward a decade and a half...and there I was yet again having just turned twenty-six, not yet entirely proud of myself but feeling some sense of personal progress after having worked on some notable features with great directors, gifted designers and (soon to be) immortal actors.

Having cultivated a strong work ethic if not a vast body of work, I was still playing the Sorcerer's apprentice under their mentorship, willing to learn everything I could. I find so few young craftsmen today devoted to that kind of growth, ready to undergo the grind, to do whatever the game or film or production demanded to make it right. To even know the lens required for a certain shot or how to ask a director of photography how he'd like to light this set, requires a certain discipline and application of skills. Calling oneself a production designer, one has to know the rules, and be able at least to sketch the scene in question.

"Work hard. Play hard!" That was our mantra in the 1960s. And no doubt about it, there were definitely many ways that one could enjoy the downtime—the weekends and all those other wonderful lost moments.

"The Gang," (let's call them that for now) were a very close the group of friends that would meet in the pub for a drink on Saturday—a couple of pints of Guinness that would end with a single Jamison whisky being tipped into the remaining pint. Then off to lunch, usually at the San Frediano, a trendy Italian Restaurant where we'd book a large table with eight plus male and female friends…whenever the mood struck anyone in our select group of rogues. Oodles of wine were poured with each course, ending with a glass of Zambooka topped with a handful of coffee beans, then home to one of the apartments.

There we would all roll and light up, shake and bake the remains of the day, then drift out into the evening with a buzz. How did we do it? I have no idea, but we did. Then to make a cake from Afghani Red that was soaked in Brandy for a week, delicious with a cup of tea.

Mondays would always come as a challenge, but challenges to be met. Monday as I was drawing up details of an interior German Kitchen for Quiller, getting a call from Gavin that Rose, one of our "ladies who do," had imbibed in our Afghani red/brandy sponge cake and had to be rushed off to hospital (utterly buzzed) while attempting to explain that she only had "two slices of cake" with her tea…and that she was feeling very strange.

This ritual of shake and bake weekends and long hard workweeks had a rather brief shelf life…because in a year or so my work became my World. And "workaholism" is an addiction that I proudly embrace.

During that time, one of the leading production designers in film, Don Ashton, became like a father to me, in some ways replacing that incomplete relationship I had always had with my own.

I worked with Don on *The Countess from Hong Kong* with none other than the living legend, Charlie Chaplin, directing Sophia Loren and Marlon Brando. We built the boat decks and the interiors of the boat cabins as well as the dining/reception areas all on stage at Pinewood Studios. Don was a phenomenal conceptual sketch artist and was able to create atmospheres that became their own protagonists.

Knowing that he had also designed *The Bridge on the River Kwai* I wanted to hear all the stories of how they had built that eponymous bridge. Working with Don was such a period of enrichment for me. And more than that, it was an honor for all of us to work with Chaplin our director.

Charlie Chaplin, one of the 10 most famous film personalities of the 20$^{th}$ Century, was truly a living legend, as well as a comic genius. His "Tramp" series was a masterpiece of comedy. And for the entire decade and a half from 1915 to 1929, he alternated with Doug Fairbanks and (Fairbanks' wife) Mary Pickford as the #1 World Box office draws…and they were all three forever in the top ten—a dynamic box office tandem of superstars rounded out by Rudolph Valentino, John Barrymore, Buster Keaton, Lon Chaney and Marion Davies among others—a pantheon that represented nearly 50% of Hollywood film revenues in any given year.

So powerful was this terrific trio that, along with director DW Griffith, they formed United Artists in 1920, an independent production company that rivaled the major studios in industry leverage and public appeal at least until 1931 when talkies changed everything.

Early one chilly winter morning when the cold air sharpens one's senses, I was walking along the covered exterior corridor at Pinewood. Approaching me from the other end was Charlie Chaplin himself, dressed in a long beige overcoat with a dark brown winter wool Trilby Fedora hat pulled forward down across his forehead. His wife Oona held onto his arm. And, if I remember correctly, she was wearing a long dark grey coat with a scarf wrapped around her shoulders. As they both walked towards me, they smiled, acknowledging me with a hearty "good morning," and I to them. I stopped, turned and on seeing them both walk away from me, reflecting upon what a phenomenal creative life that this man had had.

Charlie Chaplin's life formed the fabric of the ultimate rags-to-riches story. On a personal level, he was both poignant and definitively the Silent Screen's most iconic figure. Groundbreaking, controversial, outspoken, visionary, he was, for decades, the cinema's most famous comedian. And Chaplin and Winston Churchill became fast friends when they met at Hurst Castle in the late 1920s. By the 1930s, with the advent of "talkies," the game for Chaplin began to change. He was a redoubtable pacifist and social activist—an expression of political fervor that his later films many of which he both directed and produced…like the *Great Dictator*, *Limelight* and *Modern Times*. If you ever get a chance to hear his last speech in *the Great Dictator* do so, for it forewarned us all of the Gathering Storm of totalitarian rule throughout Europe and the advent of WWII.

Like Carl Foreman, Chaplin was also under watch by the House Un-American Activities Committee (HUAC) for his "questionable political affiliations." And (as a British Citizen) he was banned from re-entry to the US in 1952 following a film promotion for *Limelight*. So, he ended up living mainly in Switzerland, where he spent his final years and never returned to America.

Only when he was finally honored by the Motion Picture Academy, did Charlie Chaplin finally come back to the USA for a brief stay, primarily to receive his Honorary Oscar in 1972, a much-deserved award that netted him a three-minute standing ovation.

To round out the fact that Chaplin was the consummate Renaissance man, consider his music scores for his films, all composed by him, *Lime-*

*light*, is the classic cinematic summary of Chaplin, the *auteur*—writing, directing, starring-in and composing the score for the entire film.

Aside from the experience of growing up surrounded by the songs of the music hall, Chaplin later recounted the story of that revelatory day that, "music entered my soul." Returning home from school to an empty house, he waited for hours for someone to arrive, then wandered off into the streets.

"Suddenly, there was music. Rapturous! It came from the vestibule of the White Heart corner pub, and resounded brilliantly in the empty square. The tune was 'The Honeysuckle and the Bee,' played with radiant virtuosity on a harmonium and clarinet. I had never been conscious of melody before, but this one was beautiful and lyrical, so blithe and gay, so warm and reassuring.

"I forgot my despair and crossed the road to where the musicians were. It was here that I first discovered music, or where I first learned its rare beauty, a beauty that has gladdened and haunted me from that moment."

In 1898, aged 9, Charlie began his own career in English music halls with a troupe of juvenile clog dancers called, "The Eight Lancashire Lads." The rest from there is a trip to America and an upward arc through

*The Kid and the Tramp.*

*[Left] Chaplin on the violin, circa 1971 (the consummate Renaissance man).
[Right] Chaplin receiving his Honorary Academy Award from
Jack Lemmon in 1972.*

a film career that even as early as 1916 found him becoming the most popular movie star in the world.

Legends persist. And his was indelible. So here I was working on a film directed by Charles Chaplin. And I really couldn't imagine it getting any better than this. Had I made it? Who was to say? But it felt like it at the time. I had an exciting career in film more than I had ever expected. I was only three years into this magical world of filmmaking, and the best was yet to come. Now it was time for preproduction on *The Countess from Hong Kong* and a cluster of luminescent stars that were the legends of their time.

I was given the job of drawing up the boats deck in perspective and the lifeboats themselves. It was quite a challenge but it all worked and then the interior of Sophia's onboard apartment. Brando had a hard time taking direction from Chaplin, as Chaplin was always precise, and Brando was frustrated that he wasn't allowed to just "wing it," which was what he always did best. Finally, Brando surrendered the power struggle and submitted to his every move being choreographed by his director. It made him look stiff on camera…and everyone knew the reason for it.

Sophia! Goddess! Just to be able to be within her presence on stage and seeing her walking through the corridor somehow brought me such deep feelings, not of desire but admiration—knowing all the great films that she had helped turn into legend. Back when movies were made for adults, there was no better, no more irresistibly sexy screen couple than Sophia Loren and fellow Italian (her dear friend) Marcello Mastroianni.

They were such a dynamic film duo, starring together in numerous films, including *Marriage Italian Style, La Bella Mugnala, Yesterday Today and Tomorrow, Vittorio,* and *A Special Day,* to name a few. In 1960, her acclaimed performance in Vittorio De Sica's, *Two Women* earned her a multitude of awards including Cannes, Venezia and Berlin festivals' best performance prizes, along with the distinction of being the first actress to win an Academy Award (Best Actress) for a non-English language performance.

One morning, having left the office, I was walking down the long corridor towards the glass doors that led out to an area that I often took to go for breakfast in the studio canteen. There was another entrance 90 degrees to the right. I saw Sophia open the double doors and on seeing me closed them, as I walked past the side glass door she opened it: "Good morning, Alan," she said thoughtfully, walking past me with a perfect smile on her face. Turning back as I turned to see her, she continued up the corridor. Obviously, my heart skipped a beat. Sophia had smiled at me (and called me by my name). It wasn't something a young man of my tender years would ever forget.

Memorable as well were the "chance" exchanges I also had with Marlon Brando about that time. I had a friend who lived in an apartment in Marble Arch, and Martine Beswick, an actress who appeared in *From Russia With Love* lived just above him. Brando, while he was filming *Countess,* was dating Martine's sister at the time, and I would invariably bump into them at the various clubs and restaurants that we all honed to.

Slim, trim, chiseled, and in great shape when I met him, Brando was another film icon who is often regarded as the most influential method actor of his time. He was also going through a bit of a career crisis in

1967 that only a few people in the business knew about. Already a winner of an Oscar, a Golden Globe, three BAFTAs and a Cannes "Best Actor" for such films as *Viva Zapata, On the Waterfront, Julius Caesar* and *A Streetcar Named Desire,* Brando was hitting a rough patch, marred by some questionable film choices that he would not come out of until his career got a complete reboot with his Oscar-winning performance in *The Godfather* in 1972. Still, you never would have known it from my perspective, because "Bud" Brando was always gracious, magnetic, powerfully intelligent and fun to be around whenever we did cross paths.

The week that I was to leave the film, *The Countess from Hong Kong,* Charles Spencer Chaplin KBE signed a sketch I did of him in his old bowler hat. I could see he loved it. He visibly praised what I'd done and thanked me for all the work and time I had devoted to his film.

Vernon Dixon, our set decorator on *The Countess* knew that I was going to work next in Spain, and that my film was going to be shot in Torremolinos on the Costa Del Sol where he had an apartment. That's when he told me I could rent it from him if I liked! *(If I liked?! How could I not? How could I not love the life that was unfolding for me now—a constant surprise as if it had been part of a plan designed somewhere long ago?)*

We agreed on a price. And there I was about ten days later, walking the beach, eating fresh fish that had just been cooked on a small beach fire, sampling my first bowl of *Paella* and a large green tomato salad sprinkled with a little olive oil, pepper and salt—a tasty dish that's still a favorite after all these years.

It was all so perfect at this point—working a job I loved, visiting a country I'd never seen and doing a project with industry pros on the edge of a star-studded world. Was it all as easy as this? Of course, the answer was "no!" But contrast is what makes life all the sweeter when the good things arrive.

*Charlie Chaplin directs Sophia Loren and Marlon Brando based on one of Don Ashton's set designs for* Countess from Hong Kong.

*Marlin Brando and Sophia Loren on set of* The Countess From Hong Kong.

# Seventeen

## "I Think You'll be Okay!"

*Fathom* was the film this time. Maurice Carter was art directing yet again, and Jack was his assistant. Our cast included Anthony Franciosa, Raquel Welch and Ronald Fraser. The film was directed by Leslie Martinson, who did so many TV shows that it would be easy to dismiss his work as devoid of style. But if you were to see such projects as *PT 109* and *Batman,* simplicity would always prove to be something in his favor. John Dankworth, a jazz musician, wrote the score…and would later marry and partner with chanteuse Cleo Lane.

Raquel's appearance in Fathom, stunning in her variety of coloured bikinis, was fodder for a series of saucy movie posters. And, if you remember the iconic Farrah Fawcett poster of 1977, Raquel's in 1967 was the "original." I would imagine these Raquel posters helped jump-start the adolescence of about 40 million baby-boomer boys at the very least.

Her searing eyes, her sexy toothpaste smiles and her taut athletic poses were what made this movie a guilty-pleasure. She plays dumb, acts smart, skydives and gets some great lines in this twisty, surprisingly intelligent script, beautiful Spanish location and some colorful characters.

Tony Franciosa, one of the more underrated actors of his time, made the perfect leading man for her in his own gutsy style.

It had rained hard all night, one of those relentless downpours that never seemed to end. Philip, my brother, had just arrived and was staying with me in Vernon's apartment. I heard him screaming and ran into the bathroom, only to find him writhing in shock; he had been electrocuted! We discovered that all wires in and under the house were not insulated in plastic pipe—they were bare, exposed and "hot." The imminent dangers made the apartment uninhabitable and hazardous to one's health. So, Vernon and I found another apartment near the beach.

After drawing up the treasure from the Ming Dynasty and the elusive Fire Dragon (the object of the quest) Maurice decided that it would be a good idea for me to draw up the continuity sketches for the air combat sequences as well as the ocean speed boat chases. A dear friend, Peter Medak, whom I had met in Shepperton Studios, was going to direct the 2nd unit as well as being credited as Associate Producer. Peter was signed to direct television films for MCA Universal Pictures in 1963. In 1967, he signed with Paramount Pictures to make feature films. His first such film was *Negatives* in 1968. Some of his most notable other works were *The Ruling Class* in 1972, *The Changeling* (1980), *The Krays* (1990) and *Let Him Have It* (1991).

One morning John Kohn the producer came into our Malaga office. As he and Maurice came toward me, I could see that their semi-serious conversation was about to involve yours truly.

"Alan, John would like to know if you could direct the 2nd unit, starting tomorrow?" This invitation/challenge from Maurice stopped me in my tracks.

John followed through with, "You are the only one, Alan, who knows what has to be shot."

I went silent, looked around my desk, picked up the sheets of sketches and said, "You mean these?"

The reason for this unexpected assignment was that my friend Peter had been taken to hospital, with a case of septicemia, an infection he contracted from a contaminated cactus needle. What they found out later through their own forensics was that the needle they removed had come from a cactus that the local donkey was using for a piss break every morning.

Nervous, apprehensive and just a little bit exhilarated, I arrived at the airport and was introduced to Gilbert Majeure the Alouette II helicopter pilot and his two-man crew.

In broken English and French he asked, *"Alan avez-vous été dans un hélicoptère avant? (*Alan have you been in a helicopter before?)"

I replied, *"Non, je n'ai pas. Ce sera ma première fois.* (No, I haven't. This will be my first time.)"

*"Eh bien, venez vous asseoir ici, à la porte ouverte."* (Well come and sit here in the open door.)" He responded, pointing to the camera operator's seat. With my legs dangling out he strapped me in and we took off. He took us up to 10,000 feet and let the helicopter rotate down over the ocean…while my feet seemed to skim only about four feet above the waves.

He raced us towards the oncoming cliff, almost seeming to flirt with the ridge of it. Up and up we went to the top of a mountain and the helicopter gently found its rest. Due to taking in so many deep gulps of air, I was out of breath.

Gilbert came around and undid the harness. "I think you'll be okay, let's go back to the airport and decide what you would like to shoot first." He smiled, and before I knew it we were with the continuity script girl and looking at the sketches.

The ocean and boat-to-boat chase would be first shot in the sequence, followed by the air-to-air combat sequence. In a white suit and a wig Philip was Raquel's stand in. He cursed me for days as the plane flights made him sick, but was mollified a few days later with a pretty decent paycheck.

I spent the next five weeks in the air, twisting and turning and finally achieving what we did with the help of Gilbert. We formed a fast friendship out of those weekly junkets, and it saddened me greatly when I learned two years later that Gilbert had been killed during the filming of the *Battle of Britain* in Ireland in 1969.

Apparently during a dogfight in the air, a Biplane's wing broke off as it flew overhead and smashed into the blades of Gilbert's helicopter chopping them in half and causing the chopper to plunge down into Dublin Bay. Gilbert, his co-pilot and a famous Director of Photography named Skeets Kelly all perished as the copter broke into pieces…and sadly their bodies were never retrieved from the murky depths of the Bay.

Towards the end of this production, I met two rather lovely ladies in Malaga: Carol and Marion. Carol's mother had a small village home up in the mountains, and Marion, Carol's buddy, had been a member of the cast on The Dave Clark Five film *Catch Me If You Can*.

Driving or walking through the streets and lanes, I remember being surprised by the intricate design of the black and white pebbled narrow lanes in the small mountain village. Then when we all went to Granada and approached the Alhambra Palace, there again were the stones laid out in multifarious intricate patterns. It truly took our collective breath away as we passed through one architectural arched corridor, patios and exquisite rooms, sweeping along a seemingly infinite network of fountains—all of which combined to create an enchantment of Moorish Design.

The Alhambra Palace was added to the city of Granada area within the ramparts in the 9th century, which implied that the castle became a military fortress with a view over the entire city. In spite of this, it was not until the arrival of the first king of the Nasrid Dynasty, Mohammed Ben Al-Hamar (Mohammed I) in the 13th century that the royal residence was established in the Alhambra. This event heralded the beginning of the Alhambra's most glorious period and marked the Moors most enduring inroads into Spain.

Prior to arriving back in London, I had yet another call from Maurice Fowler (my original Art Director on *The Victors*) asking me if I would I like to meet him in Nairobi in two weeks…and was I free? He asked. I replied that I happened to be. And since I was, I accepted.

*Kenya!* I thought. *Can this be real?* The year was 1967 and I was already back in London. I went to meet Henry Hathaway who was going to direct *The Last Safari* with my friend Jamie Granger's father Stewart Granger.

Hathaway had just finished directing Steve McQueen and Karl Malden in the prequel to *The Carpetbaggers,* a film called *Nevada Smith* and one of my favorites some years earlier, *Niagara,* Marilyn Monroe's breakout film also starring Joseph Cotten.

When I arrived in my dark brown suede trench coat, I think he was surprised at the length of my hair but admitted that he liked the style of my coat. He told me a little bit about the film and said that he would meet me in the African bush, and that I had better make certain I had all the necessary inoculations. (And there were several.)

After I finished meeting with Henry, I went into another hotel room, signed my contract, picked up my ticket, and the deal was done. A week later, I was off. I had very little time to say hello or goodbye to my friends. I did find out, however that Gabriella Licudi was going to be co-starring in the film. Arguably one of the hottest actresses in town in 1967, this Casablanca born British beauty was just the screen fare for some big hits such as *Casino Royale* and many others. She and I had already been friends for a considerable time, so it was wonderful to have such a lovely spirit onboard for the film.

We met for a lunch a few days before we took off, and both expressed how excited we were to be able to go and be among all the wildlife in the Serengeti. (Little did I know how close I would be, but I'd find out soon enough.)

When I arrived in Kenya a few days later, Maurice Fowler was already there waiting for me at the Keekorok Lodge in the Maasai Mara…and so the new adventure began.

*Raquel and Richard Briers in a scene from* Fathom.

# Eighteen

# A Uniformity of the Law in Nature

The next four months in the African Bush working with my crew, was an experience no one could entirely prepare for. A young white Boer farmer, Bute Donhauser became my construction manager, forty Maasai tribesmen became my laborers, twelve Kirikuu carpenters and one Jelure driver—all these disparate elements and more combined to create a real shift in consciousness for the young man who was about to be given the responsibility of a lifetime...to that point!

I was resting in the Nairobi hotel only to be awakened to the fact that a pilot of a Cessna 350 plane was waiting for me in the lobby. Up and out, flying across the Savannah to Keekorok Lodge and standing there as we landed was Maurice. I still had not rested. I was shown into my lodge room. The aroma of the oils they used to protect the wood still lingers somewhere within me.

The head of this lodge was a great bearded Maasai who became my guide to the Mara. It was the first lodge to be built situated in the direct path of the migration of the African herds, and the wildlife was so abundant.

With virtually no rest, I took a quick shower and joined Maurice, who drove us in a Toyota Jeep through twelve miles of dirt track roads where I saw my very first giraffe and zebra. In the distance I could see looming up an outcrop of rather large boulders sufficiently daunting to bring the Jeep to a stop. Maurice pointed out what seemed to be a pack of wild dogs, some of the ugliest canines I'd ever seen.

"Whatever you do," Maurice cautioned gravely, "do not think you can get anywhere close to them. Stay far away, and do not dismount. They are incredibly dangerous!" Caution given and duly noted, we drove on, gingerly navigating a patch of road that was tricky driving at best.

Along the way, I quickly learned that Nature has a power that is both astonishing and humbling all at once. It is a bond that unites man to the world he lives in and awakens some vestigial sense of self inside us all. I know that I discovered an intense joy, because it was during that time that I found each day carries with it a primal awareness of our connectedness to the natural world. I know I found it early on … through the unique relationship with my crew or with a pride of lions or a herd of Cape buffalo, or hippos…or the zebras, gazelles, giraffes and cheetahs—so many African animals that formed a living landscape of flourishing life as far as the eye could see. Implicit with all this was the silent understanding that I belonged there with them. I was a living cell on that body. It was a discovery of myself, within myself and outside of myself, that brought on a shared consciousness and inside it a new silent joy.

Now, for a London street kid with very little exposure to the primal essence of all life, I experienced a rush I had never known before: *a uniformity of the Law in Nature,* something akin to what the first explorers must have felt. Had the world been a stranger to me until then? Maybe not! But, upon reflection, I know that this is what was happening within my soul's perception, and this "powerful play" of Nature was definitely a tectonic shift in my consciousness that united me to all that was below, above and surrounding my being on that primeval Continent…called Africa!

On this same day and our first foray into the bush, we approached a river and stopped. Maurice got out and proceeded to tell me that this is where we were going to build our set—a ferry, a village, a chief's hut and an expanded meeting compound. He then gave me a small drawing saying as he handed it to me that, for reference, there were a couple of books in the Lodge that I could have, while he (Maurice) was going back to Nairobi to find various props for the village."

"Well Maurice," I was moved to ask, "…who is going to help me here?"

"There is a young farmer who will be arriving tomorrow, and he will be your construction coordinator. He will have arranged everything, so have no worries," Maurice assured me.

That was that, or so I thought. And I only saw Maurice five times again during the four months that I lived in Kenya. The next day just before Maurice got ready to leave, we were both sitting in the shade of a large Thorn tree, selecting dressing details from the two books he had brought along. An open backed old green Toyota truck approached us and stopped. Standing in the back were two impressive African men classically dressed in old safari jackets, hats and vests. Both were Maasai, Doctari and Tigisi, and both were holding rifles. Out of the cab just behind them stepped Bute Donhauser, my construction coordinator. (I'll have to give the man one thing: he knew how to make an entrance.)

Later that day, Maurice flew back to Nairobi, while Bute with his two-man entourage drove us all down to the river. As I was going to spearhead the project, I asked every single question I could in order to build on this out-of-the-way location, our village and ferry. That evening we shared stories of our upbringings and all the steps that had led us to this moment in time: splitting a bottle of good red wine while looking out to see elephants drinking and showering at the waterhole in front of us.

The next day a flatbed truck arrived at the river with a bulldozer on it. A road was established, along with an area for the village huts alongside the riverbank, the chief's area and a landing strip for a small plane—our own little pocket of "civilization."

I was able to sleep one more night at the Lodge. Then Bute set up a campsite not far from the river. My forty Maasai laborers came with two cows, twelve Kirikuu carpenters and my driver, a very tall, blue-black, compassionate Jelure fisherman. (This was to be my crew for the next twelve weeks.)

The Maasai are considered among the tallest people in the world, with an average height of 6 feet 3 inches. The Maasai meet most of their food needs through their herding of cattle, along with several indigenously grown root vegetables. They eat the meat, drink the milk and also the blood of the oxen. Although the Maasai's entire way of life is historically dependent upon their cattle, more recently, with their herds dwindling, the Maasai have grown dependent on food such as sorghum, rice, potatoes and cabbage known to the Maasai as goat leaves.

One abandoned tradition of the Maasai tribesman is that each young man is supposed to kill a lion before he is circumcised. Since roving lion prides were constantly at odds with the indigenous tribes, lion hunting over the generations had not only become a cleansing ritual but also a matter of survival. Now, however, all lion hunting has been banned in East Africa. Increasing concern regarding lion populations has given rise to at least one program that promotes accepting compensation when a lion kills some of a tribe's livestock, rather than hunting and killing the predator.

Inside that is a tradition as old as time (and one that is hard to resist). Even now, killing a lion gives one great status inside the Maasai community. Their music traditionally consists of rhythms provided by a chorus of vocalists singing harmonies while a song leader, or *olaranyani* sings the melody. Women chant lullabies, hum songs, and compose melodies praising their sons.

In all their melodic mantras, the Maasai often chant *Nambas,* which are a set of call-and-response patterns, a seeming repetition of nonsensical phrases and monophonic melodies. Phrases are repeated following each verse being sung on a descending scale, and in the process of singing the females often respond to their own verses, creating a kind of chorus for their own work. When many Maasai women gather together, they sing and dance among themselves. Polyandry (the custom whereby a woman takes many husbands) was also practiced until the middle of last century. In the old Maasai tradition, a woman married not only her husband but also the entire age group. Men were expected to give up their bed to a visiting age-mate guest. The woman decides strictly on her own if she will join the visiting male…so the power was always in her hands to accept or reject the proposal.

In the Serengeti today, this practice has been abandoned. But apparently the practice of polyandry was still in force when I was there, because upon my arrival, the Maasai offered me a beautiful tall young woman who was covered in red mud on her forehead and ornate beads around her neck and arms. They were proud of their gesture, though not offended when I declined their "generous" offer. Doctari was listening to the young woman as she pointed to me, finally admitting through his laughter: "She thinks you're ugly Mr. Alan!"

On the very first night I spent in camp, I was jolted out of my cot by some deep animal grunts and snorts just as an immense shadow loomed to one side of my tent. Upon peering out, I saw a huge hippopotamus, and I froze. Out of some unexpected respect for my position as "boss man," the locals thought I would want to be off by myself. But with the "hippo encounter," they immediately moved my tent further into the camp.

We lived like this at this location for approximately five weeks, sometimes returning to the Lodge for a good night's sleep and a hot bath. We ordered supplies and food from a crank-generated shortwave radio that we also used to communicate with the production office in Nairobi. I had my own cook, whom I called *Peche*, later to find out that it actually did mean "cook." He would always bring me a pot of tea at the set by the river around 3 p.m. There I would sit and often see some of the men fish and catch large headed squeaking catfish for their dinner.

The village was almost complete, but we still had to distress it to give it that "timeworn" patina. I told the crew to get red dirt and turn it into semi liquid mud and splash it on the base of all the huts, this gave it the look that was required. The Ferry was ready to take the guiding rope across the river to attach to a huge tree on the far bank, well, not too far. There were huge hippos that would, upon mating, sound like speedboats hurtling through the river. Nobody was willing to swim the rope across, so guess who decided to set a "good example?!" (What was I thinking?)

I attached a smaller line to the large guide rope and swam as fast as I could to the other side. As I was tying the rope around the tree I heard that all-too-familiar call: "Hey, Kid!"

As I looked up from my derring-do there was Henry Hathaway, Gabriela, Ted Moore the DP, Stewart Granger and Jamie standing on the other side.

I swam back and stood looking up at them, not receiving quite the accolades I'd expected.

"Don't you ever let me see you do that again, Kid!" Henry said as I climbed up to greet them in my skimpy red briefs. He then shifted from his stern Dutch uncle to address the issue at hand. "So, Kid, it is looking great! But I have to make a change over there in the chief's area. I want to move his tribal council center closer to his hut. Do you have the sketch and plan that Maurice gave you?"

"Yes, in my tent, sir," I replied.

"Then go get it, Kid!" (Gabriela would tell me months later how cute I looked running away from them in those little red briefs while Henry looked on, smoking his green cigar and laughing.)

I returned in a few minutes and handed Hathaway the small sketch, which didn't seem to net the desired result.

"This is it?! That's all?!" He made a face as if he'd just eaten bad eggs. "This is all he gave you?! You're my art director now. Let's walk over to the chief's area, and I'll show you what I would like." He took another chomp on his "stogie" and motioned to the others to follow.

During the first few weeks, the Maasai had become very protective of me, and two of them would always accompany me as I walked down to the river location. For certain reasons I could not define, I had earned their respect. (I suppose that not trying is perhaps the key to earning such camaraderie.)

The Maasai are a marvelous lot. They are unique among the world's tribes in that they have never assimilated into society as we define it. When they dance, the men jump and rise high, higher and higher in a ritualized attempt to outdo themselves. I tried to mimic their graceful movements, but couldn't get anywhere near their height. And apparently my ineptitude struck their funny bone, because every time I tried, they would all burst into hysterical laughter.

Out of tradition and some tribal belief in its potency, they would all drink from the blood of a freshly slaughtered cow. One day for their food one of them took a huge Panga knife pressed just below the cow's neck, punched it quickly and killed it in one stroke. I turned away as they began to disembowel the beast, channeling the blood into a special gourd.

Once a week, Bute would go into the wild and return with a small antelope to feed the crew and the carpenters. The meat was extremely rich and lean. Early in the morning as the sun began to rise I would often get into my Jeep and drive to catch a glimpse of a pride of lions. Fascinated and feeling connected, I would sit there and observe them for a while, feeling somehow immersed in their feral energy, noting the doting mothers so tender with their young. One day we were driving back from Nairobi and we passed a mother zebra giving birth. We lingered there too long and the baby decided we were its mother. It tried to follow us, but the loyalty didn't last long. Of course, we left, and the young zebra returned to its own mother.

A sand river ran parallel to our camp. Sometimes Peche would dig a hole in it, and in the evening it would be full of water. Hot and tired from a long day's work, it was just the perfect place to bathe. I was there enjoying my evening bath when I heard two throaty growls that would unsettle just about anyone with half a mind.

Reluctantly but carefully, I looked back over my shoulder, and upon turning saw two young male lions standing only about 20 yards away. Knowing that 20 yards could be covered in about two seconds, I got up very slowly and walked naked into the camp where all the Maasai were having their food. Apparently, my nude flight from the curious young lions was fodder for their version of farce. There was so much laughter I thought it would never stop, and then just as quickly two Maasai Morans (male warriors) took up their spears and chased the lions away.

*Photo of bathing in the river. Courtesy of Jamie Stewart Granger.*

There was one incident though where Doctari was making me a Rungu, a wooden throwing club that is especially associated with the Morans who traditionally used them in warfare and for hunting, along with the Panga, a form of machete which, when finished, looks like a small sword.

There was a Kikuyu driver wanting a tin of spam for himself and continued to argue with me for it, even though I offered to share it. Doctari picked up the Rungu and smashed the driver across his head. All hell broke loose, and a melee ensued, which was shortly put to rest, as my driver being the size he was managed to break up the fight. The injured man was placed into my jeep and became my responsibility. And as I was indirectly the cause of this, I alone drove him into the pitch of night through the bush and up to the lodge.

Upon arriving, I discovered that the head Maasai didn't seem too concerned about all the blood that was splattered all over me, or the wound on the man's head—they were only concerned because it was illegal and very dangerous to drive through the pampas at night.

Mazima Springs, a crystal-clear flowing waterway, was fed by the melting snows of the majestic Mount Kilimanjaro. The waters were clear as glass, but their depths were replete with hippos—friendly faces weighing a ton and just waiting around the bottom to make a meal of anything that happened to swim or stroke by. (Otherwise, they would just wait for nightfall to come on land to eat the variety of plant life, munching on them without a second thought about us.)

Finding the location a perfect spot, we took a position set back from the bank and built a tree house. Once we'd completed construction, we climbed up to sleep in it believing ourselves to be safe from predators or any kind of incursion; that was our first mistake. On waking in the morning, I realized that I couldn't find my shoes. After scrambling around a bit, I discovered that the chattering monkeys in the trees above us had found them a point of fascination, and had pinched them and run off to test them out as new toys.

In our new Rift valley location my construction chief, Bute, had to cut a road from the top escarpment down through the jungle to a base area where Hathaway wanted to establish a village. Henry, upon arriving with the crew, saw the village from the top of the escarpment and called down to me. I ran up the narrow path we had also cut into the two hundred feet high face of the hillside.

"Looks great, Kid. Now let's talk about the next set," Henry quickly observed. "Now I want you to take a baobab tree and place it as close to the edge of the rocks as you can to the location we agreed to take by the river. Do you think you can do that?" he asked, then smiled and drifted away.

I looked over at Bute, quizzically. "A baobab? Aren't they huge?"

They were, and we knew it. But that was the challenge—always to make things work. "Let's go find one we can handle," Bute replied with a broad grin.

Assignment made; assignment accepted. Now I had to find that tree and leave the safe haven of our encampment to do it. I told the prop master not to add any paraffin to ignite those two huts for the burn. "They have been fire-retarded," I reminded him.

Bute and I located a tree. Then we drove his open backed truck up to the baobab and attached lines to it, pulling it taut enough so it would fall partially onto the flatbed area. Somehow, we managed to drive it to the location and, with a winch, pulled it into position very close to an outcrop of rock. (Believe me when I tell you that only one large crowbar held it upright!) I looked down below to see three crocodiles, one at least 20-feeet long, basking in the shallows of the river hoping that the tree would stay there until the crew arrived in the morning.

Upon our return to the Rift valley encampment, we were horrified to discover that half the village had been razed, burnt to the ground. The prop master had entirely ignored my request and added paraffin to the roof of every single hut. Where was he, I had to wonder. He was nowhere to be found. As it turned out, I wouldn't have to reprimand him, or give him his notice. The deed had already been done.

Henry saw me walking down towards him and said, "Hey ,Kid, I fired the prop man. I want to shoot the village tomorrow. Can you rebuild it for me?"

"I'll certainly try!" I answered, knowing the job ahead would leave me with a sleepless night and a bunch of unanswered questions.

That night, my crew all worked by lamplight and in the pre-dawn morning, there it stood—half a village rebuilt. I looked up and there was Henry Hathaway, looking down at me from the edge of the escarpment. The crew came down the jungle road and I climbed up the narrow path to my tent.

I was awakened around 11 a.m. by a young PA who said, "Henry wants to see you," then quickly closed the tent flap.

Pulling myself together after about four hours sleep, I stumbled down the path to the set and up to meet with Henry. Beaming, he simply regarded me, smiled and said "Thank you, Kid! Thank you!" It was just about all he said, a bit of terse praise, later echoed more effusively by Stewart Granger and members of the cast.

I pointed to Bute and some of the Kirikuu and emphasized, "We have to thank those lads, too!"

For reasons probably lost to me now as these days, I travel light, I had brought my wind-up record player with me from England and would occasionally play music on it for the crew. The Maasai loved to hear the Beach Boys "Good Vibrations" and would continue to really enjoy their dance, jumping high and requesting encores again and again.

Doing a doodle for them in my sketch pad, I tried to describe a satellite as it moved slowly across the star-studded sky. I was trying to explain it for what it was.

Simon, one of the carpenters on our last day, said, "Master Alan, you do not smell anymore!" I'd never realized that when we first met my body odor was as unpleasant to them, as theirs was to me. My hair was now very red, and my body so tanned, I was smelling like a jungle buck with the sweet bouquet of the Serengeti upon me.

I learned while I was in Kenya exactly how their President Jomo Kenyatta had come into power after the bloody Mau Mau rebellion, which he in fact had led. (Like Menachem Begin before him and Nelson

Mandela after him, Kenyatta, too, had gone from "freedom fighter" to president, doffing the mantle of terrorist and donning the aura of the leader of a nation.)

In retrospect, so many farmers had died and others lost their fertile resource-rich land that supplied England and Europe with so much food during the war with Germany, that it was a devastation from which they never quite recovered. The local people were given an acre, each of those farms, and thus the country went into famine relief. Thousands who held English passports were given the choice to stay and accept the new regime, or to leave and return to England now that the land had become the nation of Kenya.

Many, many more tales came from this trip. What an experience. I have wonderful memories of the morning Savannah winds drifting through thorn trees as I sat in the jeep perilously close to a restive lion pride.

I flew down to South Africa and met cousin Michael in Johannesburg. He took me to see Victoria Falls (in what is now Zambia). From there we took off south to Durban where I visited and spent time with my mother's brother Frank who was a very successful construction engineer. I was very put off however to see just how his wife treated the home help and how inhumanely the black Africans were treated by the whites. Apartheid was in full fettle back in the late 1960s. And even the mixed races—Indians, Arabs and Asians or blacks with whites—were looked upon by both black and whites with both contempt and distrust.

One evening though we were hit by shattering shafts of lightning followed by deafening thunderclaps that cut into the sky and did not cease until the early dawn: the gods of Creation bidding farewell to an Africa in flux.

After working with Henry Hathaway in Africa, I sat having breakfast with Karl Malden one morning in Pinewood studios canteen. We talked about our experiences with Henry and his countless films. Best known for his Westerns, especially ones starring Randolph Scott and John Wayne, he also directed Gary Cooper in seven films, one of which he spent some time in India supervising filming of scenes for *The Lives of a Bengal Lancer* (1935). This film was an unexpectedly huge hit and received seven Academy Award nominations, including one for Best Picture. Oddly enough, it turned out to be Hathaway's only Oscar nomination for Best Director. Just to let you know a little more of the man who I walked with in the African bush, here are a few of the films he directed:

In 1925, Henry began working in silent films as an assistant to notable directors such as Victor Fleming and Josef von Sternberg and made the transition to sound with them. He was the assistant director to Fred Niblo in the 1925 version of *Ben Hur* starring Francis X. Bushman and Ramon Novarro. During the remainder of the 1920s, he learned his craft as an assistant, helping direct future stars such as Gary Cooper, Marlene Dietrich and Fay Wray, That was the first few years. Much later he moved over to 20th Century Fox where he directed the studio's biggest male star, Tyrone Power, in *Johnny Apollo (*1940) and *Brigham Young* (1940). Then, he went back to Paramount to direct John Wayne in *The Shepherd of the Hills* (1941).

During the 1940s, he began making films in a semi documentary vein, often using the film noir style. These included *The House on 92nd Street* (1945) for which he received a Best Director nomination from the New York Film Critics Circle. He returned to adventure films with *Down to the Sea in Ships* (1949). He was reunited with Tyrone Power for *The Black Rose (1950). The Desert Fox: The Story of Rommel* (1951). He also directed Marilyn Monroe in the film noir classic, *Niagara* (1953) something I'd mentioned before ... and *White Witch Doctor* (1953) with Susan Hayward and Robert Mitchum. He was reunited with Cooper and Susan Hayward on *Garden of Evil* (1954), a Western with a surprisingly gritty plot.

At nights during and after the evening meal Henry shared so many jokes and funny anecdotes and would have us all in fits of laughter with recounting the antics of the some of the leading men and ladies who had starred in so many of his films. Henry was truly the director's director, and I'll always remember him fondly with that trademark big green cigar in his mouth leaning into the camera:

"Turn over ... Ready ... Steady ... Go!"

*Henry Hathaway (middle) confers with Kas Garras and Stewart Granger on the next shot for* The Last Safari.

# Nineteen

## Alpha. Omega. Cinecittá. And Two Close Brushes with Death

**By the spring of 1968,** I no longer had my Fiat. I had loaned it to my brother Philip upon his return from Spain, and soon after it became a memory—crashed, smashed…and totaled! In London I no longer had a place to rest my head. So temporarily at least—and without intending to—I had become a gypsy. But it wasn't quite as apocalyptic as it might had seemed. Since I had returned from filming in Africa, I'd saved money I had made from my work on *The Last Safari* and bought myself a dark green Alfa Romeo/*Giulia Sprint GT.* So… I was a gypsy with a very hot sports car. ☺

One afternoon while having lunch in Casserole Restaurant I met Kiki Byrne who had been the costume designer on *Fathom*. Kiki lived just off Kings Road and invited me to stay in her guest room. By that time, Kiki had become a successful fashion designer, and her main competition happened to be Mary Quant. Along with her high-fashion designs, Kiki had garnered considerable success as a film costume designer. She created the golden bikini worn by Margaret Nolan in the very sensual title sequences of the 1964 James Bond film *Goldfinger*, that her then boyfriend, Robert Brownjohn designed. Another film that she costumed for was *Perfect Friday*, and she collaborated with Gina Fratini on Anthony Newley's stage production of *Stop the World: I Want to Get Off*.

It was at this time that I first met Rachel, the remarkable woman who has been my life companion these past 47 years. I ran up some stairs and knocked on my friend's door. And no sooner had I done so than this stunning young woman I did not know flung the door open wide. I asked if my friend was in. He wasn't. But I found myself confessing to this beautiful stranger that I was only stopping in order to use the bathroom.

Somewhat amused, she let me in. I made a quick phone call and, upon leaving, was moved to tell her: "You should not let anyone you do not know in again." (For reasons I could not explain at the time, I felt protective of her. They would be revealed to me in detail a bit further down the line.)

A few days later, Robert Brownjohn had arrived back from New York and promptly kicked me out of the guest room. The timing was one of pure synchronicity, since Bill Hutchinson had just called me for a booking, and I was out of the door and on my way to Rome, Italy and my next adventure.

I took my new Alfa Romeo, driving it "from London to Rome." And what an unforgettable drive it turned out to be! Packing lightly, I left Chelsea at 5 a.m., took the ferry from Dover to Cherbourg, drove down through the picturesque French countryside, and arrived at Lake Lucerne, Switzerland precisely at 5:45 p.m., that same evening.

The next morning, I woke up to rain, and it pelted rain all the way down to Rome. And yet here I was during the entire drive absolutely in "the zone," that feeling race-drivers tell me they get when you and the car are totally one within every change of the gear and turn on the road to *Caput Mundi!*

As I drew nearer to Rome (and lacking anything remotely resembling GPS) I wondered how I was going to find the Via Veneto? I had arranged to meet Bill at a hotel along what amounts to being Rome's main drag, and I was virtually flying by the seat of my pants. Somehow, I managed to navigate my way straight towards Rome *vis-à-vis* the Via Veneto archway just after 6 p.m. that same evening. And since there are no accidents, I had to look upon it as fortuitous that everything just fell into place. Perhaps not surprisingly, the rain stopped the moment I got there.

What a scene appeared before my eyes as I drove slowly, looking for the hotel. (Was it on the right or the left?) So many well-turned-out people walking and sitting at the sidewalk cafés, coffee bars and restaurants—all of them styled to the nines. That night I read the screenplay, and followed Bill early the next day with the Alfa navigating in the ancient chariot ruts along the classic Apian Way—past the aqueducts, old Roman tombs, catacombs and statues, canopy pines and down through the gates of *Cinecittá* film studios.

This was going to be my reality for the next four months on a film called *The Adventures of Gerard* based on the "Brigadier Gerard" stories by

*My 1968 Alfa Romeo Giulia Sprint GT*

Arthur Conan Doyle. The film was to be directed by Jerzy Skolimowski, someone I remembered seeing as an actor in Roman Polanski's *Knife in the Water*. The cast included the great stage actor Peter McEnery, the beautiful Claudia Cardinale, Mark Burns, Norman Rossington, and Jack Hawkins, with Eli Wallach as Napoleon. It was an adventure/comedy, and the adventure seemed far more satirical than serious, set in the time of the Napoleonic Wars.

Our office complex was on the corner of one of the studio buildings, a space I shared with Bill's son Tim, Ken Muggleston, the set dresser, and Alessandro Alberti. Hutchinson mentioned that there was much to see here at Cinecittá, suggesting that I at least join with Tim and take a walk. We went through the plaster shop and there, hanging on the walls, were molds of most of all the ancient columns, caps and details from the smallest to the largest. Then we walked onto the back lot to see the set that was built for Franco Zeffirelli's *Romeo and Juliet*. It is so hard to describe what lay before us—the streets, squares, fountains and a church—we had just stepped back in time into the 14$^{th}$ century city of Verona.

Back on the drawing board, I started to design and draw up the Napoleon army camp that was set around an old bullring and a water mill. A large head at my shoulder height passed my window. I thought this was weird. So, I ran outside, and there was a giant of a man on a

*Peter McEnery, Eli Wallach and Claudia Cardinale in*
The Adventures of Gerard.

small Moped that seemed so out of place. More than curious I followed him as he went into an open stage.

I stood. And there to my utter surprise was Federico Fellini, my Master hero director, setting up a shot on a candlelit set of naked male and female extras in a large tub of water. This was one of his sets for Fellini/ *Satyricon.*

Norman Rossington, who I shared an apartment with in Piazza Santa Maria in Trastevere, had been in the Beatles' first film *A Hard Day's Night* as their "Roady." Peter, Norman, Mark and I used to hang out some evenings at a local pizza parlor, which tended to be a bit more atmospheric in Italy (and with far better pizza).

Once, on a lark, we all dressed in costume of the French Lieutenants (and these three great actors, who had all done Shakespeare most of their careers) spontaneously reciting from the works of the Bard, and continuing to do so during the course of the evening—all to the utter delight of the locals, only a few of whom understood English.

Norman had recently received *The White Album* from John Lennon, and on Sunday we placed the record player on our balcony and broadcast it out over the Piazza Santa Maria for the rest of the day. The Plaza was filled with people of all ages from that area, including many tourists. What began as a spontaneous concert, carried over into the night with a wild kind of "street bash" and people rollicking to the Beatles great new sounds!

*Meyer's Handbook of Ornament,* the art department reference bible, was there on every corner that I turned in the city of Rome. And in a short time, I was standing with my hands on the 2,000-year-old doors built by Hadrian for the Pantheon. Even after 1800 years, they still opened and closed. Bernini's fountains, Michelangelo's *Pietá,* his frescoes on the Sistine Chapel, which I since rediscovered having read *The Agony and The Ecstasy,* along with 400 of Michelangelo's personal letters—all these and more formed the moveable feast that soon became the Rome of my long held fantasies. It was one of his last works, as he was 84 when he was finally commissioned to design St. Peter's Basilica in the Vatican, passing from this earth age 88 in 1564. He was a Renaissance sculptor, painter, architect and poet who exerted an unparalleled influence on the development of Western art.

Browsing through all the architectural wonders that still stand—like the Coliseum and the Forum—the cultural antiquity of past human ages made me thankful that the film world had enabled me to travel and see all that I was able to see in such a new light.

We built various sets in the studio, and on locations in a mountain area where we created a battlefield. In Anzio, where I ran the construction and design of the Napoleon camp, we set up in marshland beyond the beaches of Anzio.

It was fairly easy to clear and create a lake for the water mill. The director, Jerzy Skolimowski, arrived and took a walk around the bullring we had built. After a brief reconnoiter, he stopped, turned to me and observed, "Alan, I do not like those green trees."

The "green trees" that so offended Skolimowski's sensibilities were part of a forest that rimmed the area. I ordered three water tanks and loaded them with three large sacks of coloured powder. The trees were sprayed for two days and suddenly it was pre-autumn. Everything had turned golden and red, and Jerzy was more than content and ready to shoot the following day.

I was asked by production to go to look for a river in Sicily, as they could not find a shallow enough river for Peter to ride his horse through. I was told that a car would be waiting for me and that I would be safe. I drove around various areas and, whenever I stopped, there was always the same car behind me that I had seen since leaving the airport. I spent three days unable to find a river that would work.

Upon arriving back at the airport, I was suddenly made aware that there was nowhere for me to leave the car. I took my bag, acknowledging the two silent men who were now standing outside of their car. And they in turn acknowledged me for the first time with broad toothpaste grins and a hearty wave. On arriving back at the studio, the production manager told me that they were from a Mafia family and had been told to make certain I was safe.

After we had completed the film, Norman drove with me along the winding Italian roads, twisting and undulating up and down through the mountain tunnels of Italy and into France. We had decided to go back to London via Paris.

We by-passed Dijon and were on an auto route that had just turned into a wide freeway when I saw a farmer with his donkey cart trudging across the freeway 200 yards ahead of us. Another car was approaching going the other way—no time to decide! I double-clutched, downshifted, decelerated then just as quickly double-clutched and accelerated, somehow causing the Alfa to jump to the left and then back to the right just as a French ambulance sped past us, missing the Alfa by maybe an inch. Norman almost fainted as the car was a right-hand drive, and all he could see was the fast approaching vehicle as it came looming towards him barely missing the left side of the Alfa.

After that "close encounter," we pulled off to the side of the road, opened the trunk and drank the remaining half bottle of single malt. Today, I still have no idea how my car did what it did. But for that brief nanosecond of time, the Hand of Grace turned me into Juan Fangio… and it managed to save our butts.

After arriving home on the 22nd of December, I was invited by Don Ashton and his two daughters, Lorraine and Marilyn (now close friends), for dinner on Christmas Eve.

In the morning, Marilyn took one look at me and exclaimed, "You're yellow, Alan!" After that she called her father, Don, who immediately got me to a doctor. The doctor quickly diagnosed me as having contracted jaundice—the wrong diagnosis, as it turned out. It was actually contagious Hepatitis A, no doubt from all the oysters in the restaurant where I'd spent most of my lunches when working on Napoleon's camp. (So much for eating shellfish in Anzio!)

In a sort of left-handed blessing, I was well cared for during my recovery. Don would not let me leave. In fact, he made every effort to see to it that I was looked after day and night. I spent literally three long months in the attic bedroom, being tended to and cared for by Marilyn.

My mother came to visit me once. While I lay there in and out of consciousness for the first three weeks, there were times when I thought I was hearing a beautiful voice. Maybe it was just my state of being at that time. There was a feeling that I was not going to get through the disease: that was when those silent thoughts drifted in and out.

One afternoon, as I lay in bed, a deep enveloping voice began to speak. *"Make your life equal to those of the laws of Nature. You are one with Creation's Eternal Gift."* I questioned the reality of the voice, and yet I knew that I had heard it. I did not mention this to Don, Marilyn or Lorraine at the time.

There was a change coming in my life, and I began to slowly understand that there was no limit to the depth of my feelings of love, and that there could even be an inner unspoken, silent joy that I might be able to tap into.

# Twenty

## "The Lion" in Provence

By the time I was able to leave Don Ashton's Georgian retreat three months later, I was a rake. That entire quarter of a year had nearly done me in. Bone-thin and slow to regain any real semblance of vitality, I drove to Shepperton Studios, where Peter Murton had called me into pre-production on *The Lion in Winter*. In the office complex, I found Ted Clements and Peter James in conference again, this time with a scenic artist named Peter Melrose.

Anthony Harvey was to direct. The film's marquee cast, virtually thrown together in two weeks, would star Katharine Hepburn and Peter O'Toole (this was my third film with Peter). The rest of the ensemble for this make-work piece would feature the introduction of newcomers Anthony Hopkins, Timothy Dalton and Nigel Terry, plus Jane Merrow, John Castle and Nigel Stock. Anthony Hopkins, in a 2008 interview, mentioned that Katharine, upon meeting him, said: "You've got a good pair of shoulders, a good head, good eyes, and a good voice…that's all you need. Don't act. Just say the lines. It works. Just watch Spencer Tracy, that's what he does. That's what all the best ones do."

The plot: It's Christmas at the English-held castle at Chinon (France) in 1183, and King Henry II is planning to announce his successor to the throne. The jockeying for the crown, though, is complex and fraught with manipulations. Henry has three sons and wants his boy Prince John to jump the line of succession and assume the throne of England. Henry's wife, Queen Eleanor of Aquitaine, has other ideas. She believes their son, Prince Richard, should assume his rightful role as heir apparent. As the family, with their opposing agendas, gathers for the holiday, each tries to make the recalcitrant king opt for their favorite. The plotters and schemers soon find themselves entangled in a web of old grudges and open wounds, until no one in the play can trust anyone else. It was, in truth, a fairly accurate reflection of history in that Henry's sons all plotted against him at one time or another, and John and Geoffrey actually waged an open rebellion against the king on two different occasions.

The first responsibility that Peter Murton gave me was to research and design the furniture depictive of that period of the 12$^{th}$ century. I had to work closely with Peter James, break down the script with him and decide what additional furniture we would require. I went to the Victoria and Albert Museum not too far from where I was living at the time with Peter Young and Bill Muldoon. It was a great apartment in Artillery Mansions, Westminster—replete with classic architecture, rich surroundings and a pretty hefty price tag.

The museum had a voluminous, wide-ranging library that was ideal for archives and research. I spent hours going through ancient scrolls, leather bound manuscripts that had woodcut prints, etchings and pen drawings of the chests, chairs and tables that we needed. The museum kindly allowed me access to them and even made copies for me. Peter Murton agreed with the producers Joseph E. Levine and Martin Poll that the furniture should be made from Beech wood. My working drawings went to a group of carpenters selected by Gus Walker our construction manager for their carving skills. The majority of the chests had intricately designed detail depictive of the period, and these master craftsman had

*One of the nine Beech Wood chests that I detailed*

just the tradition of excellence to pull it off. The carts and wagons that I had drawn up were to be built in Ireland once we arrived there.

Again, I was surrounded by reference books of England's castles. We all arrived in Ireland, set up shop at Bray studios where we conceived and constructed many interiors for the castle. My first job was to draw the plans and elevations for the large high walled castle and courtyard set that was going to be built on the back lot of the studio. On the first day of our shoot when all the extras came in, Peter O'Toole and Katharine came out to meet Timothy Dalton who was playing a very young King Phillip II (Philippe Augustus) of France. The greeting had such verisimilitude that I felt as if I had been right there in the time of Henry II. Everything in Bray went so smoothly…well almost.

We had built a castle window on a twenty-foot-high platform. From the point of view of this window we were able to look down onto the wagons and carts as they left through the arched castle gate. There was a cry on the headphones, "Alan, the cart will not turn! The wheels are locking!!"

Oh my god! I realized: I had really screwed up! I didn't make the turn on the axle and central shaft at the right angle. I went down and immediately detected the difficulty and showed the horse wranglers that the only way at this point to make it work and not hold up the shoot was to just move the cart more in line with the arched gate and drawbridge. Approved from the high tower, it worked; there was no more delay.

Weather was also an issue because it could be bloody cold on the set, especially in the mornings. Due to Peter having to get out of bed and break the ice on a bowl to rinse his face, we kept a sub-zero stage where we had built Henry's bedroom chamber. It was freezing in there. And I remember after two takes Peter, chilled to the bone and shaking, finally saying, "That's it! Next?"

Being the art department assistant on stage for most of the shots, I witnessed Katharine's tears as they flowed freely throughout some key scenes. I imagined they came from the silent pain that she must have truly felt due to her loss of her dear friend Spencer Tracy.

Peter Murton had gone ahead to Arles to hook up with a French art director named Gilbert Margerie. There they were creating a garden at the Abbaye de Montmajour, an old monastery, and at Tarascon Castle where they were building a boat dock for the Queen's barge to arrive with considerable ceremony. On arriving at the Abbey, I was struck with a *déjà vu* moment over the tower, and tried to recall why it was so familiar? Back in the hotel that evening I pulled from one of the bookshelves an anthology on Vincent van Gogh's best works. There they were: sketches of the monastery. On Sunday, I walked to where I thought that he might have stood to make those drawings. I read that Vincent discovered it two weeks after his arrival in Arles and expressed a desire to go there soon to paint.

The very first location was at Carcassonne Castle, where Anthony Hopkins was going to joust for his introductory sequence. He said he would not require the stunt man and would undertake the joust himself. Well you might easily guess what happened (and it did): Upon first contact, Tony fell off the horse and managed to injure himself. (End of actor doing his own stunt.)

It was the season of the Mistral winds. They were blowing hard as the stunning red globe of the sun rose. I was introduced to our scenic artist who was painting the newly built garden walls. He shook my hand, and greeted me "*bonjour,*" and promptly removed his wig that was keeping his bald head warm, a candid moment that was rather endearing.

He was such a great character…as were so many more of our French crew. There was a young couple who had turned their farm into a restaurant for us. And Manitas de Plata, the world-famous Gypsy guitarist, would sometimes grace us with his presence and play…as did some of his sons, Jacques, Maurice, and Tonino Baliardo, as well as their wives and daughters. (Not nearly as famous as their father at the time, this was the group who later formed the core ensemble for the Gypsy Kings, the radical flamenco band that became the rage of the late 1980s and early '90s.)

Those evenings always ended with us laughing and gyrating around the dancers trying to capture movements of Flamenco. For me, Flamenco is by far the most sensual form of dancing where male and female engage in a kind of rhythmic mating ritual that borders on controlled violence.

Back in the castle, the interior hall was used for a banquet with fires burning in a central pit. And three Irish wolfhounds were scrounging for the chicken that the extras were instructed to throw to them.

Later that day, after the filming, I had climbed up onto a roof where a small bell tower had been constructed. As I sat there making certain it was going to work, Katharine, in her red tunic, had seen me and started to climb the ladder. I mentioned, as she was in costume, that it might not be safe for her to try to climb up the ladder.

Rather than be offended, Katharine smiled and said, "You are so right, Alan." She stepped down and walked away, disappearing through an arch. (I didn't know that she knew my name! But as it turned out, that was just the kind of woman she was; she knew the names of virtually all the crew, the French as well as the English.)

On the first day of shooting at Tarascon Castle, Katharine was on "the Royal Barge" that we had built, being rowed towards what was once our landing dock. There had been torrential rains in the mountains the previous night, and when we arrived in the morning to light the beacon on the dock, all had disappeared underneath the floodwaters. Queen Eleanor's boat docked on the bank and Katharine stepped down with the grace of a queen, as she truly was.

There were, in retrospect, rumors that floated about concerning flare-ups and personality conflicts during the production. They were largely apocryphal. There was, however, one row between Hepburn and O'Toole that got pretty vocal and (as we Brits say) she pretty much "tore a strip off him."

So…upon the next day's shoot, Peter (as only Peter O'Toole could do) showed up for the scene covered in fake bandages and limping on a crutch. The sight of him arriving "wounded" broke Katharine up with laughter, and she forgave him on the spot. Problem solved. Production continued unencumbered. This was such great fun and all a part of the burn of what goes on behind the camera. Peter, however, did not stop there with his pranks.

In the latter days of the production, there was one scene toward the end of the film where Henry II, feeling vengeful towards his sons, decides to imprison them. In that pivotal scene, the king, in a fatalistic mood, storms across the battlements to have all three tossed into the dungeon. I was below looking up, and upon the call to "action," Peter started to walk. With his every step, I, along with the rest of the crew, heard the clanging sound of a bell.

Peter came down the stone stairs and opened his cloak to reveal an old bronze bell, then went to his trailer and came and stood in the door and showed me a bunch of ancient keys on a big old iron key ring. With a broad kid's grin he said, "Look at these, Alan…opens all the old ancient locks! " He said, still laughing and went back inside the trailer and rang the bronze bell.

One hour later, as we were wrapping up for the night, the first AD said he'd been instructed that we could not leave, "until the bell and keys were returned." To make sure this happened, he escorted me to Peter's trailer, and we knocked on the door. Peter opened the door and stood looking down at us both.

I asked him if he could let us have what he thought was now his, because we could not leave until he did. His smiled, looked beyond us to the producer and crew, and went into the trailer. He came back and handed them to us.

"I would truly love to keep the bell," he said with a huge Peter grin. So, finally, we were able to leave…mission accomplished. It had been another rewarding experience, and it was our last day there.

Whenever I'm asked what my favorite film was to work on, I will always reply *The Lion in Winter*. It had awe-inspiring dialogue, directing, acting, lighting and design.

The Oscars, BAFTA Awards and Golden Globes all reflected the brilliance of the production. It was nominated for Nine Academy Awards, including best director and best Actor and Actress. It won three for best Actress (Hepburn in a first and only tie with Barbra Streisand for *Funny Girl*), a Best Adapted Screenplay for James Goldman, and a Best Musical Score (for John Barry). It was nominated for 8 BAFTAs and won for Best Picture and Best Actress. And Peter O'Toole won a Golden Globe for Best Actor in a drama.

Beyond the Awards, it was a transcendent experience, the kind that possesses that "lightning in a bottle" one only captures once or twice in a lifetime.

I was designing commercials many years later in Los Angeles for director Klaus Obermeyer, who knew that I had worked on *The Lion in Winter*. He handed a phone to me, and as I listened to the voice on the other end, I imagined that I was once again "talking to Queen Eleanor."

It was his grandmother, and her voice imprint was exactly the same as Kat's…and with good reason. In fact, she was Katharine Hepburn's sister, Marion. The similarity was something of a haunting delight.

*My "Research Den" for The Lion in Winter.*

*Katharine Hepburn in repose as Eleanor of Aquitaine.*

*Peter O'Toole as Henry II, at a turning point in the plot.*

All of this combined with a complete immersion in the French countryside made filming "Lion" perhaps my most cherished production experience. There is an ineffable charm in the South of France where the land invites you into its sanctuary. It is the eternal beauty I now know as Provence. More than charm and picture-postcard beauty, it is also rich in tradition, history, and some lucid memories kept intact.

*The legendary cast, including Nigel Terry, John Castle, Anthony Hopkins, Jane Merrow, Katharine Hepburn, Peter O'Toole and Timothy Dalton.*

*The castle courtyard in "Chinon" for The Lion in Winter.*

## Twenty-One

## Where am I?

**There were always those times** when I wondered when would I work again. It is an insecurity innate to being self-employed and freelance—even in the burgeoning English film community of late 1960s. Fortunately, I did not have to wait long after *The Lion in Winter*, as Harry Saltzman, producer of the immensely popular James Bond films, was so taken with Don's sets that he asked him to redesign the interior of his house, and a short time later Don called me. It was the beginning of a new chapter in Don's career, since he was told by another financier that if his sketches were able get him the job, he would buy him a Rolls Royce. So, the white doves disappeared from above the garage and the Rolls rolled in.

    A call went out from Don to a group of us…and soon enough there we all were in his new design office that he had created above the garage. John Graysmark, Norman Reynolds, Alan Tompkins, Peter Childs and Stewart Craig—all gentlemen who became very accomplished and successful in the world of film design, with a few Oscars between them—were on the drawing boards every time they got the chance.

Don had made the decision to go into the world of hotel interior design, and subsequently became a wealthy man for taking that very deliberate detour in his career. We were drawing up furniture, hotel reception areas, bars, salons, bedrooms and dining rooms for the Mandarin in Hong Kong, and the Sheratons in Bangkok, Cairo and London.

May 1968, Sandhurst, Hampshire, accounted for the time and place where Peter Hall and Peter Murton agreed to take a small suburban house and use it for Rod Steiger and Claire Bloom's home in *Three into Two Won't Go,* a cult film in its time. It came from the pen of Edna O'Brien and was based upon Andrea Newman's novel…also a literary cult favorite. In the story, Claire Bloom is an angst-ridden middle-aged woman who is going through the daily drone of her days, unhappily married and apparently barren. The backdrop for the drama is the onset of the 'Technological Revolution, in which old values and certainties are challenged. This is the stage for the central character, played by Judy Geeson, a youngish mistress caught in a love triangle with Bloom and Steiger. This was a role that was a radical departure from the typical prim behavior of contemporary heroines of that period.

The script called for approximately a week of nights, so Peter and I talked about the translights that Ted Haworth used on *Half a Sixpence.* Photographs were taken around the house at night and the entire house was surrounded with the translights. Walter Lassally, the DP at the time, had the lighting department set lamps behind the windows in the backdrops.

You could cut the atmosphere on the set with a knife, as Rod and Claire were themselves going through problems from a marriage that had been unraveling for some time. This, in turn, added to the intensity of their scenes together. It was fascinating to witness Rod Steiger's mannerisms on camera and see that they were almost exactly the same off stage—not rare in this business since so many actors often just end up playing themselves. And I sensed this was Steiger playing Steiger in a day-for-night bit of irony.

This was Peter Hall's first film, which was a departure from his utter command of the British theatre. In fact, at that time of the making of this film, Peter was also the creator and artistic director of The Royal Shakespeare Company, Stratford-upon-Avon from 1960 to 1968. Later in 1973, after leaving the RSC, he took over direction of The National Theatre from Lord Laurence Olivier. He continued to be the single most influential force in modern British theatre, a distinction for which he was knighted in 1977.

As regards his first foray into film, the writing kept the dark intensity of the original novel, the directing, acting and the camera work was brilliant, and the film stayed true to itself. The actors, despite their personal difficulties (or perhaps partly due to them), were critically acclaimed for their performances. Again, it was a fulfilling creative experience to be able to work with all the talent that had gathered on this production.

*Judy Geeson, Rod Steiger, Claire Bloom in* Three into Two Won't Go.

April 4, 1968, I did not mention that prior to starting work on the above film, Martin Luther King Jr. had been assassinated. He was shot while standing on a hotel balcony in Memphis, Tennessee. A single shot fired by James Earl Ray from over 200 feet away at a nearby motel struck King in the neck. He died an hour later at St. Joseph's Hospital. That assassination reverberated powerfully around the world, especially in American cities. The tragedy sparked unrest in Washington, Chicago, Baltimore, Detroit and elsewhere. The following week, riots broke out in dozens of cities from Philadelphia to LA, warranting the intervention of the National Guard.

The death of America's leading civil rights advocate sparked a wave of rioting in the black communities in major cities around the United States. In England, the reaction was one of disbelief—mine included. The reaction on this side of the pond at least was one of shock and dismay over the fact that America was turning into a demi-war zone. Hadn't we just got over the horrors of Kennedy's death in November 1963? What was happening over there?!

For us, in trendy London, life was going on splendidly and seemed to be getting better every day. The London scene continued to flourish. Fashions seemed to change by the week in new and exciting ways. New friends were made, and "England was Swinging," now more than ever before.

One Saturday morning in the summer of '68, Peter Young took me to a new "men's fashion store" and introduced me to a 25-year-old fashion maven named Manolo Blahnik…who in turn persuaded me that a blue checkered jacket really looked great on me. I loved it, so I bought it.

Manolo had moved to London from Paris to work as a buyer at the fashion boutique, Zapata, and had just started writing for *L'Uomo Vogue,* an Italian men's version of *Vogue.* And yes! During that particular time Manolo, as a designer, soon opened his first flagship store that remains to this very day on Old Church Street in the fashionable Chelsea district of London! There, in 1971, he formed and tooled my first high-heeled Western boots—custom made just for me! The rest is history, for he became and still is a world-famous shoe designer, and a symbol of pure classic style for the 21st century, having recently opened a store in the famous old Burlington Arcade.

The summer of 1968 was also a tempestuous time in American history. Both the Vietnam War and the anti-war movement were peaking, and Martin Luther King Jr. had been assassinated in the spring, igniting riots across the country. In the face of this unrest, President Lyndon B. Johnson decided not to seek a second term in the upcoming presidential election. Robert Kennedy, John's younger brother and former U.S. Attorney General, stepped into this breach and experienced a groundswell of support. At the time, Kennedy was perceived by many to be the only person in American politics capable of uniting the people. He was beloved by the minority community for his integrity and devotion to the civil rights cause. After winning California's primary, Kennedy was in the prime position to receive the democratic nomination and face off against Richard Nixon in the general election. Then almost on cue tragedy struck again.

On June 5th, after winning the California presidential primary and announcing to his cheering supporters that the country was ready to end its fractious division, Senator Robert Kennedy was shot at the Ambassador Hotel in Los Angeles. Kennedy was shot three times with an Iver Johnson .22 caliber revolver by 22 year-old Palestinian Sirhan Sirhan. He died a day later.

On our side of the Pond, we were collectively dumbstruck by yet another inexplicable atrocity and found it distressingly hard to comprehend. (What was going on in America? Would it ever recover? We could only hope.)

# Twenty-Two

## "Come and Sit with Me, Alan"

*Nicholas and Alexandra,* a film set completely in Russia, was soon to be my life for two years to the very day. I spent one year in Sam Spiegel's office in Dover Street, London and a year in Madrid in two diametrically diverse environments.

James Goldman, who had written the popular play and (later) the screenplay for *The Lion in Winter,* was assigned to do the script, and ended up laboring on draft after draft as directors came and went.

George Stevens, Joseph Mankiewicz and Charles Jarrot were all attached to the project at one point. Sam Spiegel had asked Anthony Harvey, who had directed *The Lion in Winter,* to direct the film. Tony brought Peter Murton onboard who, in turn, put his team together. I had been given my own room with a drawing board and began to help Peter break down the script.

The tragic story of Nicholas II (Nicholas Romanov) the last Tsar of Russia was set against the backdrop of both World War I and the Bolshevik Revolution (in 1917). The script takes an inside look into the private lives of Nicholas, his wife Alexandra, their daughters, and the painful secret about their hemophiliac son and heir apparent, Alexei, which bound the imperial couple into a cycle of codependency with the psychic healer, Orthodox priest, and picaresque charlatan Rasputin. This in turn led to the rapid unraveling of the Romanov Dynasty, the Bolshevik/Menshevik power struggle for the soul of Russia, and the eventual execution of the entire royal family.

When I began to understand that I was actually in the offices of Sam Spiegel, it became apparent that I had again somehow landed in the presence of one of the industry's most esteemed film producers. Already an industry icon, Sam had won his first Academy Award for Best Picture as sole producer on *The African Queen* in 1952. In 1954, he won again for Elia Kazan's *On the Waterfront* and twice again as sole producer for his two collaborations with British director David Lean, *The Bridge on the River Kwai* (1957) and *Lawrence of Arabia* (1962). In 1963, Sam was awarded the Irving Thalberg Memorial Award at that year's Oscars for his many contributions to the world of cinema. So here I was, along with Peter, under the career umbrella of two great masters of film at the height of their popularity.

Out of respect for Designer Vincent Korda—one of the most acclaimed designers of the 1940s and brother of the notable director Alexander Korda—Sam Spiegel had asked him to come to Dover Street and be an advisor for this highly visible period piece. One day Vincent asked me if I would like to come to his home and help him find a particular reference. I was awestruck by his extensive library—one that included shelf upon shelf of all types of books. Then, seeing posters throughout the corridor walls of many of the films he had worked on, I was moved to an even greater level of respect. From 1931 until 1964 Vincent Korda had made indelible contributions to a total of 50 productions: *The Four Feathers, Things to Come, The Third Man, Bonnie Prince Charlie* and *The Thief of Bagdad* (for which he won an Oscar for Art Direction) were a few of the many which bore the imprint of his conceptual genius. Vincent had also art directed the *Longest Day, That Hamilton Woman* and *The Jungle Book*, for which he was also nominated for an Oscar.

I was drawing up the plan and elevations of the interior of the Winter Palace when Vincent came into the room and stood behind me. He moved to one side and said a couple of things that stuck with me forever: "Alan, there is nothing without light…" and "Remember to always be a good politician. Say the right thing at the right time and not the wrong thing at the wrong time."

It was so many years later, when I was production-designing and art directing films and commercials, that Vincent's words hit home with me. My set design allowed for beams, breaks in walls, the depth of windows and dimensions required for great light on the sets. I always liked to ask the directors of photography what direction they would like to light the set from so that I could allow for openings and windows for them.

As occasionally happens with films "in development," along the way Anthony Harvey had been let go "due to creative differences" with the producer. And Spiegel was running into budgetary and contract restraints that prevented him from casting some of his first choices for key parts, including Peter O'Toole for the role of Nicholas and Vanessa Redgrave to play Alexandra. However, in a good turn, Peter Goldman, after seeing *Patton*, recommended that Spiegel hire Franklin J. Schaffner to direct the film, which he did. And it turned out to be the right choice, because Schaffner actually won the Best Director Oscar for *Patton* while he was filming *Nicholas and Alexandra*.

A little history on Franklin Schaffner, who died at an early age of 69. He was one of the most innovative creative minds in the early days of American network television, utilizing a moving camera in the days when most television directors kept the camera static. His eye for visuals was developed in the dozens of live television programs he directed on prestigious shows such as *Studio One* in Hollywood (1948) and Playhouse 90 (1956). His visual sense came to be one of the important attributes of his work in feature films, such as the trek taken across the desert by the astronauts in the first reel of *Planet of the Apes* (1968). In addition to his Oscar and DGA Awards for *Patton* in 1970, he also won Sylvania Awards in 1953 and 1954, Emmy Awards in 1954, 1955 and 1962 and a Variety Critics Poll Award in 1960.

In one of the scenes in the film, Tsar Nicholas was with his army somewhere in Siberia. Peter and Vincent thought that the train from Inverness to Fort William when the snow arrived would play well as Siberia. From Scotland the plan was to then go and scout the towns in Northern England to look for industrial slum areas that might work for Russian street locations.

As I travelled from Inverness on the train through the highlands, it began to snow. We stopped at a lone station, and I went to the isolated red phone booth and called Peter to let him know that I thought it would work perfectly for Siberia. On turning around, the train was leaving, and I ended up walking in the snow, wearing Manolo's boots, approximately seven miles to Fort William where someone had kindly left my bag at the station master's office.

During this period, Anne King, a woman I had been in a relationship with a few years earlier, came back from New York and introduced me to Mort Schuman. Mort was a tall, striking man with a great head of hair and a commanding personality who, at that time, was in a London show *Jacques Brel is Alive and Well Living in Paris,* that he also wrote and directed. Either on his own, or teamed with song writing partner Doc Pomus, Mort had by that time authored some of the most lasting songs in pop music, including "Save the Last Dance for Me," "Teenager in Love," and Elvis Presley's "Little Sister."

In this case "Last Dance" alone had already played across the airwaves over four million times, as Mort continued to write songs and music numbers for such clients as Janis Joplin, Andy Williams, and the group, Small Faces, among others.

Lorraine Ashton would hold Sunday lunches at her father's home. And on weekends, I found myself driving Mortimer and even Peter Lawford down to Apsley House, where Don always prepared a nonpareil

Sunday feast. One made even richer by the fact that you never knew with whom you would be sitting down to share the sumptuous repasts, rich coffees and fabulous desserts—each one featuring the large antique silver coffee pot and renaissance assortment of gourmet sweets.

One cold Sunday, I helped light the fires in the lounge, and Frank Sinatra was singing away on the record player while Marilyn and Lorraine were both helping Don prepare the lunch in the kitchen. As had become customary, I was expecting Mort to arrive within the hour with a date. When the front doorbell rang, I ran to open it and, to my surprise, there was Bumble Dawson...and behind her, removing her headscarf, was none other than Ava Gardner. No one had mentioned that Bumble would be bringing Ava!

I took their coats and Ava looked at me and asked, in a soft voice, if I could change the music. Remembering that she and Sinatra had been married, and even though they had been divorced for over a decade, I could virtually feel the ache in her sigh and immediately obliged her wish.

With the flip of a disc, we managed to let Frank Sinatra segue into Nina Simone and, upon hearing the changeover, Ava turned and smiled: "I like her, thank you."

Bumble (Beatrice) Dawson had worked on many successful films such as *The Prince and the Show Girl*, *The Servant*, *The L-Shaped Room* and *Tom Jones*. She had been nominated for an Oscar and three BAFTA's and was held in high regard in her profession.

Ava had just returned from filming *The Night of the Iguana* with John Huston and Richard Burton, and was currently working with Roddy McDowell at Pinewood on *The Devil's Widow*. Roddy was the next to arrive, cordial and charming as always. Lunch was again a fabulous feast, replete with luminaries and shiny dialogue...and eventually we all transported into the lounge for coffee.

Ava sat in a cozy armchair by the fireplace and, lowering those penetrating cobalt-blue eyes at me said, "Come and sit with me, Alan." And she said it in a way, as only Ava could, that precluded equivocation.

I looked around and wondered where? (I didn't have to wonder long.) Ava pointed to the floor in between her legs and placed a cushion there. How dumb of me not to realize as she ran her fingers through my hair and fingered my neck that I might very well have missed out on an amorous invitation.

*Ava Gardner*

As I handed Bumble and Ava their coats, Bumble quietly asked me, "Alan, are you not coming with us?" It was a lovely thought, though an academic consideration, as I was naïvely unaware that I could possibly fall in favor with one of the goddesses of the silver screen. Sweet dreams!

Bumble knew that I was working with Sam Spiegel and (perhaps deliberately) interrupted the enchanted moment by asking if I could introduce her to him. I did try, but Spiegel had already committed to Yvonne Blake who later won an Oscar for her gorgeous flamboyant period costumes.

Rachel and I were going steady at this time, and she helped me to find an apartment in Chelsea on Ashburnham Road. I left Peter and Bill in Westminster, and exchanged the Alfa Romeo Giulia for a blue four door Giulia. I had entered many new milestones in my life, and yet the best adventure was yet to come: finishing that filmic masterpiece called *Nicholas and Alexandra,* and all those strange and wonderful moments that came with it.

*Sam Spiegel, receiving his Best Picture Oscar for* On the Waterfront.

# Twenty-Three

# Two Years to the Day!

**Well...** *Tempus Fugit* as they say in Latin. (Time *does* fly.) And soon enough what began as a few months' assignment on *Nicholas and Alexandra,* turned out to be a two-year gig.

We began by casting various actors to play Nicholas. I had set up on a small stage in St. John's Wood a simple drape and Victorian desk. I was surprised to see Max Von Sydow being tested for the role of the Tsar. Having seen him when I was at college in *Through a Glass Darkly, Wild Strawberries* and *The Magician,* I was very aware of his work. He had already established himself in that unique class of actors looked up to as a role model for others to follow. But Sam Spiegel had his own ideas about the personality of Nicholas II, and cast Michael Jayston, who bore a far greater physical resemblance to Nicholas II than Von Sydow (or just about anyone else).

Spain was now the country that our producer had decided upon, with Madrid as the principal venue for the film. Before leaving England to go onsite, I left my new Alfa to be resprayed with the father of Tony Hicks (of the Hollies). This turned out not to be a good move for reasons

I will explain later. (But never leave something you like in the hands of someone you barely know. Lesson learned.)

As is often the case in creating a film, much of the first year on *Nicholas and Alexandra* was devoted to pre-production, design and development. And in the one year that I spent in Dover Street, I remember that few if any of the drawings we originally drew up ever reached the designs that finally went on stage in Madrid.

On July 16th, 1969 I was with a group of friends and saw the Apollo 11 lift off from Florida's Cape Canaveral in sight of vast crowds of people who camped there to watch the launch. I mention this here because it was one of the most significant scientific achievements of our time. And I was surprised to note that we, in Europe, seemed far more intrigued by the event than they did in the USA.

The crew journeyed to the moon for four days, achieved lunar orbit and separated the two spacecraft on July 20th. As the crew descended to the surface, they could see landmarks below passing by several seconds early and they reported to Mission Control that they would be several miles away from their planned landing area. Subsequently, the Eagle's computer displayed several program alarms due to its hard drive having been overloaded with tasks and needing to reboot. Mission Control guidance officer Steve Bales with assistance from computer engineer Jack Garman told the crew they were okay to go to the surface.

Neil Armstrong took over the landing himself when he saw that the computer was guiding them to a boulder-filled landing zone. The Lunar Landing was achieved at 4:14 p.m. EDT (2014 GMT) with only 25 seconds of fuel left. Armstrong announced, "Houston, Tranquility Base here. The Eagle has landed." Capsule communicator and astronaut Charles Duke responded from Earth: "Roger … Tranquility, we copy you on the ground. You've got a bunch of guys about to turn blue. We're breathing again. Thanks a lot."

The schedule called for the astronauts to sleep before the first moonwalk, but they elected to go outside early because they felt they would not be able to sleep. In view of a black-and-white television camera transmitting his movements live to Earth, Armstrong descended Eagle's lander and touched his left foot upon the surface at 10:56 p.m. EDT July 20 02:56 GMT July 21. His first words were… "That's one small step for a man, one giant leap for mankind."

On arriving into the city of Madrid, I rented a top floor attic apartment in the Plaza Mayor from Peter Beale's mother. It was a rustic interior but perfect for my needs…and the view was quite nearly spectacular. Every morning during the workweek, I would take a bus from that attic apartment to go the studio. Rachel had gone to Greece for approximately two months and wanted to come and see me before returning home to England.

Movie star gorgeous on her worst of days, Rachel had come back from the Aegean so tanned with her blonde, sun-bleached hair that, wherever she went, she would literally stop the show. That became even more evident when we went to dinner that night, because while we were walking to the restaurant, I turned around to discover that we were being followed by at least forty men and boys. In Spain, at least, this was a time when young women were still wearing white gloves and being chaperoned. So, this kind of public appearance was considered both bold and brassy, as well as being somewhat depictive of celebrity.

Now, I have to mention at this point that John Box, renowned for his work as the production designer on *Lawrence of Arabia*, was signed by Sam Spiegel to be the second unit director. One evening over dinner, Peter Murton sadly confided to me that he had been fired…for reasons no one could seem to explain.

Up to that point, the general consensus was that his designs had been so brilliant that one could only surmise it had been a total political move on behalf of John Box wanting to design the film. I also had to observe that Sam Spiegel just seemed to be one of those producers who found it necessary to make burnt offerings of terminated staff to drive his production ahead, which (it had been widely rumored) led to his breakup with David Lean.

Distressed over his dismissal, I said to Peter that I thought I should leave. But he encouraged me to stay, informing me that Franklin, the director, had specifically wanted me to stay, as I had now sketched out most of the continuity graphics for him. I still had to complete the plans and elevations of the interior of the Central Hall and had yet to draw the full-size details of the metal stair railing area of the Central Staircase in the imperial palace. The top-landing radius was not an easy thing to do.

So, I sadly said goodbye to Peter and stayed on with John Box, who had now become our Production Designer. Not surprisingly, John revised the sets that were already under construction, overseen by Ernie and Jack, who both received an Art Director credit.

After completing the details of the Central Hall, I was given the responsibility of drawing up the farmhouse at Tobolsk. Located in the Russian Urals, it was the winter refuge where the Tsar's family was taken to sequester them from the rising tide of the Bolshevik Revolution.

John and Gus went with me into a mountain area outside of Madrid, and we located its position close to a group of old pine trees. I went there a few times until it was completed, and as winter set in, it snowed heavily. While there, I purchased some great knee-high leather Spanish lace up boots, and later returned to review the effect of the weather on our set.

While driving up the hill, I first saw the pine trees laden white, then our fiberglass wooden walls that surrounded the farm topped with snow. Upon opening the large wooden gates, I was delighted to discover, nestled below and in front of me, the perfect snow-crested farmhouse: Icicles were hanging from the wood gutters, and it looked as if it had been there for a few hundred years.

To render the setting even more ideal, on the first day of the shoot, the land and trees and surrounding terrain were ensconced in an icy mist.

The prop department was spraying the paraffin wax with water on the gates to create more ice as the troops arrived with the family in a wagon.

Back in the studios I had also finished my drawings for the interior of the farm, something to match the exterior, but with a soul of its own.

Once filming commenced on *Nicholas and Alexandra,* I became the Art Department standby on stage and location for almost every frame of the film, except the second unit. I would make a small plan of every set, place alphabetical numbers around the walls and call Franklin around 6 a.m. From there, he would then let me know which walls to replace and which to take out. I would arrive at the studios at 7 a.m. with my assistants and reset the walls. Then Freddie Young and his crew would arrive at 8 a.m. to see by the new configuration where to set the lights. The actors then came on stage at 8.45 a.m. And Franklin, without fail, would arrive at nine, place his shot list on the camera…and the day would begin.

Despite a rather complex set of negotiations and some last-minute casting collapses, the production ended up with a stellar list of actors with formidable box office performance! Michael Redgrave, Laurence Olivier, John McEnery, Michael Jayston, Janet Suzman, Jack Hawkins, Ania Marson and Harry Andrews—these were just a few members of the luminary cast, capped off by the chameleon Tom Baker who was surprisingly convincing as Rasputin. Mr. Spiegel had an acting coach pre-rehearse all the actors' scenes with them prior to coming onto the set. No doubt from his past experience and the tightness of the schedule he had decided it was necessary to smooth out the dialogue.

One afternoon on stage to my surprise I came across none other than producer and superagent Mim Scala with Gavin Hodge, both standing talking to the 2nd AD. They were on their way to Morocco to record ethnic music of the Ganoua. The recordings were the first of this secret sect. And now, even 45 years later, the Ganoua festival in Esouera Morocco attracts tens of thousands of fans to an electric mix of world music that is always ahead of the curve.

At the time, they spent the night with us, and then took off the next morning in Mim's Jeep cannily well-equipped with everything you could imagine strapped to it. Upon reflection, I truly had no idea how they found our remote Madrid studio…then again "connected people" know how and when to connect. It is what makes them who they are.

One morning deep into the production, I came down with an agonizingly painful toothache and had to leave the stage. Upon returning, the First AD, Pepi, informed me that Sam Spiegel wanted to see me. At this point, I need to explain that there are two types of producers for a film. The first type—the one most directors prefer—are those who set up everything in the beginning of the production, secure the funding and then disappear, leaving it to the director and crew to work their magic. The second type were those who were involved in every aspect of production from the wooing of the actors and directors down to the final cut. Sam Spiegel was the quintessential Type-Two producer; hence the reason for my trepidation.

Expecting trouble or something worse, I climbed the stairs to Sam Spiegel's office, only to be greeted by his secretary's worried face and being told that Sam was waiting for me.

"Where were you, Alan?" he said to me from across his desk. "I came down to the stage and you were not there!"

I told him that I had to go to the dentist. "Well next time you leave the stage, you must come and tell me. You are my eyes." He was compassionate in the way he expressed it. More than that, he wanted me there. He had that much faith in me; that was the responsibility of my job and his words did not hit me until much later. Entrusted with that kind of confidence and faith from the man who had put all this together, I made certain from that point on, there was nothing that I missed—be it the creases in the drapes, placement of props or even an extra in the wrong position.

I was behind Franklin when we were on the location we were using for the Russian Duma. Upon the action, I ended shouting, "Cut!" (I had done so for a reason.)

Franklin turned and looked up at me, saying "This better be good, Alan," and smiled.

I replied: "The man in front had worn his glasses for the last three takes." He looked at continuity and she looked at me. I nodded a yes, she nodded back yes and we continued.

The most emotional scene was obviously the day we were going to re-enact the family being shot. The set of the basement in the original house in Ekaterinburg, Siberia—where the Tsar, Tsarina, the four daughters and young Prince Alexei were to be executed—was finally made ready.

I stood next to Franklin that morning as the actors were led into the room and arranged (as the Royal Family had been) seated and standing... told as they were that it would be for a "photo."

This was followed by a pregnant silence that was meant to be intense. And immediately upon the call for "Action," the Bolshevik Officer and his operatives marched in through the door and immediately started to shoot. The moment was so startling and the verisimilitude was so utterly palpable that, upon the call to "cut," the four daughters—Ania Marson, Lynne Frederick, Candace Glendenning, and Fiona Fullerton—had all dissolved into tears, and we had to wait at least an hour so that they could wipe their tears away, change their costumes, and steady themselves. Three more takes: the remaining close ups, additional coverage it was a difficult draining day for all.

On the last day of the shoot, Freddie Young approached me, removed his light meter, placed it around my neck and said: "Alan, this is for you, you may need it one day." Such a gift and I still have it—the same one he used on *Lawrence of Arabia, Lord Jim, Doctor Zhivago, Ryan's Daughter* and many more. (I learned so much from him.)

One day Freddie told me to slightly close my eyes…and I did as he asked. "This is what the camera sees!" He emphasized, and that was when it struck me. In other words, the camera saw the larger picture; that left the "details to me." That meant, you could paint most of the moldings and make them become what the camera needs to see.

He taught me how to age the sets with warmer slightly darker tones in the corners and make the ceilings darker and bring the tones down from the ceilings and up from the floors. A man of superior vision that I had the opportunity to again work with and learn so much towards my future design work in film.

Earnest Day, the operator I had first met on *Lord Jim,* was another who had so much subtle control of the camera. If you see the films he has worked on, you will notice how he is uncanny in his intuition for dialogue, in such a way that renders him able to follow the emotional arc of the actors with the subtle, seemingly insignificant movements of the camera.

Often in my downtime during *Nicholas and Alexandra,* I would go to the Musco Del Prado on Sunday mornings, where I was able to enjoy so many works of Francisco Goya, El Greco, Diego Velasquez and José de Ribera…in fact, there were really too many works of art crammed together on the walls to enjoy in one sitting.

Rachel returned and stayed in Madrid for an extended period of time, becoming one of Madrid's top models—enjoying the Spanish penchant for "La Rubia" and all the fantasies that blonde women bring to the Latin masculine psyche.

We were walking to lunch one day with Jean-Claude Drouot who was playing Gilliard, Prince Alexei's guardian. We unexpectedly walked straight into Kirk Douglas, who was someone Jean-Claude had recently worked with. In a moment of sweet serendipity, we ended up having a very cool lunch with Kirk, sharing many a joke and story in that inimitable Kirk Douglas style.

Upon our return to London, Sam Spiegel surprised us by having his chauffeur at the airport with his Rolls Royce to take us home along with our large wicker trunk filled to the lid with a year's worth of collectables.

Later, upon its release and only moderate box office success, the film *Nicholas and Alexandra* was nominated for six Academy Awards. Included among them were those for Best Picture, Best Actress, Best Cinematography, Best Original Score, Best Costume Design and Best Art Direction. It won two: one for Best Costume Design and another for Best Art Direction. It also received three BAFTA nominations for Best Costume, Best Art Direction and for Janet Suzman as Best Newcomer.

I was surprised and a bit disappointed to note that, after all that time that we had won the Academy Award for best Art Direction…and yet neither John, nor Ernie nor Jack had ever called to thank me for my contributions to the success of the film. That's life! And it is the teacher. And if it taught me anything, it was this: always let others know that their work, as it related to me, would be appreciated…and to express that appreciation early and often. It is oxygen to the spirit of any creative soul. It is the very stuff of life, and what drives us to excel.

*ARJ with Ernie Day on the set of* Nicholas and Alexandra.
*The famous "Imperial Palace Staircase" recreated for the film.*

*Oscar winning costumes designed by Yvonne Blake.*

# Twenty-Four

## Shifting Gears. Saving Graces. And a Bit of Déjà vu.

It was great to be back after being away for so long. I settled into my new apartment, reconnected with friends and went to see my mother to pick up the six cases of wine I had left in her cellar. Well, more the fool me. After two years of my having been on location, I stepped down into the cellar only to discover five boxes entirely emptied of their contents—except for three bottles of the good Pinot Noir left in a sixth case. She and her friends had drunk the lot.

"I thought you had left them for me darling," she said, as I walked up the stairs from the cellar with two bottles in my hands.

"You and Harry might as well have the last bottle, Mum. Love you, bye!" I said, trying not to show that I was a little put out and also incredibly amused. A few minutes later, when I walked back to my car, I couldn't help but burst out laughing. At least I had two bottles. (It didn't matter in the final count. I didn't have that much time to enjoy them, because before you know it, I was back at work on another major motion picture.)

*Young Winston* was the film where I soon found myself employed, working again with Don Ashton at Shepperton Studios. This film covered the early years of British Prime Minister Winston Churchill, and was specifically based on his book, *My Early Life: A Roving Commission.* (Most people remember Churchill as Prime Minister, politician and statesman; he was most certainly all those things. What too often escapes notice is the fact that he was also a literary lion and one of the most prodigious English authors of the 20th century, having penned more than 40 volumes of history, philosophy, social commentary and even three novels.)

The first part of the script for *Young Winston* covered Churchill's unhappy school days, up to the death of his father. The second half covered his service as a cavalry officer in India and the Sudan, during which time he takes part in the (last official) British cavalry charge at Omdurman, his experiences as a war correspondent in the Second Boer War, during which time he is captured and escapes capture…and finally his election to Parliament at the age of 26.

Churchill was played by Simon Ward—a relative unknown at the time. But Simon looked every inch the part and was supported by a distinguished cast, including Robert Shaw as Lord Randolph Churchill, John Mills as Lord Kitchener, Anthony Hopkins as David Lloyd George and Anne Bancroft as Churchill's American mother Jennie. Other actors included Patrick Magee, Robert Hardy, Ian Holm, Edward Woodward and Jack Hawkins.

The film was written and produced by Carl Foreman, for whom I had originally worked during the time he was directing *The Victors*. Richard Attenborough, whom I also met on *The Wrong Box* and *Séance on a Wet Afternoon,* was directing this time; one of his first efforts "behind the camera."

I was getting ready to draw up the set for Randolph Churchill's reception area and office when Don asked me to go to Apsley House and measure up accurately the entrance hall area. I returned to the studio and drew it up, knowing that now the details of the Randolph Churchill's office bookcases would fit into Don's reception area. They were built-in oak and when you walked onto the stage there they were ready to move to Apsley House once the scene had been shot. This obviously was kept between Don and myself—"mum's the word" (or was).

Carl Foreman, being a writer and director, was now producing and found it very hard dealing with the freewheeling style of Richard Attenborough and his morning hour-long discussions with Gerry Turpin, the director of photography. They would stand and debate how and what to shoot, seemingly *ad infinitum* while the cast and crew waited around. One morning, Carl walked in, pulled them aside and gave them both a strong talking to. They obviously got the message, because from that day on, Attenborough arrived at the set entirely prepared.

Geoffrey Drake was also credited as Production Designer for *Young Winston,* and he was in charge of the locations to be shot in Morocco, which would represent the South African scenes. We also had locations at Sandhurst, Blenheim Palace, Chartwell House and Harrow school. At Harrow college, I met Jack Hawkins again and walked with him through a lower corridor, admiring the small Turner watercolors.

Jack had changed a bit since I'd worked with him on *The Last Safari,* as he had just survived throat cancer. He had to undergo a laryngectomy to remove the tumor, and was speaking to me through a voice throat communicator, or "voice box."

For the moment, we both stood in front of one of Sir Winston's paintings and wondered why he loved to paint. Was it in order to let go of the complex nature of politics, finding in life's nature a tranquility as he captured with his brush a golden sunset? Or was it just another world to conquer?

Later, for one of the sets, Don asked me to find and make a photographic copy of any of Winston Churchill's paintings that I was able to locate. Upon seeing them, Carl suggested to Richard Attenborough that it might be a great idea if they were used for the credits.

We went ahead and built the Houses of Parliament central chamber on stage to a certain height. Don asked me if I could draw up the hanging foreground miniature of the roof, for without it the set would not look so impressive. I had learnt how to do this on Chaplin's film and went ahead laying it out. It had to be accurate to the 'nth degree on paper. I had a print of the plan of the set that John Graysmark had drawn up. From this print I projected back the walls to a point at the distance where the miniature would be 24 feet high from the ground.

The carpenters built a highly detailed miniature from my drawing. That, in turn, was hung in the exact place that had been marked on stage. I went up the tower, and gazing through a view finder, I was more than surprised that the miniature fitted perfectly onto the set below. Parliament was complete.

That weekend, Don asked me if I would stay at Apsley House, as he had some details he wanted to complete for a restaurant in the Hong Kong Mandarin Hotel. He requested that I draw them. A short time later, I found myself once again in the attic bedroom, and on Saturday started to draw-up etched glass chessboard screen partitions for the restaurant.

Sunday arrived. Lunch was going well when the phone rang. Don listened in silence and then looked at me "The foreground miniature doesn't work…Here take the phone."

I took the phone and listened to Ronnie Taylor, the camera operator. "Don, he has what he thinks is the best angle."

"There is only one angle it can be shot from," I said.

Don replied, "I know. So, you better get over there."

Off I went to Shepperton. I came onto the stage, went up the tower and found the camera in the wrong position. Ron continued to argue with me and said that he had called Richard Attenborough.

"Why?" I asked and went to let Don know what was happening. The next thing I knew, Carl Foreman and our director arrived. I repeated what I had already told Ron, and suddenly an irate Don appeared.

"Where is the camera meant to be, Alan?" I showed him. He went over to the camera, took it from Ronnie and placed it directly in line with the center of the hanging ceiling model. "There gentlemen. It works there… and only there. Maybe our arrogant operator has learned something today. Alan, we are missing a great lunch. Let's get back to it!" he announced, after which time he climbed down from the tower, and we left.

Being on a production was part of the job. My social life was another matter. And it was the '70s after all. I knew that some of the gang had been in the past either reading or listening to (former Harvard Professor) Dr. Timothy Leary and tripping out. Some had told me of their experiences with LSD, and I had to admit they were fascinating.

One evening at a party, I was still a little reluctant but was persuaded by Bob Richards to go ahead and try it. "Won't hurt you," he said and slipped in the pill.

What a surprise I got, as my consciousness began to see minutest particles within all that surrounded me. It was a translucency of space and time. I won't go into further details, other than to say that before collapsing on the couch I wrote the following on a small piece of paper: *I believe that what I have experienced is divine.* Then I slipped the note under a cushion where I would eventually pass out.

Upon waking in the morning, I immediately looked under the cushion and read what I had written the previous night. Bob and the others were waking up to find me a convert to "the vibe."

"Bob, if I can experience what I did by taking a pill, I have to be able to experience it by taking nothing, for it exists. Look what I wrote last night," I said, in a moment of crystalline revelation.

"It was just a trip," Bob dismissed my zeal. "Make a coffee, and go back to sleep." After that, he snuggled up to his date and went back to sleep.

Monday morning, I seemed to float on four wheels to the studio and somehow glided the pencil across the plan and elevations of a coal mine.

Due to the fact that I had earlier recovered from hepatitis, I was almost teetotal. One evening in the studio Churchill Bar, I drank two

Carlsberg Specials: small drinks, but oh so strong! While driving home a little later, I noticed that the carburetor on my Alfa was playing up, so I punched it just as I was going over Richmond Bridge. Then out of the corner of my eye, I saw two policemen in a car put on their helmets and give chase.

Once they caught up with me, they checked me out for the British equivalent of a DUI, and had me get out and walk the line. As a result, I ended up in the Richmond police station.

Fortunately, these were the "good old days" when humanity still trumped agenda. Taking pity on me, the two arresting officers told me to walk it off, have some coffee and come back in an hour. I walked across Richmond Green to where I knew my director's beautiful home was, opened the gate and knocked on the door. Lucky for me Attenborough was at least a bit understanding…

"What are you doing here, Alan?" a slightly shocked Richard asked. I explained what had happened, and his lovely wife (forever) Sheila made me a pot of coffee. The combination of coffee, walk and company worked, because about an hour later I was back in the police station, receiving a citation and was told to appear before the magistrate the following week.

To my surprise (and utter chagrin), the judge the following week turned out to be my director's wife—the very same one who had made me the sobering pot of coffee. When she told me I was going to lose my license for a year, I immediately said: "I am working with your husband on *Young Winston*. How will I get to work?"

She replied, without missing a beat, "I'm sure you'll find a way, Mr. Roderick-Jones."

Rachel was now living with me, and we were planning to get married. So, we talked over my options. As it turned out, according to British law, I wasn't allowed to drive a car for a year. But there was no restriction to my coming to work "on a motorcycle," was there? Bob Richards had a Harley Davidson. So, Rachel and I decided that buying one was decidedly my best option.

*With the Harley outside the art department at Pinewood Studios.*

A week later, with no license, I was learning to drive a Duo Glide Harley in "all-weathers" to the studio—even finding myself on a few mornings racing Charlton Heston at 6 a.m. down the M6 motorway in his Green E-Type Jaguar convertible to Pinewood Studios. (I think he was prepping before he went to Spain to direct *Anthony and Cleopatra*…)

Once underway—and once Foreman and Attenborough put some of the rough patches in the production behind them—the end result was a film that earned international kudos for excellence in filmmaking and good box office numbers as well.

If you have an opportunity to view *Young Winston,* you will see Simon Ward give a profound rendition of Winston Churchill's first speech to the House of Commons in Parliament. The film was nominated for Academy Awards for Best Screenplay, Best Art Direction (for Donald M. Ashton, Geoffrey Drake, John Graysmark, William Hutchinson, Peter James) and Best Costume Design (for Anthony Mendleson).

To everyone's surprise, Don began dating Lorraine's closest friend Joanne, and later married her, taking off for Hong Kong where they lived

*Richard Attenborough and Carl Foreman on the set of Young Winston, 1972.*

*Simon Ward as a young Winston Churchill in the "office" that went to Don's Apsley House.*

for 20 years, eventually becoming Asia's most successful interior designer for major hotels throughout all of Southeast Asia (some of which I was privileged to help him with). His last public appearance was at an 80th birthday celebration for Lord Attenborough in 2003. By then, Don was severely disabled by Parkinson's disease, but Richard Attenborough introduced him to the audience as "one of the legendary and all-time great designers of the cinema."

The audience gave him a spontaneous standing ovation that lasted for a couple of minutes. Stylish and elegant at all times, Don had more than a passing resemblance to Rex Harrison. He loved beautiful clothes and always wore the latest styles with panache. True to himself, he was able to put as much style in his clothes as he did in his interior designs. No question he was definitely the most profound fashion influence on my life. And he was a great mentor and father figure to me in all things. Sadly, Don passed away in September of 2004, and I still miss him. And yet his creations are with us still…

*Don Ashton. Dear friend and mentor. Art Director and Production Designer on* Young Winston, Bridge on the River Kwai, A Countess from Hong Kong, Masquerade *and so many other films.*

Travelling my first time to India in 1982 and making several stops along the way, I arrived around midnight at a hotel in Bangkok, Thailand, signed in and went straight to bed. When I woke up, I had such a weird feeling of *déjà vu* that I thought I might have died and come back as someone else. (Where was I, after all? My surroundings looked so familiar.) I went down to the lobby, and there again was a reception area I knew only too well. Immediately I recognized that I was standing in the Sheraton Hotel in Bangkok, some of which I had drawn up and detailed for Don.

# Twenty-Five

## What is the Truth?

After *Young Winston* wrapped, I continued to design for the photographers at Roby Montgomery's company—doing small sets that were for various kitchen, yogurt, butter and furniture companies, *The Sunday Times* Weekend Magazine and Typhoo Tea Chimpanzee commercials with Syd Robson directing.

("I only asked for one lump," if you remember that one? Hilarious… as a golf ball plops into a cup of tea.)

And it was at this point where something called *synchronicity* came into play in my life. The concept of synchronicity was originally developed by Swiss psychologist and Freud star acolyte, Carl Gustav Jung. Jung coined the term to describe what he called "meaningful coincidences" if they occur with no causal relationship, yet seem to be meaningfully related." He variously described synchronicity as "the causal connecting principle," i.e. a pattern of connection that cannot be explained by conventional, efficient causality.

Rachel and I had that kind of meaningful *coincidence,* in the purest sense of the word—a coalescent string of events without apparent cause. My mother, who had made suits for Queen Mary, wife of George V, was called the "Queen of Clapham Junction," because every time she made the Queen's suits, she made one for herself.

Rachel's grandfather, who had been King George V's personal Church of England Minister, was also a famous cricketer known as "Gilly." Later, in a somewhat unofficial but accepted line of tradition, Rachel's father, Peter, became George VI's personal Anglican Minister.

Rachel was born in Windsor Great Park. And a few days after her birth, Queen Mary dropped by to pay her respects, noting somewhat ironically that, "Maybe we could call her Phillipa," since Princess Elizabeth had recently been going out with a young Greek/Danish royal named Philip. Two years later, when George VI died, Peter then became young Queen Elizabeth's Anglican Minister and spiritual advisor. So, the tradition, and the connection, carried through.

Something of a sign of the times, Stephen Gillingham, Rachel's cousin had, two years prior to 1971, taken a trek on the "hippie trail" across to India, where everyone from the Beatles to Shirley MacLaine had come across his or her spiritual guide and mentor. On his return, Stephen had mentioned to Rachel, somewhat rhapsodically, that he'd come across this young 12-year-old Guru…and that it had changed his life.

Rachel responded with a kind of characteristic healthy skepticism, something like, "There are so many gurus. If you still have him in a year, let me know."

I had no idea that they had been in touch with each other. Rachel went off in the morning to what I assumed was work, and I did not see her again for at least 24 hours.

Bob, Peter and I were just enjoying a post-dinner conversation after a repast at San Frediano, when Rachel came home, visibly moved to tears. "I have seen him," she said, through eyes still pooling up with emotion. And when I asked her who? "The one we have all been waiting for!" she replied.

A silence followed; this was not like Rachel. I looked at Peter. Bob lowered his eyes, and we all exchanged glances as Rachel then said, "I can see Light!" She then disappeared back into the bedroom and did not come out.

The following morning before I had awakened, she was gone again. I wondered where, and I took off on the Harley for the last week's work on *Young Winston*.

Rachel and I had been planning to get married. So, this sudden transformation came as something of a shock, especially when she announced that we could not. When I asked her why, she took a moment to think about it, and finally said, "You are not high enough."

You can imagine my reaction. "Not high enough!?" I protested. "I've smoked 'hash.' I've taken LSD. Why?"

Rachel's father came that evening and sat with us as she tried to explain why at this time she could not go through with it. I later found out she had picked up her cousin Stephen, plus four friends, in her Mini Minor and had driven to Heathrow Airport, along with many others, to welcome the young 12-year-old Guru, Prem Rawat.

We decided that we would still live together, and six months later I picked her up from a modeling job, she suddenly shouted, "Stop!"

I pulled over. Rachel jumped off the bike and ran over to a young man who was pinning a poster of a young boy on a telegraph pole. She was clearly over-the-moon about the poster and asked me if I would go with her to Westminster Hall to see… "him!" It turned out to be Prem Rawat.

I did go along with Peter Young and John Kearns. As it was difficult to understand his English, all I remembered was that he said these seven unforgettable words: "Whatever this Knowledge touches it makes perfect." In a way it was a soul summons, because even if I may not have recognized it, every cell on my body seemed to…because somehow this infused my entire being. It was as if I had been waiting all my life to hear this. They gave out a number where he would be the next few days before going to America. On phoning, I found myself in my Duke of Windsor suit and my loafers on the Harley driving to a small house in the country.

As I got off my Harley, I was greeted by Robin Heslop, who was far more interested in the bike than he was in me. Robin then began to ask me why I had come, and I replied that I was not certain but wanted to listen more to try to understand what this experience of Knowledge was, even though Rachel had tried to explain it to me.

As I listened to him and a woman they called a Mahatma (or "Great Soul"), I noted that I was hearing meanings, interpretations—maybe even the truths—that were hidden in the homilies I had been taught by my Jesuit Priests. One, for example, that Robin mentioned was a quote from the Bible: "If you receive what I have to give, you understand. If you do not then I shall speak in parables and similies."

I asked how one even begins to reach that level of consciousness where the parables disappear. He concluded and made it very clear that this young boy, Prem Rawat, was giving the same experience that all past Masters—male and female—had given throughout the ages. I listened to others who had received that experience, and everyone to the person had expressed the same pure truth through their inner voices that I had been hearing from Rachel.

I drove home that evening and spent a considerable time with Rachel, hoping she could clarify more for me, then made a point to return early the next morning. And well, as they say: "When the student is ready, the Teacher will appear."

Prem Rawat came the next day and met with us in the garden—just a very small group of souls, but every one willing to learn. I was going to ask him a question when precisely the same question came from a man in our group named Bruce, a query that the young master answered perfectly. He then looked at me and smiled. I lowered my hand and in one breath seemed to ask him if I, too, could receive Knowledge.

"Listen a little more so you may understand," he replied in his broken English.

The next day, I sat in a room with eight other people of ages varying from 20 to about 50. The female Mahatma began to explain to us the details of Prem Rawat's early life. He was born in the foothills of the Himalayas. His father Shri Hans was a revered Master known for the ability to put you in touch with your eternal self. Shri Hans had four sons. Prem was the youngest who, even at the age of three, would counsel people to meditate.

When he reached the age of eight, his father—knowing he had grown ill—asked his four sons if they would like to receive Knowledge. The boys received the experience of Knowledge…and knowing he'd passed his mastery along to the next generation, Shri Hans shed this mortal coil and moved to the next dimension.

At the memorial ceremony, thousands came to pay their respects. Young Prem Rawat, asleep by the side of the stage, suddenly awoke as if jolted by a lightning bolt, strode over to the microphones and started to speak with what caught everyone there as a sense of destiny.

"Many times, have I come. This time I come with more power than ever before. But what can I do unless men come to me with love in their hearts and a desire to know peace and Truth?" (Even thinking back on hearing this story and those words that came from a eight-year-old boy, I was dumbfounded: "Really!?" Speechless.)

It was then that the Mahatma informed us that, at the age of 12, Prem told his mother he had to leave—that the world was waiting.

I listened, and I could hear myself questioning: If a young eight-year-old could say what he did, then why not me? After all, what did I have to lose? Who was this young boy of 12? If he was the Messenger, so be it! If he wasn't, he wasn't. So, why not embrace the notion?

Opening myself up to the process, I received the four techniques that came to be my four noble truths. I know I mentioned that, as a child, I had seen The Light and ran to tell Granny. Even now, at this point in my life, I was able to see there within when I brought my awareness to the center of my forehead, I was struck by a vibrant Blue Light cupping my hands up to my ear to hear the Silence within, and there it was: The Peace that Passes all Understanding.

I was being shown how to set free a soft liquid oasis that flowed from within (there is a well within you that never dries) from the area of the Pineal Gland, infusing every part of me and awakening me to the awareness that inside the stillness of my breath dwelled my eternal soul.

Those early mantras from Genesis instilled in me so many times by priests… "In the beginning was the word, the word was with God and the word was God," had their sources inside the collective consciousness of us all. I understood then and even more as years went by that we are all One…always had been and would always be so. One Being. Being one with Creation, that word, that inner vibration…what C.G. Jung called the *Numinosum,* the universal collective will.

I seemed to be so uncertain as to why I was now having an inner feeling of knowing, an awareness of life's perfection. (Could I call it the Truth?) As I drove the Harley all the way home, filled with what I now term as "grace," I still found myself wondering: *Why me?*

On walking into the Potters Pub on Kings Road I said, "Drinks are on me." Gavin Hodge sitting with Jane Lumb, Peter Mines and Eugene between them asked me if I was okay.

Somewhat stupidly I replied: "I now know what we have been looking for…Ah, yes!" And "Fuck off!" … And "Give us all a break!"

My curt reply and sudden withdrawal brought cascades of laugher around the pub, along with several jibes from the bench.

"What have you been taking?" Gavin asked, with a wide smile while taking the glass from my hand. "I want some," he said, taking a large gulp of ale.

That evening I placed a cushion on the floor, sat cross-legged for the first time, and began to focus on my breathing. My breath became like a slow-moving piston within.

Of course, my mind fought back: *Why are you doing this? Get up! Stop this nonsense!* And yet despite my own "head games," the more I focused on the movement of my breath the more I was able to dismiss the noise of the mindless voice until there was just a silence.

It was a silence that I could hear—a silence that resounded, inside and out. It flowed through me like a perfect cleansing of every cell. The sound of the outside traffic was there no longer. I was experiencing for the first time an unknown joy that absolutely streamed from within. If you had asked me if I truly understood what I had just received, I would have had to answer no. And yet, I could not deny that an absolute unspoken consciousness had opened gates to awareness...*an awareness of absolute Truth*. I was on a trip without so much as taking a pill. The Messenger had come to me unknown and not requested. It came "without a bell" and lifted me up into life's unspeakable Truth.

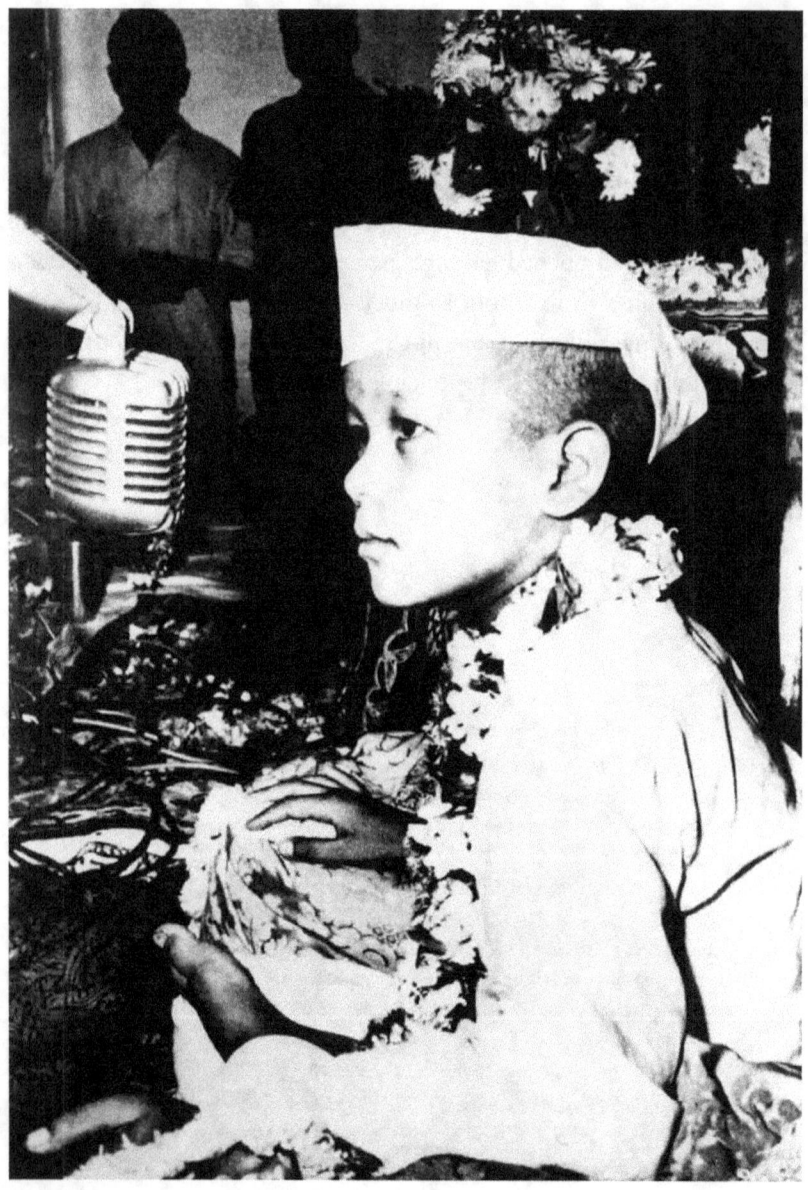

*Prem Rawat at the age of 8-1/2.*

# Twenty-Six

## A Conscious Unfolding

**Given my Catholic upbringing** I already had a Bible, but decided at this point in my young adulthood to make a personal study of comparative religion. So, I gathered together copies of *The Vedas, The Quran* and *The Upanishads*.

*The Vedas* are the oldest and most sacred texts of any religion that still exists today. In fact, these texts date roughly from 1700 to 1100 BC and include the *Circum-Vedic Codices* as well as a redaction from the *Samhitas* dating all the way back from 1000 to 500 BC. The combined text comprised a Vedic period, spanning nearly two millenniums encompassing both The Bronze Age and The Iron Age.

*The Upanishads* are a collection of religious texts, written in Sanskrit that form a major part of the Hindu scriptures. They were written between the 8th and 6th centuries BC, though the name Upanishad is sometimes extended to cover many later writings based on the Vedanta philosophy.

According to traditional Islamic beliefs, the Quran was revealed to Muhammad, starting one night during the month of Ramadan in 610 AD, when he, at the age of 40, received the first revelation from the

Archangel Gabriel, who had given him the responsibility of inscribing these messages to give to mankind. (Note: This is the same Gabriel who also appeared to Jesus's mother Mary, and 33 years later at the Tomb of Jesus. [In more ways than one Gabriel really got around!]) In fact, that sequence of events makes Islam the youngest surviving religion, which may go far to explain its rather aggressive expansionist expression of itself.

Still living with Rachel in Chelsea, I studied this compilation of texts and, over a period of time, gleaned from these amazing scriptures one fact: almost to the one, they were transcribed not by the masters who revealed the teachings but by their disciples and scribes after the masters departed. They were all giving the same message: what we are truly looking for is within us. So, day by day it seemed Creation had opened the Universal Book for me—one that I was consciously reading and learning from moment by moment. This was truly a gift that had been bestowed upon me.

*The Vedas* were beyond anything I had ever read, for they talked about battles in the air. In the purely metaphorical context, they paralleled the Lucifer rebellion in Heaven, the angelic combats led by Michael—the ultimate spiritual schism between good and evil. Yet the ancient texts themselves took it a few steps further, referring specifically to incredible "flying ships" that visited our planet over six thousand years ago—interstellar crafts called the *Vimanas*.

One lunchtime in Casserole Restaurant on Kings Road in Chelsea, Rachel and I were talking over the possibility of finding a weekend retreat to get out of London. As it was, we just wanted to get away from the hustle of the city. Sitting opposite us was Sir Charles Mark Palmer. Charles was my age, a fifth generation Baronet and a British aristocrat who put together one of the first modeling agencies devoted to the male image… and who later adopted a somewhat eccentric alternative lifestyle, travelling around Britain in a horse-drawn carriage.

When we first met Mark, we had overheard him talking about selling his farm in Wales. So, I went over and introduced myself, telling him that

Rachel and I had taken an interest in seeing the farm he had just spoken about.

"Come this weekend, can you?" he replied, and we both agreed to go. By now my driving license had been returned to me, and I had bought a VW Bus. We used it explicitly for the journey. It had a red exterior, a painted black interior and Rachel had covered all the seating with a kind of woven Greek fabric.

At Tintern Abbey, deep along the Wye Valley, we stopped for tea and crumpets. *Abaty Tyndyrn* (Welsh for Tintern Abbey) was founded by Walter de Clare, Lord of Chepstow in 1131. It is situated adjacent to the village of Tintern on the Welsh bank of the River Wye, which at this point forms the border between Monmouthshire in Wales to the West and Gloucestershire in England to the East.

The Abbey fell into ruin after Henry VIII split with the Catholic Church in 1534, formed the Church of England and sacked all the monasteries, razing many of them to the ground. We took our time and walked through these once beautiful buildings, feeling the presence of the *Carta Caritatis* (Charter of Love) monks who had led lives of obedience, poverty, chastity, silence, prayer and work.

Upon arriving in the small ancient castle Welsh town of Montgomery, we inquired at the post office for directions to The Grove, Mark's farm. Meandering through narrow roads, we came across a red telephone box at the end of the hedge row lane, turned right and within three minutes we turned into The Grove—and were greeted by an old open barn shrouded by a huge elm tree, a covered barn, a railway truck on blocks and a small red brick farm house. After knocking on the door, one could not help but notice the well-worn stone threshold and the big gap under the old wooden paneled front door.

This was a small old house with wattle and daub walls, woven lattices of wooden strips were daubed with a sticky material usually made of some combination of wet soil, clay, sand, animal dung and straw, structured within old ship beams that were found on the beaches of Ireland

and Scotland after the Spanish Armada had been sunk and damaged by Sir Francis Drake. These were the careworn qualities that rendered it eccentric and, at the same time, lovely and unique.

Mark took us up to the top of a hill that overlooked the 20 acres and the valley beyond. At that point, I asked him how much he was asking for the farm. "£9,000, all in. There is, however, one other person interested," Mark said.

I could see the questioning expression on Rachel's face, indicating she maybe really liked the farm and all the valley surrounding us. So, I asked him if he would take £9,250. He accepted, and (in keeping with an old English tradition) I placed a silver coin into my palm, spat into my hand and we shook—it was a deal.

Back in London we had to make a gargantuan commitment, not only to a complete life change, but also to conclude, for my part, that I would let go of work for a while and, instead of a weekend retreat, convert this newfound cottage into our combined home.

Rachel and I both sold our apartments. And, upon learning that we were off to Wales, Ian Quarrie volunteered to help us move. Later, he and I, after hours of running up and down the stairs to Rachel's Nottingham Hill attic apartment, could barely move.

Exhausted, we all rested that evening. We took off the next morning, Rachel driving the crammed-to-the-roof VW Bus while Ian and I followed in the rented truck—all of us heading to an uncharted future in the lush verdant hills of Wales.

I had recently given my signed drawings away to a prop house and only realized a little while later how stupid that had been—especially the ones of Chaplin and Hepburn, who were classics in their time. Upon going back to ask for them, of course they were gone, no doubt hanging on the walls of the man who owned the rental company.

Once we settled in, we quickly realized that we would have to really clean up the interior. That meant rebuilding the walls, sanding the beams and a generally overhauling the small bedrooms, making a real bathroom and getting rid of the rats that fed on the remains of the sheep's jaw bones Mark had put in place to line the garden paths (essential, prior to our moving in).

We bought a beautiful Jersey cow and bantam chickens that had a penchant for roosting in the trees. We made our own bread and various wines from the pear tree and even from dark purple rose petals. The locals were happy to know that we were not going to be just weekenders, and we soon came to be known as "Jones, The Grove."

Then, one day, I had a telegram. How they found me, I have no idea, but there it was, handed to me by the local postman. Jack Maxsted had a request for me from Franklin Schaffner, who was going to direct *Papillon* in Jamaica. He was asking if I would like to join them if I was free. Also, what was I doing on a farm in Wales?

I called Jack and found out that Tony Masters was the production designer and that Franklin had personally requested that I be on film. It sounded like too good an opportunity to pass up. I did not want to leave Rachel, but adventure (and some considerable augmentation to our income) beckoned—not to mention a great career experience. She finally said that it would be okay. Go!

I went back to London and stayed with my brother in Richmond for two weeks, going to Jack's home studio and finding research for the Devil's Island hospital. Having completed my research, I drew up preliminary plans and elevations, went back to The Grove, and within a week was on my way to Jamaica. We had two weeks prior to my leaving the farm, so we contacted a local Montgomery builder who agreed to go ahead with installing the bathroom.

Rachel continued to sand down the beams, and I placed extra dry wall in the bedrooms. It seemed to be an endless process and turned out to be quite expensive. Still we pressed on…painted and wondered if we had made the right move.

As I drove away up the lane, I felt definite pangs of guilt over leaving my darling girl behind to deal with all the renovations. But the film bug still had a bite to which I had not yet grown immune. It contained challenges to the creative spirit that, once heightened, are never quite left undone.

*Rachel still at home on "the farm." With so much left to be done.*

# Twenty-Seven

## Papillon *and the* "Rasta Man"

**Montego Bay Studios, small and dirty,** formed the base of our first impression when our production team was shown our quarters. Our office complex was comprised of a series of small offices you could just about swing a cat in, and a small cat at that. So, when we went to see the Bond Penthouse suite that their art department was in, envy struck a chord. Jack and Ernie said we would be fine—the bonus for us all being that Jim Moynahan, Terry Ackland-Snow and I shared a beautiful villa high in the hills with a breathtaking ocean view, a pool and a cook who loved to torture our palates with the spiciest Jamaican pickles on all of planet Earth!

More design research was required: this time, regarding the solitary confinement cells for the scenes where they were going to place Steve McQueen (as Henri Charrière). There was ample photographic background from which to glean inspiration. And as the pencil began to draw the cells, I wondered how anyone could design anything so tortuous as this in which to confine another human being.

In the mornings, I would go and check out the construction in the carpenter and plaster shops, only to walk out feeling rather stoned, as they were all smoking the biggest Reefers; those Rastas! The sobriquet, "Rastas," referenced the Rastafarians, a rather cool religion started up by Marcus Garvey in 1931. Whatever its original intent, Rastafarianism soon became an arcane spiritual sect that, in its way, initiated a unique form of "black power," one that embraced an Abrahamic religion closer to the pure Aramaic scripts.

They were easy to spot: All wore dreadlocks, rejected traditional medicine and smoked prodigious amounts of weed in what amounted to a cannabis counterculture. They were also, in equal measure, a socio-political movement decades ahead of their time.

For my part, I understood their journey. I certainly remember having a reaction from all my old friends, as Alan was no longer the guy who always seemed to be in the company of beautiful women at poolside.

I'd become a creature more detached—this apparently due to the new consciousness I had embraced and the newfound understanding I had for this life. The Rastas would often come in the evening and sit with me on the lawn outside my office—just so they could hear about my new experience, passing me a joint, which I sometimes declined.

I was asked to go on the hunt for an area where McQueen, as Papillon, could jump off a cliff into the ocean. I took photographs from a cliff side not too far away from the studio that, I thought, worked perfectly.

Franklin Schaffner, who had yet to arrive, requested that I should take a plane, fly around all the islands and pinpoint a great location, as he was not too happy about the one I had found.

Who was I to argue? (He was the Director, after all.) So…off I went in a twin-engine Cessna, flying only a few hundred feet above sea level, combing all the islands of the Caribbean, walking into teargas on the streets of Antigua and finally ending-up in Cuba. To the surprise of Tony Masters, the closest location I had found was the one finally selected. So, it was a bit of a wild goose chase that left us with the original choice to begin with. I had a great time though with my pilot, as he meandered through some phenomenal cloud formations, ducking and diving and flying low over so many exotic Islands.

At this point, I was really missing Rachel and began to write her every day. On returning, she told me how upset the postman was that he had to drive down our lane and deliver my daily missives. One of my early letters had been the cause of many a laugh with our friends John and Joanie Gilbert, with whom I'd spent time with at the London BAFTA celebration. (In March of 2019 John's father, Lewis Gilbert had been recognized for his life achievements in film. And that provided the opportunity for us to enjoy the recollection.)

Recalling our times together, we were still laughing over "harvest the cobnuts for money," passages—due to the fact that, during one point of pre-production, we did not get paid for six weeks. So, I penned a letter to Rachel, expressing the notion that the small trees would produce enough nuts to enable her to sell them and help make ends meet—a letter that she showed to John and Joanie while I was away.

Smiling even now as I write this, I note the irony of the request, since there obviously weren't any cobnuts on the trees, and if there had been, it wouldn't have amounted to enough even for a couple of pounds.

Anyway, Rachel had decided to go to India with many others on three jumbo jets to spend time with Prem Rawat in his hometown of Prem Nagar—a rather large village in the Dehradun District of Uttarakhand, India. It was a spiritual journey that seemed a fortuitous contrast to what I had been experiencing with the pre-production group prior to filming *Papillon*.

Over dinner one evening in our villa, Jim brought up the issue that Jack had mentioned that morning. Production was cutting back and would either have to let him or Terry go. They both explained to me they had already brought their families tickets to come and be with them. I was not really getting on too well with Tony Masters, since he seemed to heartily disapprove of my keeping company with the Rastas, spending my evenings in spiritual conference and smoking a bit of weed. So…

willing to "take a bullet" for my friends, I went out the very next morning to speak to Jack and Ernie, letting them know that I was aware of the situation. I also made mention of the fact that—even though I was probably there due to being with Franklin every day on *Nicholas and Alexandra*—maybe I should be the one to go.

When I returned to discuss the issue with Tony, I did not see any expression of concern cross his face; so, the decision was made.

If only I had known, the very morning I was to leave, that Franklin Schaffner would be arriving, I would have stayed on an extra day in order to thank him for considering me. Lesley Tompkins flew in to replace me as the stand by Art Department rep on camera.

I took off from Jamaica with a sense of finality and, given the rather strained dynamic, perhaps even one of relief. Although I still had a passion for the film business, it wasn't so much that I was leaving a production as it was that I had something much better to look forward to. And for the first time in a very long time, it felt like I was going home.

*Scenes from* Papillon, *including the "solitary confinement cells" I had researched and drafted.*

# Twenty-Eight

## *Somewhere Over the Rainbow: I Am Okay*

**Having returned from Jamaica** and *Papillon*, I was reminded of the old Calypso song written by Roaring Lion in 1933, whose lyrics, still ringing in my ears, go something like this:

> *If you want to be happy for the rest of your life*
> *Never make a pretty woman your wife.*
> *So from my personal point of view*
> *Get an ugly woman to marry you…*

It was great to be back to "Jones, The Grove," and to my lovely Rachel, who had done a yeoman's job of turning our farm into an idyllic place to be. I was also, upon my return, made quite aware that every bachelor in the entire area had been aggressively wooing my girl.

Defying the advice of the calypso song, I officially proposed to Rachel, and we decided to get married down in Horsham where Rachel's father was the local minister. (And who better to marry us than he?)

Meanwhile, while making repairs, I nearly killed myself traversing around the corner of the barn on an old Fergie tractor. Rachel had bought a horse. And we planted our newly ploughed fields with broad beans, onions and cabbages.

Roby Montgomery and Sally came to visit a short time later and fell in love with a recently vacated farm just a short walk away from us. Almost seamlessly, it seemed, they went ahead and purchased it, eventually turning it into a comely, cozy retreat.

We also decided that we would try to make some money by having a company that sold grains, sugar, candles and our vegetables. When the field of broad beans had been picked and the cabbages were all approximately two feet in diameter, I stood on the corner in Welshpool and Newtown markets and averaged twelve pounds a day, just enough to buy some stores and coal.

One old lady, when she saw the size of the cabbage, asked me if she could just have a leaf, "Of course, you may, take two." I smiled and handed her two oversized cabbage leaves.

By this time, we'd had a phone installed at the farm. From time to time, I would get a call from Roby and I would drive down to London to work on a commercial or a still shoot. And from the subtle change of scent in the country air and the manic dip in temperature, we learned how to sense when winter was on its way. Having to commute to London the next day, I would invariably get up at 4 a.m. I would plough the field only to note, upon my return, that the ground was covered in a thick frost. Certainly, this was a teachable moment for me. I was beginning to learn how Mother Nature in her rather imperious ways teaches us how to go with the flow.

In the early mornings before sunrise, we would be awakened by a delicate run of avian melodies that came from frequent visitations by the larks. Their elevated songs would often come in sequence, rising at times into a series of short, high-pitched notes. On other occasions, if looking for a mate, their melodic strains would roll on for at least a minute in a series of trills and calls of longing.

Upon looking out the windows, we could see these beautiful birds flocking on the garden posts. Sometimes though they would soar into the sky and then return. Their singing, as they passed through the chilly currents of the sky above, would seasonally change in tone, acting as heralds to let us know that winter was on its way.

In the early spring, I invited my father up for a weekend. Frank had always loved to garden, and he was amused to the point of distraction that we still had an outside toilet box (aka outhouse) due to the fact that our house bathroom still had to be finished. At least he and I had reconnected, although the mystery remained…since he never chose to confide to me why he and my mother had divorced.

Meanwhile, I was beginning to recognize the pitfalls of becoming "the gentlemen farmer," since the job itself amounted to a lot more farming than it did the genteel lifestyle one might have seen on *Green Acres*.

Emotionally, at least for a while, I was going through a crisis of consciousness. To match my mood, late one day, the sky had turned completely black, and I was undergoing a silent meltdown, trying to understand why I had given it all up. Why had I forsaken my true life's work for a so-called "spiritual journey"?

I walked out into the fields to the top of a dell, took a deep breath and prayed. It was a deep inner prayer to Creation asking "Why? Please tell me. Tell me I am okay! Please let me know I am okay."

Demanding empirical evidence for my faith, I had asked for a "sign." And though it shames me when I think of it now…within seconds one appeared. Almost the moment the words left my mouth, a rainbow began to appear in the valley facing me. As the sky blackened, the rainbow continued to arch and stopped, touching a distant hill. I looked around and could not see the sun or any rain to give it substance.

At that point, I turned to call Rachel, when a second one began to form beneath the first. I fell to my knees and took a deep breath, quite in disbelief. *Was this real? Could this be happening?* I trembled with the silent query.

As I raised my head, the second rainbow started moving slowly towards me. In the dell below there was a large tree where the rainbow had stopped and a luminous white light shrouded it. Again, I lowered my head to touch the soil, feeling immersed in light as I sensed a sublime presence encircling me: "I am okay. Thank you! Thank you!" I heard myself say, while an inner voice seemed to reply: *I love you.*

It was after this experience that I became inspired to start writing a story about a Master in a far-off universe, a dark overlord, four neophyte princes and three princesses, each representing one of the planet's seven races. It was a fantasy series called Karas, which became a script, helped along by Lex Neal and then a game, created by one of the very first game designers, Monica Zgutowicz.

Ronnie Lane of The Faces lived on a farm not too far away from us with his wife and family. From time to time, we would all hook up, and go to a nearby brewery-pub that became our "weekend hangout." The girls would dance to the boy's music. Across the valley, Michael, our neighbor, had decided to put his farm up for sale. Bob Richards and Julie Christie had come down for the weekend, and Julie, like us, fell in love with the valley.

Julie took the next leap of faith, dashed over to Michael and, to all our surprise, bought the farm on the spot. Mark Palmer returned that weekend with his horse and cart, using it to take us through the lanes to Michael's farewell party. While we were there, Pete Townsend, Ronnie Lane and others had converted the old 16th Century barn into a dance hall. What a night, with ancient dust drifting down from the rafters, and specters stirred up as the great music and stomping resounded up through the ancient beams.

Snow was falling. Winter had arrived. And we were off to Horsham to spend Christmas and get married. I walked the cow over the hill to place it in the care of our neighbor, Mr. Munford. Then Rachel and I locked up our farm and took off to drive to London. Then, we still lived in the remnants of "radio days," and even now I still remember those BBC afternoon radio plays blasting out over the car radio as we ate fresh country cheeses layered in sandwiches made with homemade breads, and all the rich flavors of the farm.

Jonathan Mills, son of the iconic actor John Mills, and his wife, Chris Mills, had become friends of ours met through Prem Rawat's *Gift of Knowledge.* Outside their front door were three pairs of the oddest-looking shoes, so odd in fact that I thought they might be some alien fabrication. It was only later that I was told by Rennie Davis that they belonged to him, his partner Susan and his son.

They were called (Kalso) Earth Shoes—a kind of inverted clog that pushed all the weight of the stride to the back of the heel. (They supposedly strengthened the leg and are still available today.) Rennie was a former prominent American anti-Vietnam War protest leader of the 1960s. Along with Abbie Hoffman, Bobby Seale, Jerry Rubin, Tom Hayden and

*"The Grove" in the dead of winter.*

others, he was one of the Chicago Seven and later became a venture capitalist and lecturer on meditation and self-awareness.

The founder of the Foundation for a New Humanity—a technology development and venture capital company commercializing breakthrough technologies, Rennie was on a new leg of his spiritual journey. And, given his renegade beginnings and his bizarre taste in alien shoes, who would have guessed he would become one of the most significant entrepreneurs up to that time?

On December 27, 1972, Philippa Rachel Gillingham and I were married in the little Horsham Church in a ceremony presided over by Rachel's father. My darling bride looked so radiantly angelic in her long white Mexican dress. The affair was attended by Diana, Rachel's mother, my mother, Aunt Esther, Aunt Doris, my brother Phillip, Cat, Peter Mines, Bob Richards, John and Chris Mills, Peter Crisp, Anthia Izzard plus Rachel's uncle and aunt, brothers Bruce, Richard and sister Mary. They made up a good-looking family gathering, and were reflective, yet appropriately sedate. Let us not forget our dog, Jade, who was ready to give birth.

When it was done, off we drove for the honeymoon in a 16th century hotel, where Jade gave birth to two little pups on Rachel's silk scarf under the four-poster bed.

Stunningly beautiful, gifted, intelligent, this loving woman—the mother of our two children Ella and Rowan—and I have been emotionally dedicated to one another for 46 years. So, with all due respect to Roaring Lion and that silly Calypso song …from *my personal point of view,* I did the very rightest thing.

# Twenty-Nine

## "Elvis" is in the Building

**In the spring of 1973,** we had made a plan to go to Miami for an event where Prem Rawat was speaking. Afterward, we planned to drive across country with Jonathan and Chris in a classic "woody" station wagon to Los Angeles.

Just before going, we had met and befriended a couple, ultimately deciding to let them stay in The Grove rent-free, giving them the run of the place, as long as they looked after the farm and the crops that were just sprouting up.

Once we arrived at the event, we met Jacques Sandoz and many more who are still our lifetime friends. Jacques was working on the cameras filming the event and knew that I was involved in the same world of "production and entertainment." So, he suggested that when we were in Los Angeles I should connect with him at Shri Hans Productions—the reason being that they were planning a film that would cross the country to end in Houston for the Millennium celebration. And providing that things worked out, Rachel could be the female lead.

Upon arriving in Vegas, we stopped at Cesar's Palace, just to check it out. Sometimes it's all about being in the right place at the right time because, having seen Elvis Presley on the marquee outside, all commented as we walked in:"Elvis is in the building!" Laughing at the spontaneous combustion we all created by speaking the same thought at the same time, we meant it in jest. And yet, in just a few moments, we walked up a slope toward the ballroom and opened the doors only to find Elvis on stage rehearsing his rendition of, "Surrender," just as if we had conjured him.

From Caesar's Palace, we made the drive the next day from Las Vegas to LA. And after about six hours (standard travel time back then), there it sat —off in the distance: an orange pea soup of lights, looming gloomily on the horizon.

"What is that, Jonathan?" I asked as we sped down the freeway.

"That is Los Angeles," he responded.

"And we are going in there?" I asked with disbelief, looking back at Rachel and Chris. That was the last fresh air I would breathe for at least the next two months.

The time spent in Los Angeles would take up another few chapters, so to be brief Rachel and I spent considerable time dedicating our lives to helping Shri Hans Productions, living in South Beverly Hills in an apartment with the Mills and their little new baby boy.

Then we baby-sat a one-year-old for a week in old Beverly Hills, and later moved up into Topanga Canyon, where I helped architect Larry Bernstein design a Hanging Garden City. (Think Nebuchadnezzar and "The Hanging Gardens of Babylon.")

By that time, our old production acquaintance Jacques Sandoz was ready to get on the road and start filming, so we did and crossed the country to Houston. We had a great team with Mickey Cottrell working on the script, and George Goen on sound.

Mickey later went on to be an actor, producer and a highly respected publicist who made two guest appearances on *Star Trek*. Also known for his role in *My Own Private Idaho,* having his own scene that he wrote with the young prodigy River Phoenix, having (as they say) "stolen the show" in the process.

We actually all bedded down at his mother's home in Little Rock, Arkansas. Even now, I can remember what a feast she cooked for us that night, followed by breakfast the next day with her famous cheese grits.

On arriving at the Houston Astrodome, we came across Larry Bernstein, who had designed an enormous stage for the 1973 Millennium Program for Prem Rawat who, at the time and in his way, was just as hot as Elvis.

Rennie Davis was there at "The Dome" as one of the presenters and speakers at the widely publicized event for Divine Light Mission. Such had become the mythology of Prem's impact on others (and some of the pushback that followed). Rumors were already floating around that the Astrodome would somehow take off and launch into outer space. So wild had become the speculation that Rennie was quoted in *Texas Monthly* Magazine as saying, "This city is going to be remembered through all ages of human civilization." (Even Rachel's parents, who were in Charleston, South Carolina at the time, arrived for the big day.)

We bid farewell to all our friends and headed back to the farm. What a nasty little surprise we had waiting for us there.

The family we had allowed to stay had decided to let all our furniture go to a charity! This included the bed from Becket, the antique clock that Rachel bought for me and worst of all the locked wicker chest that we had placed in the barn loft had been broken into. This chest had many of our personal belongings, photographs of Rachel's modeling days—even our silverware. What upset me most was the fact that my mother's diamond ring was gone.

Of course, we asked them to leave and settled back in, spending considerable time readjusting to the very small quarters of the farmhouse. The rooms were small and somewhat less furnished than they had been before. And, of course, Oscar Wilde was right: "No good deed will go unpunished." Part of life's journey was having discernment, and this was a lesson well learned.

# Thirty

## Our Miraculous Gift

**One day Rachel came to me** with that wondrous sparkle in her eyes that she got when she was about to tell me something special. That's when she held me, kissed me and informed me she was pregnant. If it was possible by that time in our relationship, our life together was filled with that synergy of perfect loving that is hard to put into words.

In the days of that summer our well would very often dry up. We looked at that as an opportunity to walk across the field to Julie Christie's farm. Julie, lovely woman that she is, would have us over for a bath and tea, not necessarily in that order.

In time, Julie moved out, and Jonathan and Leslie Heal moved in to set up shop. As they were both artists, the move was something of a working retreat. And I do remember that for some strange reason Jonathan had a fascination with pigs and seemed, of all things, to enjoy chauffeuring them around in his car. On more than one occasion, we would see him cruising down the lane in his Morris Minor convertible with a big sow sitting in the back, her nose set into the wind.

At one point, and in the interest of improved growing methods, I had borrowed a neighboring farmer's muck spreader and towed it over to a pig farm. On the way back, the axle of the muck spreader collapsed, and I went to farmer Mumford who kindly lent me his.

I was knee deep in pig muck I was loading from one spreader to the other and who should come along but Rachel and Chrissy in the Morris Minor convertible, not even allowing a glance to pass my way as they drove straight by. Rachel told me that she said to Chris: "Don't even look!" And so, they pretended not to notice me (although we all admitted later that they did). All's well that ends well. And I got some small measure of poetic justice later that summer when the half-acre of comfrey that I'd "fertilized" grew as high as your shoulder.

Winter came early in that second year (1974), and the narrow lanes in the glittering frost had closed up surprisingly early. Snow was thick on the ground and shrouded the lane hedges. As the wind blew, it lightly cascaded in a soft mantle down into the edge of the snow-white fields. That's when I suggested to Rachel that I should take our mare and ride up over the hill into Montgomery to get supplies.

Rachel was skeptical, and with reason. "First let me see you handle her. You are not going anywhere without my knowing you can ride her."

I saddled up, mounted the horse and immediately she took off up the field, turned in the far corner and headed back to Rachel. By that time, I was struggling to get my feet into the stirrups when the mare planted her front legs and I flew over her head and landed on my back, all the wind taken out of me. That was the end of my equestrian fantasy. I hiked over the hill and back into Montgomery on foot. (It took a very long time. I was so ready for the hot waters of a bath.) Life as a farmer in Powys was never without an adventure. In truth there were virtually too many to count.

Rachel's mother and father came over to visit in the dead of winter. Not surprisingly, the lane was frozen over for their arrival, and as it dipped down a hill to the farm I laid out a roll of wire to allow a vehicle to gain traction.

Apparently, I had done too good a job, because in a short amount of time as we were taking tea, there was a knock on the old wooden front door...standing there was our neighborly gentry with his usual bit of Sisal tied tightly around his old slicker.

"Well, Mr. Alan, I need your help. It seems my back axle has been jammed. Your wire has wrapped around it, and it's locked." He said it so imploringly in his low Welsh brogue that I was immediately moved to help him. And so, for the next three hours in the freezing weather, I lay under his Land Rover and cut away the wire little by little with my small wire cutters. Lying under the Rover snipping away, it occurred to me that life always is the unexpected teacher.

The American poet and essayist Ralph Waldo Emerson once wrote that: "*Life is a train of moods like a string of beads that, as we pass through them, prove to be many coloured lenses each painting the world its own hue, and each shows only what lies in its focus.*" What lay in focus were my hands. They were frozen, and yet we completed the mission.

It was Christmas day, and we had gone over to Roby and Sally's for tea and cake, along with Patrick and Richard, two local friends. A log fire was burning...uninformed about some of the "ingredients" involved in the baking, I had unwittingly eaten a large slice of spiked Christmas cake. Rachel decided she wanted to go for a walk, so we all wrapped up against the cold weather and took off across the fields and up a long steep hill in front of us.

Halfway up the hill, Rachel stopped (that was enough for her). So, we walked back down to the old farmhouse. Her instincts proved to be fortuitous, because as we were enjoying the mince pies and watching *The Magnificent Seven* playing on the TV, Rachel's water broke, so we sped back to the farm. Patrick and Richard were upstairs taking her pulse, knowing we had to get her off to the hospital in a hurry.

Out of some parallax bit of reasoning, doubtless influenced by the Christmas cake, I decided that I ought to milk the cow...as I had no idea when I would be back. To add to the confusion as we drove off, I was concentrating very hard on staying on the road. Understandably, Rachel was growing agitated, saying, " Hurry up! Hurry up!" ...all to someone who was unwittingly on a cannabis slowdown.

As we sped along, psychedelic images of the same tree kept reappearing, prompting me to ask the question: "Didn't we just pass that tree?"

Not the right query for Rachel who screamed, "Just get me there!" prompting me to drop off Richard and Patrick and drive to the Newtown Hospital, where several hours later our darling petit beautiful bundle arrived.

The doctors kept Rachel in hospital, fortifying her with a quart of Mackeson a day for ten days. It is a potent, if not pleasant, stout containing lactose—a sugar derived from milk. And it is supposed to help women nursing their children. So, Rachel took it all in, though to this day I'm not at all certain whether she sucked it all in just so she could bring Ella Rain home, or how many pints I guzzled down.

It had been a stark rainy night when Ella arrived and on Rachel's return to the farm we thought about a name to call her. One of Rachel's favorite books as a child had been *Ella Kari* by Anna Riwkin-Brick & Elly Jannes. So, we thought it only fitting to call her Ella Rain, our beautiful small miraculous gift.

How our lives now changed with little Ella. The cold winter winds would flow through the valley and pound the outer brick walls of her bedroom. So, I reinsulated it as best I could, which did help, at least for a while.

A short time later, I received a call from Anthony Pratt, who was designing a film on the life of young William Shakespeare. I went down and signed on and agreed that I would do the research with the Royal Court Company and then draw up the plans and elevations of the Roundhouse Theatre to be built on stage at Shepperton Studios.

Rachel and I both agreed that Patrick, a Cockney lad from London, could come to The Grove with his wife Jeanette, their small red headed son and their young Down syndrome baby. Housed there, they could tend the farm, plough, plant, milk our cow and generally look after the homestead.

Stephen, who had also been at the Shri Hans productions in LA, invited us to stay with him and his family in a large rectory in the Limehouse a district in East London. The district derives its name from the *limekilns* that were on the banks of the Thames River at least as early as the 14th century. The term, "Limey," for Englishman, was thought to be derived from the sailors of Limehouse and from the unrelated term, "lime-juicer," due to the insertion of lime-juice in the grog of the seamen to prevent scurvy. Later, it became a derogatory nickname used to describe sailors in the British Royal Navy…and finally Brits themselves.

One rather uncomfortable adjustment to city life was that Ella, in her pram, was now constantly bombarded by the continuous rumble of the trucks on commercial roads. This was such a jarring contrast to the bucolic tranquility of the countryside…the calming silence, the birds, the sheep in the meadow and the gentle chilly breezes.

While there, I met with the actor Sam Wanamaker who ran the Globe Theatre Company in London. He is credited as the person most responsible for the modern recreation of Shakespeare's Globe Theatre. To this day, his contributions are commemorated by the flourishing of the eponymous Sam Wanamaker Playhouse.

Having spent the most enlightening afternoon with Sam (and learning more new things about theatre concepts than I ever thought I would), I left with all the research that I required—even rough plans and paintings of the old London Theatre.

It was a tough few months for Rachel, as we moved so many times, and now she was pregnant again. To complicate matters further, the film was cancelled due to a collapse of funding, and we eventually found our selves back at the farm.

It seemed that almost as soon as we got back to The Grove, the phone rang. On the other end was Olivia Trinidad Arias, the lovely woman we had met in Los Angeles, inquiring to see if we were coming down to

London. It just so happened that we were going to visit Rachel's parents that weekend. So, we told her: "Yes."

Her reply was a spontaneous invitation and announcement: "Do come and see us. I am married," she declared, obviously over-the-moon. I replied by asking her to whom? It was the logical follow-up question but one from which she demurred.

"You will see when you come and have lunch with us tomorrow."

So, the next day, we drove back to London, parked the Renault on a little Georgian terrace off the Kings Road, stepped up to the front door and rang the bell. And who opened the door? George Harrison! (Yes, *that* George Harrison…of the Beatles.)

"My god! You married George Harrison!?" were the first words that came out of our mouths, much to Olivia's amusement and delight.

They invited us to come and stay with them a few times at Friar Park. We walked the 30-acre estate, spend time with George in his studio and learned the history of Frank Crisp's Victorian manor. One cold day, they drove up from Henley to The Grove and spent the night with us (from a castle to a diminutive comfy cottage).

Upon reestablishing ourselves back at the farm late in the spring, we discovered this large pool in an old quarry that was filled with goldfish (koi?) of all colours. We went a few times with Julie to swim there. It amounted to a small lake in the Welsh hills where no one would ever disturb us.

We would also picnic and skinny dip in another lake. And Peter Lyle, whom we had also met in Los Angeles, eventually came to stay. His visitation was followed by those from Alan Thomas, Michael Nouri and even Mum dropped in for a visit.

There is really nothing more celebrated by all the farmers in the hills and valleys than a glorious summer replete with the fresh golden glow from stacks of wheat in the fields after the harvest.

Now that we were getting ready for the next little one to arrive, Patrick kindly agreed that he and his family would leave so that we could have the farmhouse to ourselves.

*Alan, Rachel and Baby Ella down on the farm.*

*Ella on my back as we took off to collect some wood.*

# Thirty-One

## Under the Rainbow. Over the Moon.

There were two local midwives and a doctor with us on the day that our beautiful new soul, our son, arrived in the hills of Wales. All was dark. It was going to be a natural birth. One nurse fed the cat. The other came up now and again to the bedroom to see how Rachel was faring, and I sat on the edge of the bed holding her hand.

When that moment came for the delivery, the doctor guided the baby's head and Rachel placed her fingers under the armpits and gently brought him to us.

I went to get up and fell as my leg had just gone dead. Shaking it off, I went into the bathroom, prepared a small tin bath with a thermometer at 98° Fahrenheit water, set it down and waited while the doctor gave me the little new born baby. And as I placed him in the bath, I saw that we now had a little boy.

He cried when I lifted him out and then went silent when I placed him back into the water. I gently brought him over to Rachel and opened the curtains. And right over the house I could see a beautiful rainbow—a propitious welcome for this little one we would call Rowan, a name synonymous with a sacred sense of nature.

Patrick and Richard had been looking after Ella, and upon returning she jumped on the bed. Rachel gave her Rowan, and Ella reflexively exclaimed: "A baby for Ella!" She was blissed out.

Rowan is the name of the mountain ashes native throughout the cool temperate regions of the Northern Hemisphere—with the greatest diversity of species in the mountains of western China and the Himalayas. George Harrison had given us a little phial of Vibuthi that Sai Baba had manifested for him, and we placed a small trace of it on Rowan's forehead.

By now it was October. The house was not well heated, and we did not think we should stay for another cold winter with the little ones. Still, just to be sure, I hooked up the cart to the tractor and went off on a few runs collecting as much firewood as I could find. Then there was a call, this time from John Barry (the designer, not the music composer).

I had met John a few times but had never had the opportunity to work with him. So, I was delighted by his spontaneous call to check my "availability." Was I free? If so would I like to come down to Elstree Studios to meet with him?

"I am working on a sci-fi project, Alan, and I think you would be great for this film."

It had been a long time since I had seen John. So, I practically had to reintroduce myself when I arrived at the studio. I think the combination of my beard, my brown well-weathered Trilby and long dark brown wool overcoat made me look alien, perhaps a bit sinister, and altogether a different person from the one they remembered. Catching a glimpse of my new incarnation, John said, "You look like a Mos Eisley Rebel," laughing. "Good to see you, Alan!"

I sensed from the beginning that this might be something special since John had assembled the best draftsmen in the industry to plan this project, including Peter Child and Reg Bream (a real master). I was to share an office with Harry Lang, who was one of three production designers on Stanley Kubrick's *2001/A Space Odyssey*. The set decorator was Roger Christian, and Leslie Dilly whom I first met while working on *Becket* ... and who was later given a credit as art director. What a surprise to see such an assembly of talent! And then I was given the script to read: It was called *Star Wars*.

Who would have even guessed that now, 40 odd years later, I would be signing my name to photographs from the sets of the film and prints of my elevations and plans—one of which I've since been told is acknowledged as one of "the most original and highly regarded sets and scenes" in the world of film—that being the now iconic Mos Eisley Cantina? All this…as an integral part of *Star Wars,* that seminal groundbreaking motion picture that has fundamentally changed the aesthetics, narrative style and economics of Hollywood filmmaking!

Once I made it back to the farm for a few days, both Rachel and I made the decision to go to London, but weren't quite sure where we would stay. So that was the big question: Aunt Doris and Esther? Mum? Dad? And finally, for a little while Roger Christian and his girlfriend shared a house with us in Battersea, only a mile walk from my mother. (But Mum never came by to see the children or Rachel, sadly averring that, "she wasn't invited.")

I had just set up my office area when John walked in with a young man in a plaid shirt and denim pants, and it was then that I was introduced to George Lucas. I mentioned that I had read his script and spoke of "The Force," and how similar the content was to Joseph Campbell's *Hero with a Thousand Faces* and other works. I also mentioned that I was writing a story about a Master and a Dark Overlord. George did not reply but smiled as John showed me a small sketch and plan of the "Cantina." We had a brief brainstorming session, and I was left to put it together. What I did not know at that time was all the props and sets going to Morocco were being prepared, finished, and readied to be shipped.

While perusing the sets and watching some of the cast being fitted into their costumes, I met Kenny Baker, as he was being fitted into

R2-D2. Anthony Daniels, as the costume sculptor, was struggling with his fitting of C-3PO.

Back on the drawing board, I laid out the plans and elevations of the Cantina, made a few prints and went ahead and made a small model at quarter inch scale. George and John came to eye it and approved. I then went down to the prop room to see what I could find to detail the bar.

Roger had purchased two 1945 jet planes and had them torn apart. I went into the interiors of the engines, showed them to John and said that I would use these along with various other containers as the center of the bar. Then I took them to the paint shop and planned to have them anodized in gold and silver. John then asked where I could place a jukebox. I showed him an area by the entrance and then drew up a simple design.

Meanwhile, the corridor sets that Peter Childs had drawn were already under construction. Next for me was the Mos-Eisley garage. John had given me a sketch of a circular rooftop that was going to Morocco. At first, I did not see what it represented, until John explained that below it was the garage. Before John left for Morocco, he showed me his ideas. We then co-designed the garage, and I proceeded to draw it, including all the details and then scrambled around to find all kinds of metal elements to dress it.

A photograph of Luke's Skyhopper arrived from John Dykstra's Hollywood shop, and I drew it up, as it was set up to sit in the rear of the garage. When George was recruiting people for the SFX work on our film, he approached Doug Trumbull who pointed him towards Dykstra. Dykstra led Industrial Light & Magic's developmental crew that designed the computer-controlled motion control camera systems responsible for many of the film's ground-breaking effects, i.e. all the air to air combat sequences.

At this point I would like to mention that my hero at that time was Ralph McQuarrie, a phenomenally talented artist and illustrator. In 1975, George had just completed his second draft of *Star Wars*. Coming off the huge success of his film *American Graffiti,* he sold the idea to 20th

Century Fox, but the studio's executives didn't fully understand what he was trying to do, so they hesitated on moving forward with the film.

That's when Lucas turned to McQuarrie, a concept artist he had met a couple of years earlier, and commissioned him to illustrate several key scenes from the script. His illustrations helped get the film made, and ultimately shaped the overall look and feel of the *Star Wars* universe. We had copies of his original drawings pinned up on the wallboards as reference, inspiration and to glean some additional concepts.

Once production was underway, Alan Ladd Jr. ("Laddie") came in from 20$^{th}$ Century Fox and upon seeing what we had created went ahead and finalized contracts with George Lucas.

Alan Ladd. Jr. (son of the legendary leading man, Alan Ladd) had recently been brought in as Head of Worldwide Production for Fox. He soon came to be regarded as one of the industry's more visionary studio executives. Over the coming two decades, "Laddie" produced such blockbusters as *Alien, Braveheart* and *Chariots of Fire*. He instinctively recognized the potential for *Star Wars* when practically no one at that time gave this "interesting little film" a chance to do all that well at the box office. In fact, projections for its success ranged from moderate to pessimistic. So, the studio execs at Fox jumped at the chance when George relinquished the majority of his points in the film in return for retaining all licensing and merchandizing.

When the film jumped out with surprisingly high box office receipts and expanded distribution to $775 million worldwide, execs at Fox were high-fiving their decision to let Lucas have the merchandising. But in the time between 1977 and 1978, *Star Wars* sold $100 million worth of toys, all the royalties for which were kept by Lucas. And in the next 35 years *Star Wars*-themed toys, games and spinoffs generated $12 Billion in revenue, much of it going to Lucas…not to mention massive points in the sequels, *The Empire Strikes Back, Return of the Jedi*, four prequels, two additional sequels and four other sibling productions.

Once principal photography got underway, the crew took off to shoot in Morocco, and I was left taking care of the Garage and Cantina, and also dressing the exterior of the Millennium Falcon and the hangar.

Meanwhile, Rachel had a call from Olivia (Arias) Harrison. And, knowing how hard it had been for Rachel, she suggested that we come down to Friar Park and live in the Middle Lodge, as it was empty. The Lodge was lovely but very much in need of a coat of paint. So, a short time later we found ourselves there in Henley, staying in one of the three lodges. And somehow, I found time to slap my brush around on the weekends. I did manage to fall and break a rib as I tried to help Rowan down the narrow stairs. So, it got finished by a "wounded artist."

Friar Park was such a beautiful estate that George Harrison had rescued from being torn down. He was undertaking the extensive work of repairs to the old Victorian manor and overhauling the mansion of Frank Crisp. It was such a lovely, poetic retreat for Rachel and the children, who loved walking in the 30-acre gardens. The entire experience for us all was one of idyllic perfection.

*George Harrison and John Gilbert sharing a joke with me over George prepping one of his Bonsai trees.*

One day, my friend John Gilbert and I walked down to where George would often go to a lower area in the park where he worked on a few of his Bonsai trees. We sat sharing time with him and laughed a lot. His Liverpudlian humor, breezing up through the pines, had us in stitches time and again..

Back at the preproduction design group, Ted Ambrose had drawn up the Millennium Falcon and it was being assembled on stage. I had been given the responsibility to draw up and dress the details for the rim of the Falcon and its Hangar. For me, that meant going through the back lot of the studio to see what I could scrounge up. There were metallic piles of junk lying about everywhere. So, I compiled my own stack with numbers and told the prop people to pick it up and clean it. Once clean, I had it brought up to the set, and you will see on my drawing the same numbers: "please go ahead and place the junk in corresponding areas of the rim."

Dixie Dean, the painter, really made the Falcon come to life in the way he aged it, using layers and layers of various tones of paint, even oil, bought the clean wooden construction to what we all know as Han Solo's Millennium Falcon.

On returning one Sunday from the studio to Friar Park, I could hear a lot of laughter coming from the garden. I showered and went over to see a man in a light green sweat suit sharing stories with the children and having the adults in fits of laughter. George handed me a Pimm's cup, and when I asked him who the character was, he replied, "His name is Robin Williams and he's just on his way home after finishing *Popeye, the Sailor Man*. (The film *Popeye* was a live action rendition of the cartoon character, starred in by Robin and Shelley Duvall, shot by director Robert Altman and produced by Robert Evans.)

A natural, spontaneous genius wit (and just a kid at heart), Robin had us all in hysterics for at least another hour. I had no idea of the hugely successful *Mork and Mindy* TV comedy series he was doing in America. And his star only rose from there.

Upon their return from shooting in Morocco, Roger and John walked through the Cantina, the Garage then the Hangar. After entering the Hangar and after making a walk-through of the other two sets, Roger turned to me and said: "Alan, you are going to get me an Oscar."

The reason I mention this is due to the fact that my name was not on the unit list, even though I had mentioned it to Robert Watts, the production supervisor. On seeing the first screening, I did not get a credit and apparently wasn't going to receive one, until a few years later when I sent a letter to Lucasfilm, Ltd. I finally got a call one day telling me that, on the new release, I would receive a credit as "Assistant to the Production Designer," which was analogous to being a "Production Assistant" (PA). So, at that point, I couldn't tell which was more dismissive—not being recognized at all, or being damned with faint praise.

Finally, about three decades later, I saw some justice done when I had a call from John Rinzler, who was working with Lucasfilm, editing and creating various historic books on the making of *Star Wars* in San Francisco. He invited me for an interview, which then appeared as a six-page article in their *Star Wars Magazine* issue 131 (March 2012). I was described as "one of the film's unsung heroes."

The most rewarding part of any film, especially for me, is when the music is finally superimposed onto it. This makes an entire other dimension unfold and the film's scenes are now dynamically alive.

I went with Roger one morning to see the music track being laid down onto the black and white sequences running across the screen above the London Symphony Orchestra. The session was being conducted by composer John Williams, who has scored all of Steven Spielberg's and George Lucas's collective films. He is (arguably) the most revered film composer of all time.

Upon hearing the score, there is no other way to explain what I felt other than a complete sense of phenomenality. In all candor, I must admit that what has been the unparalleled success of this epic saga originally eluded us all because, whenever we would see the dailies, most of the crew wondered out loud if it would ever get released. George, though, had it all within him, while we of the art department were each dealing with what we had been individually asked to help design for the film, not knowing really how it would all come together…and it most certainly did.

In November 2018, I find myself here in San Anselmo in Northern California—the very place where George Lucas began to create his saga in 1973. It was also here that I met Lorne Peterson, who was the chief model maker on the first six *Star Wars* films, starting in 1975. During our conversation, Lorne emphasized that when he first started he was only hired for two months, thinking it would be a project of short duration. In this age of super high-tech and CGI it almost seems quaint that he remembers the way they were making the models was by using five-minute epoxy.

He was aware that there was a super glue used in the medical and pearl industry in Japan that was not available in retail. A week into ILM, he brought Super Glue into the model shop and asked everyone to stop for a moment to see what he was about to show them. He took a pencil and cantilevered it off the edge of a desk, held it down with one finger, placed a drop of the Super Glue under the pencil and removed his finger. A gasp came from around the room. And as it turned out, it revolutionized the speed with which they could continue to make the models. Lorne's two months turned into 35 years and nine films, and the rest is history

*The Mos Eisley Garage co-designed with John Barry, drawn, detailed and dressed by me.*

*Forty years later on stage at the 2017 1st Tokyo Comi Con.*

Under the Rainbow. Over the Moon • 237

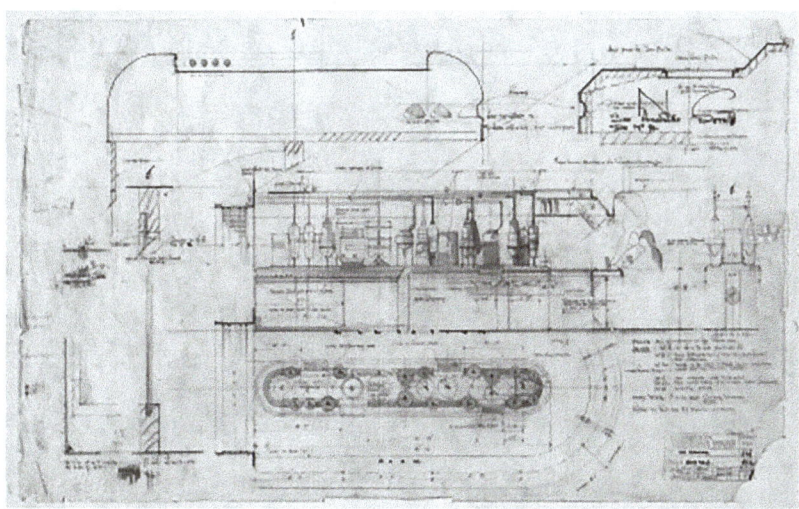

*My blueprint for the working plan and elevations for the
Mos Eisley Cantina Central Bar*

*The Rebel Strategy Grid and Control Panel—another of my designs.*

*The Millennium Falcon on stage, a rim shot, incorporating the dressing of junk from the Elstree back lot.*

# Thirty-Two

## Tehran. Tarzan. And a Leap of Faith.

**When Star Wars had finally finished** we were still living in the Middle Lodge at Friar Park. I previously directed a commercial for Gillette that had been well received by the client. Everything was happening for us in London at the time. So, it only seemed logical to remain there.

Two friends who were with the agency called again and said that they had been approached to make another commercial and asked me if I would direct it. This time though we were busting out of London and going to Tehran! (Yes! *That* Tehran, capital of Iran.)

Surprised, I questioned why? Somewhat to my frustration, I never received a direct answer from Paul other than the fact that his wife was from Iran.

The plane took off, crossed over continent after continent, and seemed to span half the globe before finally landing in Iran. Paul, who was producing for his agency, introduced me to his wife's family and we shared a dinner and another weekend lunch where I discovered for the first time the very tasty pistachio nut. We found the locations that were required, shot all the necessary film that the agency boards had showed, and got out of there pretty quickly.

Upon finding my seat on the return flight, I saw five of Paul's wife's family getting onboard with us. Then, looking at the new unit list, I noticed all their names listed as members of our crew. It became apparent to me then that this journey had all been staged just in order to help his family escape. It was 1978, and the regime of the Shah of Iran—the most pro-Western Islamic nation in the history of the Middle East—was already imperiled.

The Shah had stepped aside, an interim government had been installed, every Islamic radical had been released from the prisons (due to pressure from the Carter Administration), and radical Islam in Iran was on a rocket ride to the top.

About six months later, in January of 1979, the Ayatollah Ruhollah Khomeini took power, and anti-Americanism became the mantra of the new radical extreme government of the Ayatollah. In November of 1979, a group of Iranian college students, in support of the Islamist Revolution, seized the U.S. Embassy in Tehran by force and held 54 American diplomats and staff hostage for 444 days until January 20, 1981. Placed in prison "under suspicion of espionage," their captivity stands as the longest hostage crisis on record and one of the darkest days in modern American history.

Ben Affleck's Oscar winning film, *Argo*, was so similar in planning and context to what Paul had achieved earlier that the resemblance was uncanny. And in fact, *Argo* was based on something called the "Canadian Caper," in which the CIA operative Tony Mendez led the rescue of six U.S. diplomats from Tehran, Iran under the guise of filming a science fiction film during the 1979–1981 Iran hostage crisis.

Paul's dash for freedom presaged all that, and his anticipation of the crisis to come made it all much easier to accomplish. As it was, we did one more close-up of the talent shaving in the garden at the middle lodge, edited it, and it aired.

*Rachel and Alan on a Romantic Miami Beach interlude.*

After I returned to Henley, Rachel and I emotionally agreed that we would sell The Grove and go to live in Malibu. Even now, it seems like a wild leap of faith…never mind! It turned out to be precisely the right thing to do. At the time, it was purely a matter of gut feeling and spiritual instinct.

Prem Rawat, now sixteen, was living there, and we had also made so many new friends in California. We received a card from a woman and her husband who had previously asked us to let them know if we ever wanted to sell, since it was the only place that they had fallen in love with. We sold it to them and still were able to stay with George and Olivia in Henley until it was time to fly to California.

On the first of August, 1978, George pulled up outside of our lodge in his two-toned blue Rolls Royce, jumped out of the car, and excitedly announced (to the world) that Olivia had given birth to a beautiful boy and he was on his way to pick them both up. This beautiful new bundle

*Ella and Rowan on the gate at The Grove, a poetic farewell…*

of joy and boundless potential arrived in their family christened with the name, Dhani (which is a Hindi word that means "hamlet.")

I went to Arundel to see the masterly illustrator John Bodimeade—a friend and mentor I had worked with on my very first film, *The Victors*. I had told him about *Karas,* the script that I had been writing and asked if he might be able to help me with maybe four illustrations.

Over a pot of tea, he thoughtfully counseled me: "You will be able to do your own drawings, Alan. Just have the confidence. Since we first met through your own ability, Alan, you have become an accomplished draftsman."

We talked about many great artists like Leonardo De Vinci, Michelangelo, and Titian…and their ability to draw in all areas of art. As I said goodbye, John's wife stopped outside the front door and told me in a soft sad voice that he had cancer and would not be with us very much longer. Two weeks later, I had a call from her letting me know the sad news of John's passing.

Margaret Thatcher, the Prime Minister in 1979, had made it extremely hard to take monies out of the country. We visited Paradise Garage in Fulham, and sitting in a line were three cars: a 1962 Maserati Superleggera, a 1964 Gullwing Mercedes, and a 190 SEL Mercedes convertible. I was enamored of the green and purple Gullwing that had belonged to Gunter Sachs, Brigitte Bardot's husband, but Rachel really shunned the colour. So, we purchased the other two for £5,000.00, deciding that this would be a clever gambit to get some of our money out of the country. Anything to skirt the draconian mandates of the "Iron Lady."

It was really hard and a little sad letting go of our beautiful home in the Welsh hills, for Mother Nature with her seasons had proved to be such a teacher. It was, and always would be, our first home with the children—and thereby would forever hold a special place in our hearts.

For reasons none of us can explain through rationale or common logic, instinct takes over at a cellular level when emotions are involved. I remember, even to this day, that when I was holding Rowan in my arms and waved a goodbye across the road to my mother in Clapham Junction, I knew at some level (and yet did not know) that it would be the very last time I would ever lay eyes on her. Even so, that image of her waving goodbye to us remains as clear as a crystal and with me even to this day.

Upon deciding to depart the UK for the US, we were able to obtain a year's visiting visa to the United States. George wondered out loud why we were going, and said that we could always stay in the Middle Lodge if we had wanted to do so.

Decision made, we flew to Miami for a three-day *Holi* festival and to see some old friends. *Holi* is the Hindu spring festival celebrated in India

*(Top) A 1963 Maserati Superleggera.
(Bottom) Rowan and Ella deciding whether or not to drive our Mercedes 190 SEL Convertible. (Parked outside the Middle Lodge at Fair Park.)*

and Nepal, known as the "festival of colours" or the "festival of love." The festival signifies the victory of good over evil, the arrival of spring and end of winter, for many it's a festive day to meet others.

There was coloured water that was sprayed from a canon by Prem Rawat with laser lights flashing over the gathered throng of five thousand men women and children all dressed in white. Ella and Rowan just loved their new rainbow coloured t-shirts and pants.

A friend knew that we were coming to Malibu and mentioned that we could stay with her until we were able to find a home to rent. I had always wanted to have an Airstream trailer for the pure aesthetic value, if nothing else. We purchased a 30-foot silver bullet, towed it and placed it on Susan's property in Ramirez Canyon. We had only been there for two weeks when a letter from the canyon committee signed by Barbra Streisand and Mick Fleetwood requested that we please remove our shiny object from the hill. (Well, if you're going to offend people, why not pick something shiny?)

A few days later, we found a home to rent and just as quickly leased out the Airstream. Settled in, I started make contacts in the various studios to see if I could find work.

I went to Universal Studios to see Ted Haworth, from *Half a Sixpence,* who was designing a film there. When I arrived at the art department (and to my surprise) Ted introduced me to his team as one of the most accomplished draftsmen, but said I could not help because I was not in the union. After that, I went to Paramount, Warner Brothers and Twentieth Century Fox, where I was always given the same response: "See if you can somehow join the union."

I visited the old David O. Selznick Studios where they had made *Gone with the Wind, Citizen Kane, Duel in the Sun* and so many other legendary films. As I walked around I saw two old stages where the walls were lifted for the light, the prop rooms full of so many great models of galleons, Sinbad the Sailor's ships, crates still filled with the props that were used by Orson Wells on *Citizen Kane,* and bungalows used by Vivian Lee, Leslie Howard, Clark Gable and Bette Davis.

When the new owners purchased these legendary studios, I was surprised that they so utterly lacked a sense of history and totally dismantled the old stages, destroying most of the props. I thought they might have at least created a museum in one of them; it wouldn't have taken that much. But "new brooms" can be ruthless…and devoid of sentiment. (They did, however, keep the bungalows. And I saw Orson Welles a few times sitting in his favorite corner of his favorite restaurant on Melrose Avenue having lunch.)

Henry Hathaway, the director I had worked with in Africa, invited me over for lunch at his club and introduced me to various producer friends: Brian Eatwell, a production designer friend was now living in LA. To my surprise, Danny, who was the friend at Chelsea art school who introduced me to our world of film, was also living in Malibu.

I continued to write the screenplay for *Karas,* but we ran out of money, so I stood with the Mexican lads on the corner of Point Dume and was able to get work at $6 an hour in order to feed the family. (It was a humbling experience, but one that gave me perspective on the life of the hard-working men from South of the border who would send most of their earnings back to their families—legal or not—as we had yet to be awarded our Green Cards.) I will never begrudge anyone the right to make a life in any way they are able: R-E-S-P-E-C-T is totally due!

After a few weeks, the cars—the Maserati and the Mercedes—arrived. At that point, we were the ultimate paradox of elegant deprivation. We were not certain if we should immediately sell them. Then the call came from Brian Eatwell. He was going to Brazil on a film called *Savage Harvest,* and he needed someone to go to Africa and art direct that section of the script. Knowing I had already worked there, he wondered whether I would be willing to fly to Kenya the following week? (There was no question—of course I would. The first break had arrived.)

I had to leave Rachel and the children behind and went off to spend five weeks in an area outside of Nairobi. The work was not as intense as my previous job there, but it paid the bills and broke the ice for me in LA.

Upon my return, I had a call from Tom Shaw, who asked me with no small sense of irony: "Is your résumé real? You're very young to have worked on so many great films. Are you available to come to MGM to see me? You have been highly recommended by the producers of *Savage Harvest.*"

He did not want to discuss the project with me on the phone. "Please come," he requested cryptically. "I look forward to meeting you."

So, the next day I found myself wandering around the studio complex of MGM leading up to Tom's office. "You're younger than I imagined, Alan," he said, with a note of amusement. I asked him what this project was and he responded rather cryptically, "They'll tell you in there. Go in and meet the director, producer and the actress."

So, I did. When I walked into the office, there was Bo Derek sitting on the floor and John Derek was making notes on the script. Bo, at the time, had just starred with Dudley Moore and Julie Andrews in the movie *10*, and was one of the hottest actresses in town. Truly a 10 in her every gesture, she had replaced Farah Fawcett as the new poster girl for men to fantasize over and women to try to imitate. And imitate they did! Women were wearing cornrows and getting a tan, and there were tens of thousands of Bo clones all over America. But here I was with "the original" and getting checked out with an offhanded glance. "I like his sweater, John, he's got the job," Bo said, nodding her approval as if ordering a cup of tea.

Well, let's hear it for lightning in a bottle! Those were the very words that she said before I had even closed the door behind me. This was for the movie *Tarzan*, and even without reading the script I was scribbling a sketch in front of them, and had the job on the spot.

Tom Shaw had such an illustrious career working with director John Houston and on such legendary productions as *In Cold Blood, The Professionals, The Night of the Iguana, Lonely are the Brave,* and *Elmer Gantry* to name a few. Once again, another mentor had come into my life. And if it all seemed too good to be true, rest assured it was.

John Derek had shot from the hip by bringing me on board, and I soon came to realize that this was the way he did everything. (Sexy and spontaneous, but very often not the right way to go about it.) Perhaps it was portentous that a shocking event took place that struck me like a blow just as I'd left the meeting.

It was the 8th of December 1980, and I heard the news while driving back from my meetings. John Lennon had been shot dead by Mark David Chapman in the archway of the Dakota, his residence in New York City.

Lennon had just returned from Record Plant Studio with Yoko Ono when Chapman shot him four times in the back at close range. Lennon was pronounced dead on arrival at Roosevelt Hospital. Shortly after local news stations reported Lennon's death, crowds gathered at Roosevelt Hospital and in front of the Dakota.

I remember what a major gut-wrenching moment it was for me, because the event virtually threw me into shock. I pulled over and stopped the car. And, from a depth of both disbelief and sorrow, I shed tears. They flowed from me involuntarily and in great profusion. Why and how would anyone want to kill this beautiful soul who wrote many songs that tried to wake humanity's awareness to peace and love? Of course, I was not alone. Total disbelief spread across the globe as millions mourned John's passing. It was an unfinished symphony of a truly magnificent man.

Shock or not, life can be ruthless in pursuit of itself. As it was, I was given no time to prepare for production on *Tarzan*. Immediately, they wanted me to fly with Tom Shaw to Sri Lanka the following week. John Derek told me that they had three weeks to prep the film. I would have an Indian art director, Vincent, who would meet me there. John had already selected all the locations, and prior to leaving I had organized Peter James with whom I had worked on *The Lion in Winter* as the set decorator with Noby Clark as my construction coordinator. So, there we were, flying off to Sri Lanka. And that would be the easy part.

# Thirty-Three

## Bo-Dacious!

John Derek had been an actor in Hollywood for nearly 20 years before he turned to directing. As an actor, he was one of those leading men actually cursed by his own good looks. Stunningly handsome, Derek had given some credible performances, notably as Tom Stark in the 1949 version of the Oscar winning film, *All the Kings Men,* and as the Arab, Tasha, in Otto Preminger's *Exodus.* For the most part, however, John had been relegated to a run of lesser action-adventure movies, until he started directing in 1965, usually films starring his wives at the time, Ursula Andress and (later) Linda Evans.

Bo Derek was fourth in the line of his "goddess" wives and, due to her recent box office blowout with the blockbuster comedy *10,* was very much in demand. So, although the film was titled *Tarzan the Ape Man,* this was going to be Bo Derek's vehicle. She was even featured on the original poster, with no image of her co-star Miles O'Keefe. (In fact, Bo was also listed as Producer on the film, and the original script was titled *Me, Jane* before they decided to change it.) I also quickly learned that John preferred to be the *auteur* of his films, i.e. he liked to control everything involved in the filming and often left his crew to sort out the decisions.

Planning production for the film, I met with my art director Vincent and his team on arriving in Colombo, Sri Lanka. Tom Shaw decided that we had better go first to see all of John's selected locations. And to be sure, they were stunningly beautiful but also promised to be a logistical nightmare.

The first was in the forest above the town of Kandy, and after walking for at least eight minutes, then seeing the dark pool that was being cleared I asked Vincent what they were trying to do. They had already built a ladder up the impressive tree, and they were now trying to clear the pool—at least this was what Vincent told me. My immediate reaction was that we had better find another location. As it was set up, it was so remote that it would be virtually impossible to get a crew in there without incident. Worse, I could not see the pool ever being made clear enough for Bo to be filmed swimming in it naked!

After checking out all the sites chosen for filming, Tom and I decided we had to change them; we needed to find new locations that could be shot at least 180 degrees. This was mainly due to John only seeing what his still camera viewed, i.e. what was directly in front of him. If the camera was to turn to the left or the right, the areas were too cluttered to shoot.

I went to an island location situated just down river where Don Ashton had designed and built the bridge for the film *The Bridge on the River Kawai*. It was obvious to both of us that we would have to build steps down 12 feet and then construct a 180-foot-long bridge to the island where we would construct a native village. Vincent employed a team of Mahouts for the job. Elephants dropped the timbers we required into the river north of the island. That way, they would float down towards us and be much easier for the local workers we'd hired to drag them up onto land.

During the production, I had two teams at my disposal—one building the new selected Tarzan tree house area and another on the river island. What I did not realize was the fact that these "two teams" were from two different religions. Team One was made up of Sri Lankan Tamils who are mostly Hindus with a significant Christian population. My other group was the Sinhalese, and mostly Buddhists.

Originally called Ceylon, Sri Lanka is an island about the size of Ireland and with a complicated political and religious history. It is primarily Buddhist (72% of the population) in the North with the southern portion of the island being Tamil "Tigers," who are Hindu and Christian. The political structure of the island has always been something of a challenge as well. Or, as we say, "It's complicated."

I found that out the hard way, because when the tree location was complete, I took the men to the island location to help get it finished and suddenly came upon the Sinhalese and Tamil Tigers drawing knives on each other. After finding out the problem, I immediately took the Sinhalese lads to another location. (As it turned out this was a microcosm of problems that would roil up later, including a civil war involving Tamil rebels that broke out in 1983 and lasted for the next 26 years.)

The location we finalized was one that was going to be the set where co-star Richard Harris (as James Parker) would have his headquarter camp. The location was a reservoir with a wide field and grass banks. Vincent informed us that when they did Mosquito flushing the water would lower and then rise again, though they were not certain to what height.

That necessitated our making the decision to place the tents on top of platforms four to five feet from the ground and further back from the existing water line. I found a canvas maker and selected a soft pinky canvas, designing them with window flaps in their sides, similar in shape to the old English Army tents. We also built a walkway that would allow Bo's boat to dock alongside it.

Tom suggested that we rent a helicopter and fly north to Trincomalee to see the other ocean locations. It was Christmas Eve, and Tom, to his "peril," had earlier grown a bushy white beard. So…upon stepping out of the copter at the lodge with his white beard flowing, he suddenly found himself surrounded by children fantasizing that Santa had arrived. (We thought to disabuse them of the notion, but at that time of the year, it just seemed best to play along. So he did.)

We stayed at a hotel in Trincomalee where Arthur C. Clarke had set up home in the early fifties. Unless you have been there, it's hard to describe. But Sri Lanka is a topographical and culture wonder with fantastic scenery and a rich tradition of ancient civilizations.

One time, while scuba diving with his photographer, Mike Wilson, Clark apparently uncovered the ruined masonry, architecture and idol images of a sunken original temple including carved columns with flower insignias and stones in the form of elephant heads—spread on the shallow surrounding seabed. The complex was destroyed in colonial religious attacks between 1622 and 1624, and a fort was built at the site from its debris. A temple built in 1632, located away from the city houses, contained some of its original idols. Worldwide interest was renewed following the discovery of its underwater land ruins, sculptures and Chola bronzes by archaeologists and Clark.

I spent another few days in the helicopter, searching for areas to shoot in the river. Suddenly I looked up, and there in front of us was a cable stretching across the river. "Cable!" I shouted and the pilot just missed it.

In the evening I would write a chapter of a story for the children, and Rachel would read it to them at night. It was about a witch that had stolen a dragon's crystal eye and how the gnomes and dwarfs went on a hazardous journey to recover it for him.

John Derek's first words when he arrived were, "I hear you spent money on renting a helicopter." I emphasized that I had to in order to finalize the workable locations and make changes. I then asked if he would he like to see them.

John upon seeing them, surprised me by approving every one, and at the tree house, Bo stripped down to make certain that she could swim below and through the roots of Tarzan's tree. She took a deep breath and swam naked under and through a channel that had been cleared for her.

Then we went to see the boat that we would use for sending Bo up the river to Richard Harris's camp. When we arrived, Vincent and two local metal workers were placing the old rundown steam engine into the middle deck.

John grabbed a paintbrush and enthusiastically announced, "Lets age it down together," and started to paint the keel.

Peter James had arrived and spent time in Colombo and Kandy, finding the majority of his props. But, being the consummate professional he was, he had two large leather trunks flown down from London with the special hand props required.

As pre-production developed, it became clear that Tommy Shaw and John Derek did not agree on how the production should run. So, after a time, Tom and his daughter left us. I then not only ended up being the Art Director but also assumed the role of Chief Production Manager for the entire shoot.

The animal trainers arrived from Los Angeles with the lion, four chimpanzees and the orangutan, then spent time finding Tarzan's elephant and a python. John and Bo had previously been to the Seychelles, and had flown in from there a group of young men and girls to be our village natives.

Being there in Sri Lanka was just so rewarding in so many ways. In the mornings, one could see the rows of immaculately turned out children in their white shirts, blue and green shorts and skirts walking hand in hand to school. The hill tea plantations with the English architectural bungalows and large old plantation homes were breathtakingly beautiful. Ocean peoples lived alongside the beaches and fished to sustain their lives. You could also see the elephants as they were cleaned by their handlers and the Monks walking with their bowls held out in front to receive whatever was placed in them.

Richard Harris, John Phillip Law and Lee Canahalin soon arrived. And almost immediately, there was something of a setback when John decided that he was going to let go of his original choice of Tarzan, Lee, who had been injured prior to the shoot and did not prove to have any real chemistry with Bo. On the first day, after an amazing shot with Tarzan sitting on the lead elephant with ten other elephants following behind which triggered a dark cloud of large bats that soared above the stampede, John took me aside and asked me what I thought of Lee.

*Did my opinion really matter?* I wondered. In any event, I replied, "He looks amazingly right for the part, John."

I suspect Derek had already made up his mind before he asked me, evidenced by the fact that John fired Canahalin the next day and brought in Miles O'Keeffe to take over the role. He was a good athlete but hardly an actor to challenge the likes of a Burton, O'Toole or even a Richard Harris. However, Miles looked absolutely "shredded" without his clothes on and seemed the perfect athlete to romp through the trees.

Other than the constant attrition with cast and crew, every day was such a visually enchanted experience. It was interesting to view John directing Bo, because there was none of the typical director to actor mentoring that one might have expected. And as the daily filming wore on, it was clear to see that she truly suffered from his lack of guidance.

We had a German camera crew. And due to John's dismissing various other members of the production team during the shoot, we were down to six crew members, plus my art department and local PA's.

There were some unforgettable moments with the animals and the jungle environment. Three that trigger my memory were Miles as Tarzan being lifted by the tusks of the elephant, the chimpanzee who apparently dreaded the river being guided across by the orangutan holding his hand…and finally the jealous orangutan trying to pull Miles away from Bo as they were lying together on the bank of the river surrounded by flitting butterflies. I had cut a branch that was in Bo's face, and it was

*Top, the Classic Poster, now a collector's item.
Bottom, Bo and some of her leading men from TARZAN The Ape Man..*

*Bo and John Derek at a "talk-back."*

suddenly encircled with the yellow butterflies drawn there by the smell of the sap. Catching the image on camera was magical.

One event, more perilous than mystical, involved a real python that John Derek had decided to "employ" to replace the prop python I had put together. Showing little to no respect for Bo's seeming lack of fear, and apparently sensing she was on camera, this real Python dropped down, encircled her body and started "to squeeze" in earnest—until the animal wranglers came to remove it, saving her from being crushed to death.

During the production, I recommended to John that we should probably film an establishing shot of the village: but he did not want to. I arranged to have the fires lit and with the DP Mike Bartlett sat at dawn as the sun was rising…and we got a great shot!

Later, back in LA, I chanced to walk into the editing bay just as John was looking at that one phenomenally captivating sunrise over the village. It would have made the next sequence, but never made it into the film; ego reigned.

At one point on a Saturday, Richard Harris and I were invited up by the English dam builders to come and join them and see England play

Ireland in a rugby union match. Richard would shout: "Come on, my son!" as Ireland took the ball and scored. Ireland lost but Richard enjoyed the outing, helped by "a few jars."

Toward the end of the shoot, Rachel arrived with the children, took one rather shocked look at me and said: "You look as if you have just come out of Bergen-Belsen concentration camp! You are so thin! You have to start eating fish and chicken again!" I had been a vegetarian for the past eight years, which began when we were on the farm, but by now I was growing anemic; so, a little animal protein seemed in order.

I let Rachel have my driver, whom I later found out actually had been living in the car. He drove her and the children to many of the well-known sites while we were filming.

Rachel, Ella and Rowan had only been with me one day in Kandy when I had a call from my Aunt Esther, letting me know that my mother had died from a diabetic coma.

Sympathetic to my dilemma, John released me to go back to England. But, knowing that Mum (her eternal soul) had already left her body, I decided to stay. In my opinion, he really needed me there with him (although he might not have known it at the time). For the rest of that day, I sat in silence by the river, reflecting on the love that Irene had for my brother and me, and the sadness she had suffered in silence after being divorced by my father.

On the day of her funeral, they closed the local pub in Clapham Junction, and held a wake in her honor with an Irish band and 50 cars following the magnificent lady all the way to the crematorium! What a great send off, darling Mum! As I was no longer living in England, Philip dealt with the details…and all the family transitions from that day forward.

We finished our days in Sri Lanka and moved the remainder of the shoot to the Seychelles Islands. The extras were so excited to be returning home for a two-week shoot to their motherland, officially the French

République des Seychelles. In the Seychelles, they speak a Creole kind of French. A sovereign state in the Indian Ocean whose capital is Victoria, it sits 932 miles east of mainland East Africa. With a population of roughly 94,228, it has the smallest population of any sovereign African nation, and one of the highest Legatum Prosperity Index rankings in the Sub Sahara, reflective of quality of life.

If you have never seen crystal clear ocean water then this is where you should go to see the multicolored Parrot fish that swim within its depths: Be so careful though of the lionfish. Their scales are replete with long poisonous spikes called pteroids. Their venom is rarely fatal to healthy adults; but some species have enough venom to produce extreme discomfort for a period of several days. However, the pteroidal venom is a danger to allergic victims, as they may experience *anaphylactic shock*, a serious and often life-threatening condition that requires emergency medical treatment. Severe allergic reactions to pteroid venom include chest pain, severe breathing difficulties, a drop-in blood pressure, swelling of the tongue, sweating, runny nose, or slurred speech, such reactions can be fatal if not treated.

Establishing the final shots, we had set up on the most impressively wide exquisite sandy beach in this enchanted place. Bo was playing in the surf and Miles was about to jump from a rock in the far distance. The scene was set up so that we could see the lion in the left of frame, ever aware that the animal keepers had chained him to a stake behind the sand dunes.

I was standing right next to John as he called action. Miles started to run towards Bo. I was the only one at this point who noticed that the lion somehow had broken free from its chain and was running straight down the beach towards Bo. His paw hit her on her back, she reacted in shock and dived into the waves, luckily his claws had been removed. I started to run towards them and suddenly realized how dangerous this was and backtracked. Miles had grabbed the Lion around its neck and was struggling to hold it from darting into the ocean to get Bo. The trainers by then had seen what was going on and took over, re-leashing the angry animal just as John shouted: "Sack that lion!" Nevertheless, he did get a great shot before sending the lion home (although it was still required for three more scenes).

After a shoot, I noticed that the children were having a great time snorkeling in the shallows. I asked them, "Where is Mummy?" Rowan pointed way out to the horizon and there she was—all but disappearing on a windsurfing board. I was able to get a speedboat to go and get her, and when the boatman arrived, Rachel asked him, "How much did my husband pay you to come and get me?" Then she furthered the conversation with a query: "How much is a lesson?"

As a result, she ended up being coached back to us, having a windsurf lesson all the way to the beach. The reason she was so far away was due to having no idea how to turn the sail around. So, her adventurism nearly had her disappearing over the horizon, literally riding off into the sunset.

Looking back on the whole experience of *Tarzan, the Ape Man*, it was a rather bizarre mélange of enchantment and miscues, ending in a controversial final cut. Perhaps not surprisingly, it was one of the worst panned films of 1981, described by critic Leonard Maltin as being so bad that "even the animals performed poorly."

While visually stunning, its pace was turgid and the plotlines incomprehensible. Tarzan, however was not without its accolades. Praised (tongue in cheek) by Roger Ebert as a clumsy but endearing and "highly erotic cult classic," it managed to garner six Golden Raspberry nominations for the worst film of 1981, including John Derek for Worst Director and Miles O'Keefe for Worst New Star. And yes! Bo won the "Razzie" for Worst Performance by an Actress in a Leading Role.

In a final point of irony only Hollywood could explain, the film cleaned up at the box office. Costing a parsimonious $6.5 million to make, *Tarzan* grossed nearly $38 million in revenues, mainly due to Bo's phenomenal popularity and some pretty steamy erotica.

# Thirty-Four

## A Blank Canvas Turns into a "Triumph"

*Vice Squad,* all shot in Los Angeles, was my first introduction to Sandy Howard productions. Sandy was one of those longtime Hollywood hyphenates who really deserved the title. Producer-author-director-screenwriter, he moved to Hollywood in the 1960s to pursue a career in film. Among his film productions were *A Man Called Horse* in 1970 and *Man in the Wilderness* 1971. A native of the Bronx, New York, Sandy wrote short stories for publication in magazines like *Liberty,* and worked as a publicist for Broadway shows until he became a director for the *Howdy Doody Show* at the age of nineteen.

Later, Sandy produced the *Captain Kangaroo* show and contributed as writer on the TV series *Vice Squad.* I know he appreciated the way I understood the importance of the budget and schedule, how I made a point of prepping my crew, always ahead by at least two shots of the 1st AD's daily work sheet.

We were on vacation in Aldebrugh, England visiting Rachel's parents who had a cottage set in the fields of Suffolk that looked across to the distant ocean. The children loved to go there, as did Rachel, for her entire family would always get together for a summer vacation. They were all skilled sailors and yachtsmen and belonged to the local Yacht Club. Our two youngsters were taught to sail by their grandparents, both of whom have sadly long since passed. (But the tradition lives on, as even after all these years, we make an effort to go for the annual Gillingham family confabulation.)

While I stood trying to come up with inspiration to paint my blank canvas, a call came from Sandy Howard Productions. Derek Gibson was interested to know my schedule, as they were planning the third film in the series of *A Man Called Horse* (titled *Triumphs of a Man Called Horse*) and noted that Sandy would really like me to go on a scout to Mexico with him, director John Hough and John Alcott, the Director of Photography. We arranged a date and I changed my ticket back to the US and agreed to meet with them in Mexico City.

At the time, I was more excited about meeting and working with John than designing this project. John Alcott, BSC, was an English cinematographer best known for his four collaborations with director Stanley Kubrick: *2001 A Space Odyssey*, for which he took over as lighting cameraman from Geoffrey Unsworth in mid-shoot; *A Clockwork Orange; Barry Lyndon*, the film for which John won his Oscar; and *The Shining*, based on the Stephen King novel and starring Jack Nicholson. John, with all this illustrious work history, was, like me, unable to get into the ADG (Art Directors Guild) in America. (He did actually sue the union, won and they put him at the bottom of the roster.)

Research is the gift of any designer for the books, magazines and historical archives that need to be studied in order to bring to the screen creative values of the script's period and subject. I had never before been challenged to learn about the history of the American Indian tribes. So, the assignments I received on this film enabled me to purchase some beautiful books detailing their lives, customs and social-structures dating back to the very heart, soul and spirit of these remarkable nomadic people.

What struck me almost immediately was how developed some of their societies had become prior to colonization and the seizure of their lands. The Confederacy of the Iroquois, for example, had a hegemony that included the tribes of the Mohawk, Seneca, Onodaga, Oneida and Cayuga, covering a landmass from New Brunswick and Quebec in Canada to encompass all of New England in the US (a total area about the size of Texas and Alaska combined)—one with its own trade treaties, monetary system and even currency. The tribes under study in the *A Man Called Horse* trilogy were the Sioux, Cheyenne and Shoshone—a more nomadic people, but nonetheless fascinating and replete with their own integrity of culture.

John Daly and Sandy Howard were producing this film. John's company, Hemdale Film Corporation (later called Hemdale Communications after 1993), was an independent British-American film production company. The company was co-founded by actor David Hemmings and John Daly, creating a hybrid marquee from their combined surnames. David Hemmings left the company in 1971, and Daly purchased his stock.

Hemdale would go on to produce some of the most acclaimed films of the 1980s, often in conjunction with companies such as TriStar and Orion Pictures. Those included *Platoon* in 1986 and *The Last Emperor* in 1987—back-to-back Academy Award winners for Best Picture.

Joining us as the Associate Producer was Donald P. Borchers, known later for his work on *Children of the Corn*, 1984, and *Highlander II: The Quickening*, 1991.

Upon arriving at my hotel in Mexico City, I turned on the air conditioning, only to have the thick pollution from the city quickly pour into my room. I set up my art department in *Estudios Churubusco* (the Mexican equivalent of the lots at Warner Brothers or Paramount), whereupon opening a lock up I discovered the old tents and some props from Sandy's previous *A Man Called Horse* films.

We found the majority of the locations, and Derrick Gibson and I went to Cuernavaca. Cuernavaca was something of a hotspot for the Mexican glitterati and the largest city in the Mexican state of Morelos. It also just happened to be where director John Huston had shot *Under the Volcano*. Just outside of Cuernavaca, we drove up this wide black dirt track for approximately one and half miles and came to an area that was perfect for building what would be our fort for the US Cavalry and a small mission church.

This script had been scheduled for a five-week shoot. There was so little time and money that I suggested we have the cavalry build their fort. All agreed, and the cast was notified about its dual duties. As the cameras rolled, the gates were being hauled into position by the on-camera soldiers, one of them being yours truly.

My entire crew was comprised of locals. All were such good workers— especially Federico Farfan and his son who, without fail, were by my side for all the various complexities of the period. My prop masters were also responsible for the effects. Without them, we would not have achieved all that the art department had to accomplish.

Richard Harris arrived a couple of days later, and it was great to see him again, although he made a point of letting me know that he was now on the wagon (a teetotaler). And for the duration of this film at least, he stuck to his guns helped by a close friend.

I was driving north of Cuernavaca in search of a location for our Indian village when I decided to take a trek along a dirt road that went up hill through some piney woods. As the trees opened, to my surprise and delight, there in front of me and below sat a hidden valley sliced through by this narrow ribbon of a river and what appeared to be a herd of mustangs. (BTW, the term "mustang" for wild horse comes from the (Mexican) Spanish, *mustengo*, meaning "untamed.") This was it! I could see it there in front of me: the children playing, their mothers cooking…

and there was ample room for at least ten tepees. It was a perfect raised area for the Indian camp, and some distance beyond there was a hill for the burial site of our chief Richard.

Prior to John Alcott's crew arriving and with the help of the prop department, I laid out the tents and repainted them with various symbols of the tribe based on my studies of the Lakota (Sioux). I shared copies of my reference with the prop department and costume designer. They did such a great job of building and making all the necessary leather blankets, baskets, animal hide saddles and tribal accessories that one could not tell them from the originals. The local villagers who lived close to where we were building the fort helped me with supplying all the lumber we required—also with all the construction for the mission church, a partial adobe house that I set into a hill with a grass roof, and the Indian camp.

On the final day of the shoot, I allowed the villagers to have all the fort's timbers. As a "thank you" they invited me to their village for a feast. Unwittingly I had done them a great service because, by giving them the wood, I had enabled them to sell it and pay for an electric line all the way from the highway to their village. This upset Derrick who wanted to sell the remaining timber and get the monies back for production. Sandy, however, let it go and even followed up with a, "Great job, Alan!" It's something you always want to hear from your producer.

At the feast, I consumed my first roasted lamb in years and drank their favorite beverage called *pulque,* a *campesino* drink that was not for the faint of heart. Just like tequila, it is fermented from the juice of the maguey or agave plant. But *pulque* is the unrefined version. It's not distilled and therefore is thicker, more bitter, and more potent, with a lot more of the hallucinogenic impurities left in.

I could have used some *pulque* one afternoon during the shoot, because one of those infamous thunderstorms so characteristic of the Southwestern areas of North America came tumbling in virtually without warning. The rapidly darkening skies might have given us a hint, because in less than an hour it got darker, almost like the sky at night. But rather than shut down and run for cover, John continued to take his light values with his black and white Polaroid camera. The black storm clouds now shadowed us, and yet the darker it became the more he adjusted his lens aperture stops. When I asked him if it was going to look okay, he smiled and winked, saying, "Yes! We hope so."

Then the lightning began to strike and did so in rapid order! When it started, the sheer proximity to sets and camera equipment became a lightning rod. Suddenly under siege, we all dived into the nearest vehicles for fear of being struck; it was an intense string of moments for us all. Later, upon seeing that sequence, you could never tell that it had become so dark. John was truly a master of his craft—another mentor who sadly passed away in 1986 at age 55, crossing the street from the beach to the hotel in Cannes.

After the shoot in Mexico and completion of *Triumphs of a Man Called Horse,* it was great to be with my family again and back in Malibu. Being on location can be a very lonely life if you have a beautiful family far away. So now I had some spare time for a while to spend with Rachel, Ella and Rowan. We also finally sold the Mercedes 190 SEL.

Once back in the "Bu," I remembered, too, what a pleasant bit of synchronicity it was to bump into so many of the old western actors that had been in the John Ford and John Wayne movies...sitting with Rod Steiger again in the Cross Creek Diner with Stewart Whitman waving at us from the corner. Having done the "cowboy thing," I felt like a member of their club, sharing stories and reminiscences with some of the legends of western films.

*A more buff Richard Harris in* Triumphs of a Man Called Horse.

*Producer Sandy Howard with stars Richard Harris and Donald P. Borchers*

# Thirty-Five

## The Parthenon and "Pirate Anne"

By now, it was the spring of 1984. Another call came in from John and Bo Derek who were fresh off their box office successes with *Tarzan, The Ape Man,* and were pursuing their "next big idea." They were flying off to hunt locations for a project based on the life of the legendary buccaneer, "Pirate Anne" Bonny. Anne Bonny (no relation to Billy the Kid) was a rather foxy Irish redhead who unknowingly married a brigand and ended up becoming the swashbuckling scourge of the Caribbean for a three-year span in the early 18th century. She was captain of her own pirate vessel called *The Revenge.* Another (pretty bad) "pirate movie" had been done in 1951 on the same historical figure. That one was called *Anne of the Indies*, and starred Jean Peters and Louis Jordan. This, to be sure, had a new script and a different spin on things, and was pretty much bucking a Hollywood trend, since pirate movies had long since fallen out of favor.

Bo, of course, was going to star as this notorious swashbuckling heroine. CBS had funded this trip, and we landed in Zagreb, Croatia in order to check out their studios where we would possibly build our sets. We ended up being less than impressed by the studios and the city. In fact, both were rather stultifying. It was very much like stepping back in time to a communist controlled city, and despite the alluring film credits and low production costs, John wisely decided to give it a pass.

From that point, the joint decision was made to fly down to Dubrovnik in southern Croatia, which fronts the Adriatic Sea. It's known for its distinctive Old Town, encircled with massive stonewalls completed in the 16th century, which later in 1998-99 was attacked and shelled in the Kosovo genocide—all as part of the Serbian and Croatian strategy for a major ethnic cleansing of Albanians.

After taking a "walking tour" of the city walls, we came to the joint conclusion that this could make an ideal port for the pirate ships. Then going into the depths of the city—with its narrow streets, high arches and stone stairways—we all agreed that the film could certainly be dressed out for our period.

(Recently Rachel and I, my brother Philip and his wife, Cat, spent three days there. Upon reflection, I was fascinated to see the crowds and all the restaurants; it was a whirring hub of activity. Back in the early 1980s, when I first walked those narrow streets with John and Bo, it was literally empty.)

From Dubrovnik, John and I flew over to the ancient city of Athens. Officially acknowledged as a "city state" in 900 BC, Athens actually flourished for millennia, from about 6,000 BC to about 322 AD. During this period, it grew from a small fishing village to the most significant hub of culture and wealth in the ancient world. Here, over coffee, we decided to go first to the island of Santorini.

After we boarded the Hydrofoil, I had the mistaken impression that it was nothing more than another ordinary boat, until it finally took off and quickly rose to speeds that virtually lifted it out of the water. Skipping over the ocean at speeds of nearly 100 km per hour, we had the sensation of "flying low." We joked that it would be a great ending to the film to see Anne Bonny speed away in her newly designed galleon, but that might just have proved to be a bit too camp.

It helps to know the island's history for any number of reasons. Your first observation when you approach Santorini is that the island as it exists today is essentially what remains after an enormous volcanic eruption that destroyed the earliest settlements, razing the buildings to the ground and virtually annihilating the population.

It was the largest eruption in recorded history and occurred some 3,600 years ago at the height of the Minoan civilization. Apparently by comparison it would have made Krakatoa look like a hiccup. As an offshoot of this "tectonic shift," there sprang a giant central lagoon virtually carved by Mother Nature into a perfect square. Measuring about 7.5 by 4.3 miles, it is surrounded by steep cliffs nearly a thousand feet high and covered on three sides by terraced congeries of comely ivory cottages, villas and apartments.

In the center of the bay there still exists a constantly growing island, replete with its own active volcano. We scouted the offside of the island that sloped towards the Aegean Sea. Beautiful but structurally vapid, there wasn't anything that we thought would serve us as a setting.

What we did find most interesting were the archaeological digs, which had revealed the ancient dwellings hidden beneath the volcanic ash that, to my surprise, featured well-designed sewers, water systems and toilets. The island of Santorini, though stunningly attractive in places, would not work for the 18th century period we had in mind.

Working our swing back, we decided to head to Crete first. All three of us were interested in the history of ancient Crete and the Minoan civilization, one of the most influential civilizations of the world from 2600-1150 BC. During their peak of power, huge palace-estates had been built near Heraklion, such as the famous and superb Knossos Palace. The Minoans, known for shipbuilding, established a strong naval empire in the Mediterranean during that time. And yet this great civilization was stopped by a natural disaster: this being the huge tsunami caused by the volcanic eruption of Santorini in 1450 BC. This was the same one that also covered the northern coasts of Crete with lava ash. This was later followed by the invasion of the Achaeans and the Dorians, tribes that would eventually form the city-states of ancient Greece.

The site of Knossos was discovered in 1878 by the passionate archeologist Minos Kalokairinos, who is credited for many of the excavations there. The excavations in Knossos continued in 1900, undertaken by the English archaeologist Sir Arthur Evans (1851–1941), and his team who continued for 35 years.

When we visited the Knossos Palace, we crossed a point where we thought that its striking red columns might make a lovely setting for Pirate Anne's base. But, in this case, its own classical ionic culture would

*The Red Doric Columns of the ruined city of Knossos*

certainly tip the viewer that this was a decidedly Cretan site, a contradiction to the Caribbean motif we were trying to establish.

Finally we travelled back to Athens, and once again found ourselves walking among ancient historic buildings—many of them giving that gnawing feeling of *déjà vu*. (Had we been there in another lifetime? God only knew…literally.) Nevertheless, that is precisely what I experienced as I leaned against one of the colossal corner columns.

Among all the structures we experienced, the Parthenon is the most famous surviving building of ancient Greece and it's certainly one of the most striking structures in the world. It has stood atop the Acropolis of Athens for nearly 2,500 years and was built to give thanks to Athena, the Goddess of Wisdom. Athena was the city's patron deity for the salvation of Athens and Greece against Persia in the Peloponnesian Wars.

An architectural treasure and one of the Seven Wonders of the World, it has been eternally doted upon by the Greek government, whose artisans take great care to restore it in all of its original structural details. Awesome to see, walk around and just spend a few moments of conscious reflection on its past history. It is an experience that one must live and constantly labor to describe adequately.

One morning while were having a morning coffee in the Athens harbor, John asked me how long I thought it would take to drive to and back from the castle, pointing to an area on the map.

"About five hours" I replied.

"Why don't you go down to the dock and see how long it would take to sail there," John asked, and motioned to the boats docked below us.

In a short time, I came back and told him that we could have a 12-berth, two mast yacht, and that it would take us five days there and back.

"Let's go by boat then!" Bo excitedly said, and off we went. Having Bo constantly diving naked into the Aegean was a treat for the crew and me, as I often helped her up and into a towel as I had done in Sri Lanka. One thing you had to give to Bo was the almost childlike quality she had about doing things—she was aware and yet unimpressed with her own beauty.

We came into a harbor, anchored, and there was the setting we sought: a small castle approximately 600 yards from the mainland and, from the Oceanside, a castle wall that went up to the top of the mountain that acted as a cradle for a massive old fortress.

This proved to be the perfect location for the small castle in the bay. It was somewhere we could dock Anne's boat, build an interior on stage, and construct a tunnel that went to the mainland. Since the old fortress was at least accessible, it offered us all kinds of options.

After our brief reconnoiter through the Aegean, we made one more trip to the Isle of Capri, where John had previously arranged to see a mansion that might possibly serve as the governor's home. It was ugly though, and definitely not a choice for us.

On the flight home, John said that he had just gotten feedback from CBS, and they informed him that it was virtually impossible to get any insurance company to insure the two galleons fighting each other at oar's length. This seemed to be the *coup de grace* for an already troubled pre-production.

"I don't want to direct this film," John finally said. "They want more sex scenes in the script, and I am not going to give it to them." He paused turned to me and said, "We have an idea for another film, Alan. We're calling it *Bolero*."

Such are the vagaries of putting together a film. We ended finishing up a great vacation, pretending to scout for Pirate Anne and saw a little of our ancient world in the Aegean.

Barely had I settled back into our rented apartment when I was off again to England and back to Spain with John and Bo to look for locations for *Bolero*. This was to be a "bullfighting" movie featuring Bo as a virgin turned daring matador.

*A classic perspective of the Parthenon*

# Thirty-Six

# Let Go and Let It Flow

*Bolero* **was calling.** The production was on. That meant Spain and Madrid. It also meant my having to turn around and leave Rachel and the children yet again. This time, however, it was particularly hard. As I left them for the airport that day, I felt an overwhelming sense of love rise within me that actually brought tears to my eyes. I promised Rachel that, depending upon the schedule, I would send them tickets to join me in Madrid.

We arrived in London and scouted for a few locations, but only spent a couple of days before deciding that we would begin the work in Spain. From that point, we made a few calls to organize our crew in Madrid, and Noby Clark, my construction coordinator who worked with us on Tarzan, was scheduled to drive John and Bo down to Madrid in his new V-12 Mercedes Benz S-600.

In the meantime, I would go ahead to Madrid and set up. I would begin by immediately talking to various departments prior to John and Bo Derrick arriving. As before with *Tarzan, The Ape Man*, John would be *Bolero's* Director and Bo would be the Producer.

We travelled across the latitudes and longitudes of Spain, making location decisions as we went—knowing in that way where I would plant fields of wildflowers and mountaintops where the bull could be fastened down. We visited a village in Los Picos de Europa in northern Spain, a castle and beach in San Sebastian and finally went to Seville where we were to meet the noble *rejoneador* bullfighting brothers Angel and Rafael Peralta. I use the term, "noble," more as a nobility earned than one inherited. In truth, the Peralta brothers were from a peasant family and became, through their skills on horseback, acclaimed in their field. They allowed Bo to ride naked on horseback in their ring and taught her how to fend off the bull with a cloak.

And lest some of our readers here denounce us all for supporting a "bloodsport," *Rejoneador* is a Portuguese school of fighting bulls where the bullfighter confronts the bull on horseback, taunting the bull with *banderillas* (or long picks) but not necessarily killing the bull in the classic Spanish style of using the *muleta* (small cape) and *espada* (sword). In later incarnations in Portugal, the *rejoneo* style of fighting eventually became bloodless, eliminating "the third act" of the fight called the *faena* (or finale) as a tragic ending. Nonetheless, fighting a one-ton bull bred to kill involved some courage, daring and grace, and required "body-doubles" for both Bo and her co-star, Fabio Testi. That's where the Peralta brothers came in.

To no one's surprise, Bo had already garnered something of a reputation as an accomplished horsewoman. She had such finesse in her skill levels that her horsemanship alone carried some of the film's best scenes. The Peralta brothers supplied us with the majority of animals that we were going to need for the film and, for the most part, their choices were exceptional.

Having returned from prepping one of the locations just outside of Madrid, John approached me in the hotel lobby, "Have you seen Fabio yet?" he asked (Fabio Testi being our original leading man).

"Fabio's in the restaurant," I answered, remembering where I had just seen him.

"I think his ears are too big," John opined, his concerns were replete with subtext. Something else was at issue, and I could sense it.

*There are no perfectly handsome men,* I thought, but never got the words out of my mouth.

Jumping the shark in anticipation, John insisted: "Go in and introduce yourself to Fabio. Check him out and let me know what you think." Those were his final words before he hopped onto the elevator, leaving me with the task of prequalifying our leading man.

I went into the restaurant looking for Fabio. And as he rose to shake my hand, my first impression was that, standing in front of me was an Italian Clark Gable, an imposing handsome man with style and a resonant baritone voice. In other words, I felt he was very right for the part… that is, if John was willing to accept my opinion, which apparently, he was not.

Within a few days, we were ready to shoot. The same camera crew we had on *Tarzan* arrived from Germany. Fernando, who had worked with us on *Nicholas and Alexandra,* was now my Art Director. All was ready for that first day.

The first day in Seville, I had dressed a Moorish courtyard with silk flowers, and John said: "I can't shoot this! Those flowers… they're not real!" At that very moment, a Japanese tourist who had just walked into our area had his camera not even six inches from one of the silks.

Daring to broach a contradiction, I pointed to the man and said: "John if he can, we can."

Fortunately, John laughed at the absurdity of his own insistence and lightened up (if only for the moment). "Looks great! Thank you!"

We were in Jerez in a sherry bodega. Contained within its stonewalls were casks of sherry stacked high and running in rows, seemingly *ad infinitum.* Before explaining what happened that morning, let me begin by saying that Fabio Testi had once had an *affair de coeur* with Ursula

Andress that went deep enough for them to have cohabitated for a time. Ursula, of course, had been John Derek's second wife in a run of gorgeous leading ladies. And John Derek was, to say the least, a bit territorial where his women were concerned.

It is here that I note that John, with his stunningly handsome leading-man looks, was married to (arguably) four of the most beautiful women ever to grace the Hollywood screen…the last three being Ursula Andress, Linda Evans (of *Dynasty* fame) and Bo. Although John's split with ballerina Patti Behrs was not quite as cordial, his ties to his last three wives were almost perversely amicable—so much so that when he hit the age of 60 all three conspired to throw him a birthday party. So, in his way, John always kept close ties to his exes. There was always that *connection* (and in this case, for Fabio Testi, *consequences*).

With that as a background…as the cameras on *Bolero* started to roll, the first scene of the day was Bo being kissed by Fabio. The call of "action" came from the 1st AD, and the cry of "cut" immediately came from John.

With the first shot busted, John walked over to Fabio, who at that moment was about to kiss Bo, and stepped between them. He asked, "What is that?! Looks like a Herpes to me!" directly pointing at Fabio's lip. Fabio responded by saying that he had cut his lip that morning and that the makeup department had cleaned it up. "No!" John insisted, now growing impatient. "Come over with me into the light. Let's take look at that!"

Making an issue of Fabio's physical blemish, Derek fired him right on the set, and Fabio could not believe what John had just put him through. It was so obvious to me that he could not bear the idea of Bo being kissed by a man who had also slept with Ursula.

By that time, we were about 20 minutes from lunch break. I went to the small historical Moorish-floor replete with terrazzo tile covering every inch of it.

Needing to release some of the "on-set tension," I had the barman fill up eight rows of Sherry from the darkest to the lightest—nine small glasses in each row. Then I went back to the crew and announced that a liquid lunch, on me, was waiting in the bar. John, being a teetotaler at the time, was less than pleased to see "the boys" wandering back onto the set with wide grins and smiles across their faces.

That evening John said that he wanted me to go to Rome and find a Gypsy, as he was going to look for a new co-star for Bo and that we now were going to start production in England.

"Rome for a Gypsy, John? England?" I felt compelled to ask. "I've prepped all of Spain…and there are so many beautiful Gypsy women here. This is, after all, where they dance the Flamenco!"

Apparently, my words evaporated straight into the ether. Unheard I was on my way to Rome, and John and Bo started their search for a new leading man.

Prior to flying to Italy, I had been in touch with a couple of casting agents. And, immediately upon arriving in Rome, went right to work. Over a period of five days, I reviewed many photographs of possible actresses who could be our Gypsy girl. In my downtime, I enjoyed some fabulous lunches and dinners, drove up the Via Apia again and then (my selection of the talent in hand) flew back to Madrid.

As we came up to the second start date, there was another "slight delay," as Bo and John had mutually agreed upon their choice for her new leading man, Andrea Occhipinti, but were equally insistent that he spend some time in the gym, "toning up."

Then the decision was made. I was going ahead of them to London to do what I have always done best: find a crew and look for the manor house we absolutely needed for the opening sequences.

I did mention to John that we were not planning to film there for another nine weeks…and didn't Morocco come before England?

"No!" John insisted. He had changed his mind. First, we were going to England with no consideration of all the work that had been set up to lay the groundwork for our arrival in Spain. All was on hold, and I was definitely learning to "Let go and let it flow."

Having to reboot my pre-production planning to focus on England, I remembered that His Excellency the Baron Montague had a wonderfully expansive family estate and had a penchant for collecting classic antique cars. I managed to locate a phone number for him and called to explain exactly what we required. After our initial brief conversation, my mere mentioning of the name, Bo Derek, cinched the deal. So, I would, upon my arriving back in Mother England, drive down to Beaulieu to meet with him.

As an addition to my production team, John Fenner, a great draftsman and art director was free to work with me. Ann Hanson, a beautiful woman that I'd shared time with in the past, had recently become a set dresser and was open to being part of the crew. We were all set up with a theatre location on Richmond Green, and the estate of Baron Montagu of Beaulieu. (In the French vernacular, *Beau* ["beautiful"] and *Lieu*, ["place"] in the County of Hampshire.)

Our first morning in Beaulieu did not get off to a good start. I knew that John wanted to set up a tracking shot: this was our first day of camera ready in the manor house. I was standing and admiring the classic car we had selected when John appeared, marching towards me, seemingly on a mission. Without so much as a good morning, Alan, he launched his next run of invective straight to me (but not at me). "I have had enough! You can direct this film, Alan. I'm not going to have another Tarzan! She is fat! She cannot act, and I am going home!"

Attempting to stabilize the moment, I replied, as good-naturedly as the moment allowed: "John, good morning! What exactly are you talking about? Bo is not fat. And you are directing this film."

John paused for a couple of clicks, and then reconsidered. "Then you go and look at her and tell me she is not fat," he decided, finally calming down.

"Where is she?" I carefully queried, and he pointed to a small caravan in the field below.

I took a slow, thoughtful stroll through the tall grass towards the 1930 soft aged green caravan, knocked and entered. Bo sat completely naked on the sofa crying as her mother was applying her make up.

"Alan, John says I'm fat and he no longer wants to direct me! What am I to do?!" Shaken and stirred, she finally, sadly composed herself, soldiered up and then asked me again with tears in her eyes "What am I to do?"

I placed my arm around her as the door opened, and John was looking up towards us.

"So, what do you think? Is she fat?"

I lifted Bo's arm looked at her stunning body and tried to remain understated while answering as calmly as I could. "No, John. She does not look fat to me; not in the least."

"Then let's go shoot this shit!" John curtly replied, and quite decisively slammed the door shut behind him.

I looked at Bo's mother, and then at Bo, trying to put them at ease. "It will be okay," I emphasized. "This is our first day. He's really questioning his own ability, not yours, Bo." I then told her that I would see her on set when she was ready.

Taking a deep breath, I left them both and walked back across the field through the tall grass, truly wondering how this was all going to play out. I remembered all the events of *Tarzan*. Would this film embrace the same kind of madness as I had experienced in Sri Lanka?

Back at the set, John now sat perched on the camera dolly. Bo arrived, showing no signs of any stress, calm and collected with her mother finishing the makeup touches. The First AD showed her to her mark. Without saying a word to her, John said, "Action." And the key-grip began to push the camera dolly in slowly.

Within less than a minute John had shouted: "Cut!" He looked confused, and frustrated as he was unable to operate the wheels that moved the camera in various directions. He stepped down from the dolly and asked Mike Bartlett, the first assistant camera who was with us in Sri Lanka, for the Steadicam.

Now…on the call-sheet John Derek was listed as the Writer, Director and Cinematographer. As the Steadicam was placed on his shoulders Mike saved him from almost falling headfirst. Mike removed the Steadicam, and John asked for the four-foot high sticks.

This became a regular ritual during the filming. The rest of the film in England, Spain and Morocco was completed with the cameras mounted on sticks of various heights for every shot. From that point, no dolly tracks were placed down in any of our locations, even on those occasions when they were the obvious best choice.

Spain at last! And here we were—all the cast now augmented by one of my favorite actors from past films, that gentle giant and prodigious talent George Kennedy. In 1967, George had played the character, "Dragline," opposite Paul Newman in *Cool Hand Luke*, winning the Oscar for Best Supporting Actor, along with a nomination for a Golden Globe. He was that kind of very special man who possessed an innate ability to make everyone around him feel better for the experience.

We were ready with a first-rate crew, many of whom I had worked with on *Nicholas and Alexandra* in 1969. Sacristan was now the head of Mole Richardson Electrical that supplied all the lights, cables and trucks. So, we definitely could not do without this man who had also worked on *Lawrence of Arabia*. I had such respect for him, and having access to people like that always gives one hope.

Rachel arrived with the children. Bo immediately took a shine to Ella, and in the days that followed, shared many a moment with her.

After starting out in Madrid, we travelled North to the ancient village of *Santillan del Mar* in an area of *Picos de Europa*. A simple stroll through the narrow cobblestone streets had flung us all back in time.

Even to this day, many of the homes are still set up on two levels in what almost amounts to a medieval community tradition. In the large lower level, they brought in the family cattle in the winter, allowing the heat from their bodies to drift up to the family quarters. The village women still wash their clothes in a common covered area, replete with a roof and covered in stone where the water flows from a well into a channel made from cut stones. Ella and Rowan loved to go off by themselves, down the narrow streets to buy their favorite homemade lemon cake.

Walking the fields with the children, Rachel and I counted over 15 different species of wild flowers in one square meter. Van Gogh would have been in his element there, for the fields were a sacred canvas of wild daffodils. From the village we then went to a beach in San Sebastian to establish a shot of an old biplane landing on the sand.

In a castle close to San Sebastian, we had set up a long antique dining table for a staged dinner. All the lights were up and ready. I suggested to John that this was definitely a shot that could use a dolly-track in order to take in the entire scene. But that suggestion was dead on arrival, and more…

Off to one side in a corridor, I was approached by Sacristan. "Alan," he said, "she is going to fire me. She does *not* like me!" His deep gruff voice was laced with uncertainty (both of us knowing the subtext that "she" was our producer Bo).

"No!" I denied the thought of it. "How can she? You control all the electrical equipment and the men." That was my emphatic reply. Fatalistic to say the least, Sacristan walked away from me down the corridor and out of the building. He had a foreboding of doom and he was right.

As we were setting up the next sequence, I would have had to be deaf not to hear Sacristan's angry voice echoing throughout the castle. I searched him out, only to find that Bo had in fact fired him. With that, all the lights and equipment started to be removed.

I found Sacristan outside, announcing with a long sigh, "I have told the men they could stay or leave, but that no equipment would be brought back until the equipment had been paid for and I have been reimbursed."

The episode with Sacristan, for me, was purely a matter of *déjà vu*. It had been so typical of the many instances of spontaneous combustion that I had experienced on the set of *Tarzan* in Sri Lanka, when so many people were fired for reasons that I could never comprehend. The set of *Bolero* was becoming all this in spades…and on steroids!

Only two days earlier, I'd been dumbstruck to find out that the costume designer and his assistant had both been fired, and that the seamstress was now in charge of wardrobe. The one saving grace was that all terminated crew and cast were paid within ten days by Golan-Globus Productions and Cannon, who at least met the production's financial obligations. But work continued, sadly without my old friend Sacristan, and chaos continued to be the order of the day.

We were high on a mountain pass, and a fighting bull had been tethered for the next scene. I had a strong feeling about a steam room sequence that we were going to shoot in a few days. I pulled John aside and emphasized to him that I did not think the room we had chosen in another castle would work, as it was too big and would not hold the steam. I suggested that I could build a steam-room inside it.

This was Friday, and we were scheduled to shoot the scene on Sunday afternoon. I did a quick sketch. John approved, and I drove back to Madrid. From that point, I went ahead with the construction crew, built the small steam room and had the effects team set it up. It was completed and tested well by Sunday night.

Monday morning, I had been waiting for Angel and Rafael Peralta in the hotel lobby. We had arranged to go to a village to see how we might possibly turn the square into a bullring for the *corrida*. It was unusual for them to be late. So, when they failed to show up in the lobby, I grew concerned.

About that time, John appeared and asked me what I was doing. I said that I was going on a location scout with the Peralta brothers, and that I thought maybe their plane from Seville was late. That's when John summarily informed me that he had sacked the brothers on Friday for their apparent incompetence.

Apparently, the Peralta bull selected for the shoot that day had broken loose, and scattered the crew in a panic. Both John and Bo ended up on top of a truck, while the bull ran wild terrorizing the entire production team, trucks, craft services and all.

I was definitely taken aback, not only because John Derek had just fired the best in the business, but also because *Los Hermanos* Peralta owned all the animals that were essential for our future shoot. John then announced that he would come with me. I replied by letting him know that Fernando and Rowan, my son, were coming with me.

"Oh?! You're going on a picnic, are you?!" There was a pregnant pause triggered by the way John set up the question. By this time, my patience had been tried to the max, and I was getting a little upset.

He cocked his verbal six-gun for the very next question and then pulled the trigger on it: "Tell me, Alan, if you were me would you be happy?"

Now…if ever there had been a pointed question this was it. I tried to consider where he was going with this question. (But calculating rage is never easy.) Was it that Bo was not delivering as he expected? Was he not getting the footage he required? What was the meaning of this pointed question? In the truest feeling of friendship, I looked straight into his eyes and said, "No John, if I were you maybe I would not be happy."

"Then you are fired!" came his aggressive reply.

Rather than lose my cool, I paused for a beat, then removed a long sheet of paper from my pocket and presented it to him. "John, if you think it has been hard, this is my list for next week." With that, I ran my index finger down the list of items that was at least 18 inches long. "In that case Fernando can take over for me," I continued.

"Bo sacked Fernando yesterday!" John snapped back, as Bo, almost on cue, came striding down the stairwell.

At this point, with little left to lose, I got up as she approached and looked directly at her. "You fired Fernando. Why? I was going to send him ahead to Morocco." I then looked at them both, thanked them and walked away. Knowing that I was the only person who confided in them, and the only person who knew precisely what the schedule was to be—and had therefore become the sieve for all their discontent with the crew. I could only wonder what their next initiatives would be.

I called together the heads of the departments, thanked them for all their loyalty and apprised them of my situation. I made copies of the following week's extensive production list and bid my goodbyes. Knowing Noby wanted to sell the 600 Mercedes, I made him an offer he couldn't refuse…and he took me up on it.

Monday, we loaded the car, and Rachel and I went into the bar for a farewell drink. Sally, the costume designer (and erstwhile seamstress), walked in and told us that she had also been fired, the reason being that the script called for a monk's habit. She had secured an authentic string of monastic colours—grey, black and brown—but Bo had wanted a cardinal red. What Bo did not realize at the time was that there were pickup shots slated for that morning, and in *Santillan del Mar*.

Sally had been pressed into service as an extra in Bo's bedroom. (At that point, there were so few people left in the crew, that everyone was wearing multiple hats.)

The phone rang. Reception said it was for both Sally and me. John and Bo had remembered and they wanted Sally back. (She was all that was left in the costume department.) They also decided that they wanted me back, as the fires were not working. Naturally, I asked the first AD why the fires weren't working, and it was then that he informed me that the FX person had been fired without warning on Saturday.

With that little point of madness as the *coup de grace*, I just smiled and replied, "I have also been fired. Send my regards, and it's all there." By that point, I'd had enough. Rachel kissed me, and I put the phone down. I was brief, as I had—at long last—truly had enough!

In retrospect, I have to be honest and say that if there was a film crew equivalent of PTSD, I probably had it. (And I was by no means alone. About 85% of the crew got the same treatment.) I was shaken up, taken aback, and frankly felt betrayed, knowing how I had supported both Bo and John on all levels. At that point, I just had to let it go…let it go and flow…and wait with faith in what would be coming next.

Freed from the madness of *Bolero,* Rachel and I decided to make a leisurely return to the UK. So, we took Ella and Rowan, jumped into the S-600 Mercedes and enjoyed some sketches of Spain, driving the highways and winding roads in our "Merc" and staying in old Castles that had been converted into Parador Hotels.

We meandered up to San Sebastian, then along the French coast, where perhaps the world's most delectable asparagus is grown. We also visited Brittany, Calais and London. And during this great trip you could observe the dial of petrol drop down to empty as if it were sucking on a straw. (What a beast, but not exactly fuel-efficient!) "We are not shipping this to Malibu," Rachel said, knowing that I was thinking about how we could get it back to the States.

Flashing back to 1985 I remember that, when *Bolero* was finally released, it quickly became one of the most widely panned movies of the entire second half of the 20$^{th}$ century. The chaos and discord behind the scenes showed up in every frame of the film. Costing $7.1 million to make it grossed $8.9 million at the box office. And since you need at least three times your production budget to break even on a film, it proved to be a dead loss.

To top it off, *Bolero* nearly swept the Golden Raspberry Awards in 1985, winning six "Razzies," one each for Worst Director, Worst Screenplay, Worst Musical Score, Worst New Actress, Worst Actress in a Leading Role and the runaway winner for Worst Picture… all while garnering a nearly unprecedented 0% rating on Rotten Tomatoes.

*George Kennedy with Bo Derek in* Bolero. *Winner of six "Razzies," in 1985, including "Worst Picture."*

As a demonstrable point of contrast, a short time after returning to Malibu, I went with a friend to Ojai to meet and sit with the philosopher, author and "World Teacher," Jiddu Krishnamurti. He was in his final months (as it turned out), and we sat with a small group under the shade of a tree that Jiddu had used as a prop to rest his back. I was taken by this man whose entire life had been dedicated to what had become known as "the psychological revolution," the nature of the human mind, meditation, human relationships and bringing about a radical change in society.

His words that day rang so true to me and connected to my heart: *"It is no measure of health to be well adjusted to a profoundly sick society. The ability to observe without evaluating is the highest form of intelligence. And so, you must be able to understand the whole of life, not just one little part of life."*

He was helped to stand, walked toward his house, glanced over to me and smiled. Later that night, I drove home virtually in silence. It was soon after we had sat with Krishnamurti that he left this planet Earth, passing at his home in Ojai, California, in 1986.

In his life he stressed the need for "a revolution" to take place in the psyche of every human being and emphasized that such a radical shift in consciousness could never be brought about by any external entity, be it political, social or religious. In doing so, Jiddu reminded us that he had no allegiance to any nationality, caste, religion, or philosophy, and spent his life travelling the world, counseling individuals and speaking to groups, both large and small.

He wrote many books, among them *The First and Last Freedom, The Only Revolution,* and *Krishnamurti's Notebook.* Many of his talks and discussions have been published. His last public talk was in Madras, India, in January, a month prior to his death.

What a contrast, when I think of it now, to have finished our journey from the madness of a chaotic film production to the peace, tranquility and spiritual sense of purpose of this man. In doing this, we had gone from the ultimate illusion—the ego soup and madness of making a movie—to the only reality in this universe that made any sense. It was a revolution in consciousness and a gateway to the next level: that whatever life would hold next for us would always be a gift. Lesson learned.

*Jiddu Krishnamurti in his iconic pose the last time I saw him.*

# Thirty-Seven

## A Vibration of Times Past

When I walk onto an empty stage in one of the old major studios such as Paramount, Warner Brothers, Universal or the old Chaplin stages, I feel a presence, something akin to a vibration of times past. Countless environments that have been created by designers like me—men and women who have a vision and take the four walls or landscape they are given and create a new reality for the actors to walk through, to accept as theirs, utilize, transform and bring to life the characters in their scripts.

When sitting on stage as my crew finishes building and the set decorator and crew add the finishing touches, it feels transcendent to just be in context with a space that within hours turns into someone's wildest imaginings come true—a new reality. Life fulfills all dreams even before the words are spoken or the pencil can sketch them out on paper.

Imagine life is an empty stage: Every day is new! Creation surrounds us with its perfection. What we consciously place within those precious moments of awakening is offered to us through that gift of human nature called free will. We create our illusions moment by moment, even trying to understand what tomorrow will bring. We will never know when that next breath we take will be our last. So, I have to just flow, knowing that within that flow is the awareness of being. Like a fish in the ocean, I am constantly swimming inside a sea of creation where every breath is fulfilled. (If I just stay centered on the inner self…although sometimes it is hard, the more I focus, the easier it seems to come…that state of being.)

It was not long after the depressing misadventures of *Bolero* that I made the decision to spend more time with my family. Rachel had found a house that was on the market in a remote area known as Malibu Park, just a mile from Zuma Beach. Back then in 1983, so few people wanted to live out that far from town, and property was still reasonable to purchase.

The original property belonged to the actor LeVar Burton (noted for his role as Kunta Kinte on *Roots* and as Lt. Commander Geordi La Forge on *Star Trek/The Next Generation*). LeVar is a lovely fellow, but when we met him he had admittedly had enough of the bucolic beach life in "the Bu," and wanted to move back into the city for his work. His was one of the first one level ranch homes to be built in this remote area in 1956.

The first thing we did was redesign the façade of the home, keeping the roofline, pushing it slightly farther out and converting the old garden shed into a working studio. It was the perfect combination of structures, and it felt like "home" the moment we moved in.

I remembered that back in England I had met and designed one commercial for an American commercial director named Lee Lacy. Lee was one of the foremost commercial production houses in the US for about 30 years and also had an office in Los Angeles on Melrose Place. From the moment I walked in the door, Lee introduced me to David Tate and Donna Woodruff and said, "This is the art director I am going to use for our future work. He can sketch, do all the working drawings, and his accent will sway the clients." (That is exactly how my life in the world of commercials began.)

What a difference this was from film production. In those early years of the 1980s, there did not seem to be any real budgetary concerns, since the majority of the commercials were cost plus. If you were to go over budget, the agencies would then take care of the extra costs. (In fact, most commercials came with their own built-in "contingency fees" to cover just such an eventuality.) The majority were also filmed on stage, scarcely if ever on location. And as my reputation grew, I decided that I would have an office somewhere in the city.

Zoetrope Studios previously conceived and owned by Francis Ford Coppola and George Lucas (as American Zoetrope) had by that time become Hollywood Centre Studios. I took an office there and held onto it for fifteen years. The corner office was next door to George Burns, and most mornings I would see the legendary centenarian arrive around 10:30, get out of his chauffeur-driven limo with a big cigar in hand, walk into his office, stay for about two hours and leave, still smoking his stogy. If he saw me, he would always have a smile, a nod, and raise his cigar in salute.

The perfection of quality was of the foremost. The most important aspect of building sets is obviously the construction company with whom one creates a strong friendship and working relationship. Chris Hyde from Global Entertainment, Douglas Morris, Anthony Soja from Cinnabar, and Ernst, my very first coordinator—these men and their companies formed the core, my backup and amazing support, without whom I would have not been able to succeed. With these associations came all the carpenters, painters, and fabricators (for prop construction). And to put the finishing touches on the backings was Bill McGuire, who painted the majority of all the unique backdrops, other than those that I rented from Pacific Backings.

Many of the directors I worked with had been executives or creative directors at advertising agencies and had taken that next step to create and set up their own companies in order to direct commercials.

To name a few that asked me to work with them: I note Rick Levine, who was able to get me into the ADG—along with a list of others, including Fred Peterman, Neal Tardio, David McNamara, Peter Moss. Richard MacDonald, Brian Gibson, Robert Black, Rupert Wainwright, Caleb Deschanel, Melvin Sokolosky, Joe and John Pitka, Ken Arlidge and Klaus Obermeyer. All these directors won countless Clio awards and some Golden Lions in Cannes.

The Clio Awards were first established by Wallace A. Ross in 1959, and are named for the Greek goddess Clio, the mythological Muse known as "The Proclaimer." As such, she was the patron deity of history, poetry, great deeds and accomplishments. Each winner received a gold Georg Olden designed statuette. The competition was expanded to include work on international television and movies in 1966, and then radio ads, in the United States, in 1967.

Melvin Sokolosky was a fabulous and innovative fashion photographer famously noted for his 1963 "Bubble" series of photographs—ones that depicted fashion models "floating" in giant clear plastic bubbles suspended in midair above the River Seine in Paris. This not only won him acclaim in his field of fashion but also launched an advertising photo and design career unequalled in many areas. A winner of a record 24 Clios over his career, Melvin also became the first fashion photographer and designer commissioned to create the entire editorial photo content for a single magazine—for *McCalls Magazine* in 1973.

On stage, before starting the day, Melvin was infamous for expressing his views of his world and creative convictions to the crew (or anyone else who would listen). He loved working with Rachel as his Art Director. And, along with Danny, the two of them travelled many a mile together. I had great respect for Melvin, his creative eye and his phenomenal support team, as I did for all the directors I just mentioned.

I include among that very special group Caleb Deschanel, a cinematographer and director who has been nominated for the Academy Award

Melvin Sokolosky was a fabulous and innovative fashion photographer famously noted for his 1963 "Bubble" series of photographs.

for Best Cinematography five times, including *The Patriot, The Passion of the Christ, Never Look Away, Fly Away Home,* and *The Natural.* Winner of the National Film Critics Award for Best Cinematography for *The Black Stallion* and *Being There,* he is also the proud father of Zooey and Emily Deschanel, two young actresses also enjoying ascending career arcs of their own.

Caleb is a member of the National Film Preservation Board of the Library of Congress, representing The American Society of Cinematographers. He and Vince Arcaro had a company called Dark Light Productions, and when not away on a feature, I was his first call to design the commercials for them.

I also worked alongside many of the famous Cinematographers, including Allen Daviau, Conrad Hall, Janus Kaminski, Vilmos Zsigmond, Stephen Goldblatt, John Toll—all of whom, when not on a feature, would often be hired by various directors to be on stage with us.

I knew that I had to be more efficient with my budgeting and went with a friend to a weekend event that was called Mega Learning, a course that teaches you how to maximize the potential in both hemispheres of your brain. Well…on the plane home I swear I could feel the left and right sides of my brain moving. Within days, I found myself sketching with the phone in one ear and my hand also calculating the jobs to the penny, as we would say in England.

It was on one of the jobs for Caleb, a commercial for Lark Cigarettes for Japan in 1992, that I first met my dear friend Pierce Brosnan. Having already enjoyed a hit TV series such as *Remington Steele* and *Noble House*, and films such as *The Lawnmower Man*, Pierce had not yet stepped into the realm of the 007 James Bond Series with *Goldeneye* in 1995 and other blockbuster hits of the 1990s that would send his film career into the stratosphere.

Finding an instant connection with our similar backgrounds and interests, Pierce and I shared stories of growing up in Chelsea, Fulham and Putney. We both enjoyed painting and sketching, and today, some 25 years later, continue to share our liking for past and present masters of art, as well as mutual photographer friends like Terry O'Neill, who has photographed the rich and famous for over 50 years.*

Innumerable celebrities have been captured by Terry's vision and made iconic inside the lens of his cameras. He took some of the earliest photographs of the Rolling Stones, David Bowie and Elton John that

---

* Over the years Pierce has proven to be a true Renaissance man. As well as his illustrious career as an actor, starring in four James Bond blockbusters and critically acclaimed films such as *The Matador, Laws of Attraction* and *The Tailor of Panama*, he is also a gifted painter and uses profits from his giclée prints to benefit women's and children's charities. He also has two honorary degrees, an OBE (Order of the British Empire) and is a passionate environmental activist, working with the National Resources Defense Council (NRDC) and the International Fund for Animal Welfare (IFAW).

*Pierce Brosnan's Lark ad for Japan (right) directed by good friend Caleb Deschanel (left).*

*Pierce & Rachel, 2017.*

have all become classics. Then later, he surprised us all when he married Don Ashton's daughter Lorraine.

Many of our photo excursions and commercials took us to some of the most remote and exotic places in the world—as well as some of its most crowded and climatically challenged cities. The air pollution in Delhi, India—a quantum soup of nasty gases that comprise some of the most compromised city air on our troubled planet—turned out to be both as thick as a steam bath and insufferably noxious. I was being driven around in a wobbly, three-wheeled, yellow taxi rickshaw through the crowded city that was teaming with scooters, taxis and cows—Holy Cow!

"Holy Cow!" That memorable bit of slang was something my mother, Irene, would revert to when any event or foible of human nature took her out of her norm. It is almost innocent in retrospect. Whenever shocked or even dismayed at something that surprised her, Mum would declare, "Holy Cow!" This mildest of expletives that must have been derived from the soldiers returning from India in the late 19th century, and was used as a gentler exclamation to that more offensive Christian rail: "Holy Christ!"

While in India, I spent one week wrapped up in a space blanket in a tent at Prem Rawat's, Raj Vidya Kender Ashram. During the day it was T-shirts and then, as the sun set, sweaters and jackets went on. The temperature dropped about 20 degrees in less than an hour's time. To my utter surprise, there were thousands of men, women, and children arriving in coaches, taxis and walking with bundles on their heads to spend time listening to Prem Rawat speak. They were able to feed this amount of people three times a day from the immaculate kitchens that had been set up in the area.

I remember how I sat in front of a fire-pit as an older Sheikh stirred a large pot of Chai. I also remember having drunk three cups of his strong tea and not being able to sleep for 24 hours.

Many had travelled miles to be there and share the very special time. After setting up camp on the land, they danced and sang, obviously in a state of utter joy to be there. They also made their chapattis that they graciously shared with others.

Through the early morning haze, the sun's first light revealed the thousands of shrouded men and women walking to the ablutions…then breakfast…then a mass convergence into the area prepared for the twice-daily discourse. Once gathered, over 80,000 strong would sit in rapt attention as Prem stepped onto the stage. First, they would explode into an outcry of love and appreciation, followed by a pin-drop silence as this master began to speak. It was then that Prem revealed to them the inalterable truth that the fulfillment of mastery resides in each one of them—and that we should all pay the same measure of love and respect to one other that we were paying to a teacher such as he.

What I truly felt as I stood behind the thousands was the same feeling I had being close at his side—that once again my friend and a Master had revealed to me my innermost awareness of life. He once famously said this as a young man: "Receive this experience and get on with your life. Do not use me as a crutch."

His message was for me to set myself free: I was an eternal being within my finite frame. "The greatest challenge we face is to rise above imagination and to see reality as it is."

*Sunrise. Ready to Find a place within the area for the days discourse.*

*Prem Rawat 2015 with 185,000 plus attendees, sitting silently listening to him speak*

*Prem in Miami 5.11.2019. The Global "Ambassador of Peace," a title given to him as part of the Brussel's Declaration originally established at the European Parliament in 2011 with the goal of promoting peace.*

# Thirty-Eight

## Once in a Blue Moon

Technology is a beast with changing faces. In the 1980s, fax machines were the next big thing. So were cell-phones the size of a house-brick, cordless landline phones and the ubiquitous pager—pagers capable of annoying you 24/7/365 (and someone on the other end with a will to drive you crazy). For some reason, orchestrated by some cruel tech-god on a planet in a galaxy far, far away, production assistants were encouraged to page me with a 911 emergency page that I almost couldn't ignore. On starting a job, I would always ask to not be paged 911—that was for family only. If paged, I would acknowledge that I was obviously needed, and would appreciate it if all "business pages" came between 7 a.m. and 7 p.m. And, of course, practically nobody observed the amenities.

The creative designers and art directors in "The Agency" would send their boards to the production companies—sometimes a single bid—and then I would get the call. I would have my meeting with the director, sketch ideas there and then...and finally we would get to drafting the budget. Once approved, the agency would fly in. We would have a pre-production meeting; then work really began. As the years went by, it became far more competitive and three or four directors would be bidding for the same ad agency project.

Here is a little example of one of those typical days: Brian Gibson and Stephen Goldblatt were waiting for me as I walked toward them across the open area of a modern building in Chicago. Brian handed me a package of storyboards and explained as we went up in the elevator that they were for Wrangler Jeans. We then entered the largest conference room I had ever seen. Surrounding a massive conference table were approximately 20 different clients—some from Wrangler, as well as other agency art directors, creative group heads, account executives, account supervisors and the head of the ad agency. Wrangler was a rather huge account, and obviously this had become an important meeting!

Introductions were made all around, and as the three of us took our seats, Brian rather spontaneously announced: "I will let Alan explain how we are thinking of shooting the boards."

Nonplussed and totally caught off-guard, I nonetheless rallied, glanced at Stephen and quietly replied: "Stephen what do you think of Intro-Vision?" (Just as if we'd planned it that way.)

There was a moment of silence. Being three Brits as we were, there was always a good quick repartee between us. "Not a bad idea, go get them," Stephen replied. I laughed and fired a glance at Brian who did not say a word. I briefly studied the board and went for the one that looked like the *Raiders of the Lost Ark*.

I began to draw on the huge white board, articulating step-by-step how we would build models of the Temple and erect, on stage, only a section of the Buddha-type statue...and the rest was to be "shot at Intro-Vision!"

Explaining that a photograph of the model would be projected at 45% into a mirror that reflected back into the lens while, on stage in front of the camera, our two Indiana Jones type heroes would run down that section of the Temple that we had constructed for them.

Stephen then came up and explained how it could be lit. Brian then put-in his finishing touches to the now excited room. As we left, the CEO of the agency followed us down the corridor and excitedly told us that it had been the best meeting that he had ever witnessed and that the job was ours.

"Rule Britannia!" That was good news! So, we three English lads laughed all the way to the ground floor, and went for a long celebratory lunch.

This package was—for a designer—the cream on top of the milk. I won a Clio, as did Brian and Stephen for both spots.

I have to mention at this point that, no matter how accomplished I had become, without my crew I was incapable of achieving any of my visions for the camera. To my constant benefit, I had some wonderful set decorators, prop masters, draftsman, office assistants, and truck drivers who all went on to become art directors or art assistants. Carol Clements, Jay Malloy, John Vongt, Alan Bracket, Craig Rose, Craig Osler, Timothy Beach and many more accomplished creative souls that I shared so many hours and days with—all became rising stars and stayed in the heavens.

We were averaging about 30 shows a year. And, if for some reason two or three directors wanted me at the same time, I would try to get them into the same studio on different stages, as long as their shoot days did not overlap. Apprising everyone of the schedule, I would then agree to do the jobs.

In the spring of 1986, I held in my hands a script for a comedy-horror film directed by Richard Wenk, co-written by Wenk and Donald P. Borchers, and starring (Bond girl) Grace Jones and young Chris Makepeace. Donald, whom I met in Mexico on *Triumphs of a Man Called Horse,* introduced me to the director. And once again, I found myself in Los Angeles pulling a crew together for a five-week shoot of *Vamp.*

The scenario for *Vamp* revolved around two college fraternity pledges sent on a mission to find a stripper at a "gentleman's club" called the After Dark Club, which so happened to be home to a scourge of vampire strippers.

Grace Jones was a supermodel, singer, songwriter, record producer, and actress with that phenomenal kind of feral beauty that became the rage of the 1980s and '90s. Grace had worked with photographers such as Jean-Paul Goude, Helmut Newton, Guy Bourdin, and Hans Feurer, and had been on the covers of *GQ, Cinema, Interview, Blitz, Ebony* and *Vogue*. An agile, gifted athlete with captivating catlike moves, she was known for her distinctive androgynous persona and brazen features that became even more animated on film.

Despite her super-celebrity status, Grace was such fun to work with. And (upon my suggestion) we brought in her friend the pop art graffiti phenom Keith Haring to body-paint her, as well as matching Grace with a special chair that we had built just for her. It didn't take long for Grace Jones to develop some uncanny rapport with that chair. And I would love to know its whereabouts, because today that Haring Chair would be a collector's item worth a fortune and a bargain at the price.

On stage for another production we had built a full-size carriage of the world renowned Orient Express, and behind it in perspective were three others. Bill MacQuire, my scenic artist, had painted what looked like a domed glass portion of the station, leaving the canvas clean, with just the slightest hint of the frames of the glass, which was then backlit.

I cut a hole into the area that could be the landing and the entrance. And the verisimilitude was quite phenomenal, so much so that you truly felt as if you were standing in the station.

Ian McDonald was the director with whom I had worked many times in the past— as had Oscar winning actress and director Jodie Foster. Working on these commercials for Japanese companies, Jodi was a trooper, never took her celebrity seriously and made a point of fitting in with the cast and crew. She drove herself to work, interacted collegially with the other cast members, and got in line with the crew for lunch— qualities she shared in common with Sir Anthony Hopkins (her co-star in *Silence of the Lambs*).

It was about that time that Ian and his wife invited me to come to Spain to teach in a school of film technology that they were setting up there. Ian sadly passed away prior to it being confirmed.

*Ian McDonald on the set of the Orient Express.*

Producer Ray La Farrow, whose office was adjacent to mine, asked me if I would like to direct for his company. I was excited enough to buy him a Mont Blanc pen for the contract signing.

He offered me $250K a year, which I openly questioned, never having directed a commercial in the states…and thinking that it was a little high. He had seen the first spot I had shot at Raleigh Studios as a promo that John Toll lit prior to him becoming a very successful cinematographer. John's filmography has, since that time, spanned a wide variety of genres, including epic period dramas, comedies, science fiction, and contemporary dramas. He won the Academy Award for best cinematography in both 1994 and 1995, for *Legends of the Fall* and *Braveheart* respectively.

One of Ray's clients in New York had seen the spot and wanted me to direct the commercial for the Broadway musical *Tango Argentina,* which was about to launch in 1985. Already a hit in Europe and overseas, *Tango Argentina* broke all the rules for musicals with a simple set and dancers ranging in age from 18 to 60. It exuded that kind of magic that one encounters rarely in a lifetime.

*Commercials for the Broadway Musical,* Tango Argentina.

On stage in Broadway, I stood and observed all the stunning dancers as they twisted and stalked across the stage like mating panthers, two pairs of feet striking the floor with precision, legs incessantly intertwined, bodies twirling in a dance of sensual passion—women with women, men with men, gliding about in perfect sync with the music—while held suspended inside an erotic planet of their own.

The time I spent with the Argentinian dancers was quite emotionally rewarding for me. And the producer, upon seeing the finished cut, offered me a television special to direct with Danny Kaye. Sadly, Danny passed away, as did Ray La Farrow. So, in more than one-way, I had both gained and lost so much at once.

Another indelible recollection I have came in 1997, when I was in Washington to design a commercial for Robert Black. I remember it if for no other reason than it was the first of its kind—for that infamous male affliction called ED (and not a guy named "Ed"). It was the first nationally syndicated Viagra commercial that would have GOP Senator (and recently failed presidential candidate) Bob Dole as its spokesman. That made it unique in two ways: First, it was the first time any celebrity of any kind had ever come out and admitted he needed a little help in that area. Second, it was the first time anyone could remember that a politician was willing to tell the absolute truth.

We located an office complex that I would dress out to be Senator Dole's office. Bob was a true gentleman and invited me to come to his office and use any of his personal photographs, medals and awards. He pointed to a small-framed, handwritten note from President Dwight D. Eisenhower's personal notebook and diary from World War II.

If I remember correctly, "Ike," as Commander of the Allied forces in Europe in World War II, had written the saddest admission of command any general ever had to deal with when leading his troops into combat. In his words: "I take full responsibility for every young man who will lose his life in this campaign."

*Bob Dole for Viagra, one of the most famous commercials of the 1990s.*

I recall standing there, reading that handwritten note and, for quite a while, reflecting on the millions who had lost their lives in the insanity of combat, leaving me to wonder whether any war—no matter how just the cause—is worth the wholesale slaughter of our nation's youth. It is the same when I motor along Veteran Avenue in Los Angeles, and I drive past a sea of white crosses in the Los Angeles Memorial Cemetery. It is a brief but sad reflection on the countless fallen warriors and the families that mourn them, along with a grateful nation not yet redeemed.

By the late-1990s, I was hit with the directing bug. But the problem was that if I was now to focus on directing, then my competition would be the same directors for whom I had successfully worked in the past. So, I was faced with something of a Solomon's Dilemma: Did I want to be a constantly working art director or a struggling commercial director? I chose the former and never looked back.

(That instinct proved to be accurate, since around the year 2000, the bottom dropped out of the market for commercial film companies. Reconsolidations, budget cutbacks, and novice companies with cheaper rates cut into the traditional houses like a buzz saw. And it never regained the cachet it had enjoyed when I had started.)

I did direct one more commercial that was offered to me by Wells, Rich, & Greene, Inc. for Alka-Seltzer ("plop-plop, fizz-fizz"). Stephen Labovsky, with whom I had shared many jobs, approached me to direct the spot. They had very little monies but felt that I could help them retain their client. John "Danny" Danischewsky was someone I brought in to produce the spot with me…and on completing the project, I received a letter from Stephen.

"Once in a blue moon, a commercial comes along where everything seems to fall into place, and so becomes something that is just plain fun to boot! Such was our experience on the production of 'Drink.'"

> *My purpose in writing was to say thanks on behalf of Bob, Charlie and myself. I screened our spot today at the agency and the reception was nothing short of spectacular.*
>
> *A great deal of the credit for this flawless production must go to Danny. Such a true professional, a gifted organizer and a joy to work with. Also, please extend my appreciation to Jerry for the gorgeous film and to May for the great gear. May Eatwell, my costume designer, as well as Lori and Melanie for all their help. The entire crew was magnificent.*
>
> *Finally, I would like to personally thank you, Alan, for your sensitivity in casting and directing, your artistry with texture and design and the great little touches you brought to the spot.*
>
> *When I think about all the constraints with the budget and schedule and the complexity of the project as a whole, I*

*frankly can only marvel at the way you brought this whole thing off. It truly is a perfectly crafted spot, thanks entirely to you and your crew.*

That letter was such a mirror of the standards of perfection with which all of my team had worked. And yet, I never did direct another.

Today, upon writing about that letter, I looked up the correct spelling of Danny's last name, only to be jolted by the fact that he had passed from this plane of life on October 12th 2017. He was such a wonderful friend, and a staple in my life. There were so many times when I would call to meet in the local Thousand Oaks pub for a drink and sit with his other friends to catch up with world soccer games. A father, a grandfather and a great-grandfather, he was that longstanding friend from The Chelsea School of Art in 1961, who was unquestionably responsible for my being where I am today in this world of entertainment—he was one of my linchpins to this life, and I will always miss him. Simply irreplaceable…

I had finally, after fifteen years at the Hollywood Center studios, moved into a new office at the Culver City Old Bakery. It was Friday, and Neil Tardio was on the line asking me if I was free the following week. I looked at the schedule and said: "Yes! Why?"

He mentioned that he wanted me to go to Chicago where we were going to meet with Lee Iacocca. I knew that he was an automobile executive best known for spearheading the development of Ford Mustang and Pinto cars while at the Ford Motor Company in the 1960s. He later became a national celebrity for steering the Chrysler Corporation away from bankruptcy toward record profits in the 1980s.

"We are going to be in his office: but (a big But!) I want you to design the office to shoot on stage," he said.

"Neil! This coming week? In Detroit?" I laughingly started to process the challenge ahead.

"Yes, Alan. Do you think you could accomplish it by next Thursday? If anyone could, you could!" Neil was probing.

"Give me a couple of minutes, Neil, and I will sketch up an idea." As I picked up a clean sheet of 8" x 11" paper, Neil agreed to hang on.

I made a quick sketch, faxed it in a few moments to Geneva, to Iacocca's office, to the Agency and finally to David Schermerhorn Neil's partner in New York. David in turn gave me the name of a construction company in Detroit and a set decorator in New York. I contacted them both. And we were off and running.

As I had no image to work from for the look of Iacocca's office, I asked for both modern and mission furniture. I sent a quick plan of the set to the set company and told them to make all the walls twelve feet high. I then FedEx'd the plans and elevations with details to them that afternoon.

Monday morning, I walked towards the stage as the truck arrived with all the walls already built. I selected the molding, and the props arrived in a large truck from New York on Tuesday evening. I went to Iacocca's office and saw the large conference table that we had to duplicate—as there was nothing quite like it anywhere else.

Somehow by Wednesday evening, the set was finished, dressed, pre-lit…and ready. I had another job already booked and left Neil and the ad agency both happy and relieved over how this had all fallen into place in such a remarkably short time. That is how I worked due to all the mentors who had taught me and conveyed to me the most valuable lesson of all—just to be able to accept all that came into my daily experience and embracing it with a sense of compassionate detachment…full of positivity and devoid of fear.

Earlier, I mentioned Dark Light Productions. Even now, I recall how often Vince would call to let me know that he wanted me to come and help with the Paramount Promos for their features. He was prepping with Caleb to go to Hong Kong for a *Mission Impossible* spot. After I spent two weeks designing and creating special props, we were suddenly there in Hong Kong.

What was so great about this trip was that my son Rowan was now living and working in Shanghai. He had acquired his Master of Arts in Design out of Cal Berkeley and was with a company—AECOM Design and Planning—where he started their environmental design practice in Asia. While there, one of his primary assignments was to design one of the first wetlands ever built in China. In the few days, I was there with Rowan and we were able to spend some valuable father-son time together.

In retrospect, on drifting back to times spent on all those commercials and films over the years, it was those journeys to so many far corners of the world that, no matter how simple or elaborate, have enriched my life's experience and filled my treasure trove of recollection with priceless memories.

I have had many memorable moments of crisscrossing the Americas, eating some of the worst cooked food and having great meals with locals from the small villages chosen for our shoots. Farms and fields with cornstalks rising shoulder-high, old barns, mountain passes and deserts, bizarre locations, thunder-storms and shafts of lightning that danced across the lakes—all these and more formed the murals of my travels.

Trips to New Zealand, Mexico, Provence, all the cities of Italy, Greece and spots in Eastern Europe—these too were many trips that would fill a large prized chest, most of which were taken prior to the runaway productions going to Vancouver, Toronto, Montreal and all points North—that numbing, relentless production diaspora to Canada that hit Hollywood around the year 2000 like a draining of blood from the body.

On those many journeys when I did leave home, it was only for two or three weeks at a time, and that worked so much better for the family. Then, as the children became older, they would often work during their vacations on stage with Rachel and me.

My daughter Ella did once confided to me that, "Dad, because of how there was nothing that you could not do in the art department, I have been able to achieve what I have achieved." That is oxygen for any father, and a guaranteed life-extender.

*Three of the more than 300 commercial sets I was privileged to design over the years:*
*1) Coca Cola;*
*2) Kraft Cheeses;*
*3) Wrangler Jeans.*

# Thirty-Nine

# The Irenic Principle

Throughout the ages many have said that the mystery of life is resolved in discovering the very essence of each breath. By this discovery, it is as if the key to a universal library is then placed in one's hands. All one must do is turn this key and merely allow life's secrets to flow and reveal themselves in their own given time. With this new awareness and unfolding of mystery, we can become infused with a deep inner gratitude for each single moment of life.

I had started to write another idea for a screenplay titled at that time *Ultimately Man*—a title and concept later changed to *The Irenic Principle*. The term Irenic is from the Greek word, ei·ren·ic (κατευναστικές) named after Eirene, the goddess of Peace. So, anything *irenic* tends to promote peace, "to fulfill peace," or at least has the promise of peace.

What I wrote in the original screenplay is a fictitious tale that could one day become fact...or even a fulfillment of prophecy. A dear friend, Charles Johnson, spent a considerable amount of time with me, taking my rough outline and helping me to format the first draft. Then his son, Brian, came on board the creative roller coaster of endless pages, ending on the floor.

Now, 25 years later, our hero is a woman. It involves the portrayal of a world-renowned physicist, Dr. Jessica Peak, who has learned to collect and enhance subatomic particles called *neutrinos* whose existence has long been known to us, though their purpose has only been recently defined. Through her research and biochemical findings, Dr. Peak is certain she has discovered the ultimate weapon—a new way to break down the molecular structure of matter.

In a spontaneous reversal of the paradigm, Jessica discovers instead that she has set free the raw energy of spontaneous creation—coupling into a Universal Consciousness that propels particles into bigger building blocks of life to become atoms and molecules and larger life forms in the Universe.

She realizes that Neutrinos are a key to the secret of the creation of the universe's time-space fabric. Understanding and even knowing that she could technically develop the technology that could collect the particles of light, the raw energy, the juice that could then be directed into certain molecular codes to create life, she had discovered the raw energy of spontaneous creation. Instead, through intense world government conditions, she harnesses her newfound chemical chain derivatives to obliterate the nuclear threat on planet Earth.

One night at a party I overheard two young men speaking. I eventually engaged them by asking them if they were scientists. They both informed me that they worked at Lawrence Livermore National Laboratory.

After an in-depth conversation with the two, I came to realize that I clearly needed help in understanding the theoretical physics underlying the subject matter of my script. Within the course of the next two days, a research scientist in the field of particle physics named Charles Stevens called me saying that he had heard of my project and would like to meet with me.

Even though he was based at the Livermore Laboratory in the Bay Area, by the next day Dr. Stevens had flown himself to Los Angeles just to understand what it was that was inspiring me to write my screenplay.

During lunch, I mentioned to Charles my understanding that, "As the ocean is to a fish, so consciousness is to the universe" … and further that, "Consciousness permeates all of creation."

With that observation, Dr. Stevens concurred and added his confirmation that "Neutrinos permeate everything," also adding, "neutrinos actually pass straight through us—billions of them every second."

Given that lead-in, I posed the question, "What if neutrinos themselves are consciousness?"

At this, Charles fell silent, then responded, "I am yours. You must be 80 years ahead." So, Charles took my screenplay to analyze it for scientific accuracy of the portrayal, and to provide me his technical expertise.

On October 20, 1988, the day I finished the first draft of the screenplay, the *New York Times* ran a headline announcing the award of the Nobel Prize in Physics to three scientists for their Neutrino research. On this very same day, my daughter Ella, having already read my script, showed me a writing of noted science fiction author and futurist, Arthur C. Clarke *(2001: A Space Odyssey, The Fountains of Paradise, etc.)*. In writing a preface to one of his non-fiction works, Clarke unleashes his declaration that the day of discovery of neutrinos would begin the countdown to doomsday.

The day I sent it to DreamWorks, there appeared yet again on the front pages a scientist who theorized that neutrinos contain matter that may well be, "The Holy Grail of the Universe."

This, of course, puts us in the crux of a dilemma: are they Creation itself, or the end of all Creation? The answer, to be sure, is a resounding "Yes!" And, a resounding "No!" They are both and neither…it is our consciousness that will ultimately turn the dial.

*Neutrinos: Often called Ghosts of the Universe, they may well hold the key to all life.*

# Forty

## It is Never as One Expects

**Staggering! Some words just fit** the situation. And this is the only word that I find defines, even in the slimmest way, the memories, presentiments, forebodings and anxieties of feature film pre-productions...not just for me but for everyone. At this point, even this late in my career, I truly am amazed that any film ever gets made. Now, having stated that, I confess to having allowed hope to triumph over experience back in 1989 when I hatched a company called 360° Film Works.

I had been approached by an old associate from my London days on Kings Road. He told me that he had the financing for a script. It was called *They Come Out at Night*, and it was a Dracula spoof in the comedic tradition of *Vamp* and *Love at First Bite*. My friend further assured me that he owned the rights to it, and asked me if I would like to partner with him on the project.

Without going into the sordid details of this projected partnership, I will simply summarize by observing that it did not turn out well. One project after the other seemed to fail, mainly due to my new associate not really following through...and to my own failure to catch onto the fact that he had a shaky relationship with the truth. So, bumped and bruised but with hope in my heart, I shed the dysfunctional association and pressed on.

My friend Jonathan Mills, Sir John Mills' son, came to me with one of these projects that did find its wheels once we had rewritten it. We had Roger Daltrey on board, Pete Townshend doing the score along with John's father and sister Hayley, whom I took to Cannes for the pre-sales. At a press conference in Cannes organized by mutual friend and noted publicist Michael Dalling, John Mills afforded me one of the most eloquent acquittals of my work that I had ever heard.

When pressed by the English press to account for his decision to work with me, they asked the typical litmus test dipped (as always) in arsenic: "Sir John! How do you feel about working with a first-time director?" He stood silent for a moment, looked down at me and smiled, then looked straight at the pressman who had asked the question.

*John Mills with Director David Lean.*

"David Lean was a first-time director," he answered with his commanding soft-spoken voice and sat down with a smile. It was a comment that precluded a follow-up question. And there were none.

For my 25-day shoot, Yorkshire Television had agreed to fund the project for $4 million. I went to Pinewood Studios with Peter Murton, who was going to be my production designer. We talked about how maybe all the walls we could be made to float, just like the old days, so that I could move from one room to the other.

Back in Century City in Los Angeles, I met with my lawyer, Paul Myerson, to finalize the papers for the co-production with John Mills. I had just taken my pen out to sign the contract when Paul's secretary gingerly stepped into the room and said that there was a call from England.

Before the ink had even dried on the contract, Paul placed his hand on mine and said hesitatingly, "It's Yorkshire. They just informed me they are unable to go ahead. (Margaret) Thatcher has put all the TV stations up for grabs. They cannot go through with the four million, as they have no idea where they will be in a year."

I didn't entirely understand what it meant at the time. (There was such an air of finality about it. But I was certain it could all be resolved.)

I placed the Mont Blanc back in its case and wondered where to go and what to expect next. After all, there had already been a considerable amount of seed money invested in the past two failures. We were still having commercial storyboards sent to us from various production companies, including those from Rick Levine and Fred Peterman.

I received a call from Kevin Goetz. Kevin and his brother Michael lived on the same road as we did in Malibu and, as young boys with Rowan, would make their home movies in our garden. Kevin mentioned that they were viewing production designer reels. And Rowan, on seeing a spot that he had worked on with me, suddenly declared: "I did that with my dad!"

They had no idea that their buddy's dad was a production designer. For the next eight years or so, I worked with them on the majority of their commercials, plus all the Brinks spots—one of which was virtually cloned for a skit by the cast and crew of *Saturday Night Live*…one so closely replicated we were both amused and honored at this homage to our work.

A company in Tokyo was looking to get into film production and offered us $200,000 to develop a project that they knew we owned. It was called *The Golden Samurai,* and the plot dealt with the travels and diplomatic journey of a Samurai warrior to South Africa, during the infamous "Scramble for Africa" of 1884.

We accepted their funding and went ahead with a rewrite. We were then invited to Tokyo to meet with the company, following that up with an invitation to see a famous young actor/singer they thought would be suitable, the catch being that his uncle would fund the film.

We went to see the young man perform and found his performance quite professional. Then we were taken to meet his uncle, which turned out to be a trip into the tiger's mouth. As we were walking to his club, the street emptied and people began to bow. Right after we had enjoyed a sumptuous dinner, two black Rolls Royces pulled up alongside us as an escort for some very heavy Japanese "godfather" types sitting behind the smoked glass windows. That's when Taku Hikida, one of the producers looked visibly shaken and obviously concerned.

"Alan we cannot use his money. He is the head of the Yakuza," he nervously announced. As if his words had brought the thunder, it fortuitously began to rain, a cautionary metaphor dropped into our lap.

Looking to close the loop on our funding in other ways, my partner went to Johannesburg to meet with Film Africa to see if they would be willing to help with the African side of the film, which was something they did. By this time, we had $3 million committed from the Japanese and $4 million from Film Africa. So, it appeared on the surface at last that the film had been green-lit on both sides.

The premise of the screenplay went something like this: The fate of modern Japan is changing. The Samurai are being decommissioned around the globe. South Africa is about to become the Crown Jewel in "The African Scramble," a thinly veiled attempt by the powers of Europe to "civilize" the Dark Continent, using it as a target for colonization and economic plunder.

Framed around a set of real events in Africa in the 1880s, *Gold Thunder* is the Samurai's last Declaration of Honor to an exponentially changing world. In Japan, the Samurai clans are battling to gain favor with the new 24-year-old Emperor, Taisho Tenno. The new members of the young emperor's court are wearing western styles, and the emperor has taken pleasure in pitting the old guard against the new.

The young emperor chooses his favorite bushido warrior, Tora, to sail with a British emissary, Lord Gray, to South Africa to collect and return with a gold bullion gift from Queen Victoria, a tribute to Taisho Tenno to celebrate his reign.

Hearing of this, a rival Satsuma clan chief, Lord Yabo, (to be played by Toshiro Mifune) convinces the young emperor to send his son as well, as a goodwill gesture. Secretly Yabo has plotted to have Tora assassinated on the voyage to Africa and gain leverage for the Satsumo with the British Mission.

Anticipating this murder plot, Tora successfully fights off his attackers but is still betrayed by the ship's bible pushing skipper, Captain Rodney, who sets his crew on Tora, casting him adrift and leaving him for dead—an assassination attempt that leaves him alive but awash on an African beach.

Rescued and befriended by Zulu Prince Matchachenga, Tora quickly gains the respect of his hosts. A dark turn of fate takes hold—one that includes his romance and involvement with an English military family's daughter and an officer son. Ordered by the Zulu chief (Matchachenga's father) to fight to the death, the two friends manage to overcome obstacles—connecting at last with Lord Gray, the British Emissary who brokers the peace. This twists the next chain of events turn in their favor, which changes the dynamic of the Zulu/English wars and brings peace to their corner of the world.

I had attached a director, John Guillermin, to the project. John loved to play pool and lived only 200 yards up the road from us. I knew him from his work on *King Kong*, *The Blue Max* and *The Towering Inferno*. The development money allowed us to fly to Japan and scout the locations and meet with the new selected young actor for the lead Samurai role. Meanwhile, Taku's art director (who had worked for director Akira Kurosawa) joined us, taking us to a series of locations he had previously scouted for us to see.

Taku took the reins and guided us to various old temples, an ancient castle fortress in Kyoto, Mount Fuji and the Emperor's palace. Taku had been able to sign one of my true actor heroes, Toshiro Mifune. He had set up a press conference with Toshiro, John Guillermin, a producer-rep from the production company and myself. The phone rang, and shortly thereafter I found Mr. Mifune waiting for me in our hotel production office.

When I walked into the room, I saw before me this handsome elderly man, sitting upright in a chair. He was wearing a dark blue, pin-striped three-piece suit with a gold watch, fob and chain across the waistcoat.

If I've learned one thing in all my travels it is how to engage people from different cultures for the first time. Having encountered such a luminous figure as Toshiro Mifune for the first time, I lowered my head in respect, acknowledging Mr. Mifune for who he was. He returned the compliment. We followed with a brief conversation, joined side-by-side and walked together to the pressroom.

As we sat for some Q & A with the Japanese press, I looked across towards my lead actor. It was hard to believe that there he was, my idol from some of the classics of foreign films: *The Seven Samurai*, *Yojimbo*, *Throne Of Blood* and so many more amazing films! And I could not help but be impressed at how Mr. Mifune had been so accessible (and humble) in his willingness to play our elderly Samurai statesman in what amounted to only a supporting role. (Something to be said for the lack of ego and sense of perspective in the Japanese film community.)

Upon returning, I came to realize that John Guillermin had proven to be not easy to work with. Constantly obstructive and critical, he continued to make some demands we could not accept. We came to a joint decision with the financiers that I was to direct this script. We also knew that if we did not start shooting the opening sequence, the snow would disappear and we would be dealing with "weather challenges" virtually out of the gate.

I sketched out the storyboards and sent them to Taku, who then arranged for me to fly and meet him on location for a five-day shoot. Upon my arrival, I was welcomed by my crew, so many of whom I discovered had worked with the legendary director Akira Kurosawa (not a bad core group to start)!

Kurosawa's costume designer and art director had made and refined all the necessary costumes and props for us to work with the young Samurai. The horse wranglers had arranged a choice of three horses for me to select from for the young actor. (One could only hope he could ride…either that or at least had gotten hold of a good instructor.)

For the very first shot, we walked down to a wide apron of land by a shallow river that was completely covered with ice. When the DP asked me where I would like to place the camera, I pointed directly to the middle of the river.

Knowing that, and sensing the challenge, he mounted the camera with a fourteen-millimeter lens on a low tripod and set it before me to check the perspective. Looking through it and adjusting my line of sight, I could not believe what I was seeing: Low, over the broken ice, the flat river banks and tree line, there spread before me the perfect pallet for the Samurai to appear on the far horizon and ride directly toward us in the center of the ice-covered shallow river.

"David Lean, eat your heart out!" were the first words out of my mouth. It was a stunning shot—one that we could neither rehearse nor reshoot, as it would bring us in peril of breaking the ice. We did get it in one amazingly breathtaking shot. And at least for a moment I felt that this truly boded well for the film.

As it was, Japan (for the savvy location scout) was a feast of historical venues. So, for the next five days we travelled to ancient villages that were wonderlands of the past—with waterwheels on the side of the thatched cottages, old wood weaving looms in their attics, and a lake in front of Mount Fuji where a fisherman in his Coracle cast his net as the Samurai rode into frame. Children called to the Samurai as he caught their free-flying kite and ran along by his side, down through the tall grass slopes where he handed down the kite to a small child.

The last shot was set up at an ancient temple. An old rickshaw passed through an avenue of standing stone monuments and the Samurai rode down past camera towards the mist covered red arch. We had captured on film, with the help of a great crew, all the required footage of the period. On the last day, in front of a Temple surround by ancient pines, I walked towards a bamboo hut. Inside was an elderly woman stirring a large pot of milky sake. I bought it all from her and at the end of the day we drank a great thank you to all.

I had edited the footage up to the first week's shoot, and at that point, the film was visually stunning. But as often happens, the stock market was in trouble, the NIKKEI had just tanked. A concerned call from crestfallen Taku a day or two later slew all our dreams on the spot. With a shaking voice rife with sadness, my friend explained that the company in Japan could not go ahead with the film as the bottom had dropped out of the market in the steel industry. That meant they had lost their leverage. They were sorry but they "could not continue."

My concern was for Taku. I had discovered that he had in actual fact funded the initial five-day shoot out of his own pocket. It never is as we expect. Once again, I had been shown that I could never be attached to outcome—that I just had to surrender to the unforeseen.

Surrender, I did. And as so many things in life come full circle, in January of 2017, having been invited as a guest to speak at the 1st Comic-Con in Japan for my work on *Star Wars,* I spent an evening with Taku in Tokyo, mentioning that I had rewritten the old screenplay.

*One of the manyal panoramas available to us durring the filming of* Golden Thunder.

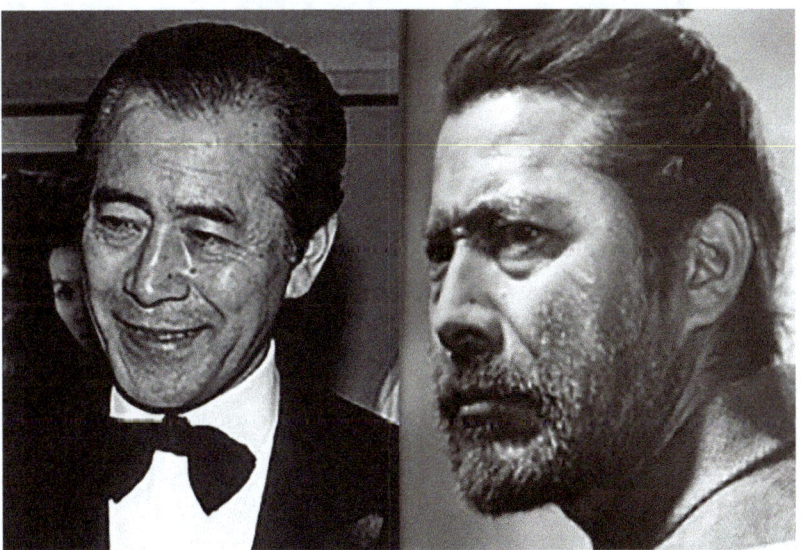

*Japanese screen legend Toshiro Mifune. (My Satsumo for Golden Thunder.)*

# Forty-One

## Legacy: Making a Difference

There is a lyric in *Into the Woods,* arguably Stephen Sondheim's most fanciful musical. And it goes like this: "Careful the things you say, children will listen. Careful the things you do, children will see…and learn." Whatever my daughter Ella and son Rowan saw and learned while they were growing up, it must have been something extraordinary. And I'd like to take credit for it, but I'm not so sure I can. They are the special souls they have become probably because we both saw the remarkable potential they showed early on. And Rachel's embodiment of love and compassion being with them 24/7 from their birth simply set them free to follow their dreams.

Having been accepted into Vassar College, my daughter Ella had made the most of her academics in her first two years by coming up with excellent grades. In many more expansive US universities, exchange programs and research grants are part of the curriculum. Vassar was no exception and, in fact, led the way on many unique academic alternatives abroad. So…the first semester of her junior year, Ella elected to go to Bali to conduct research. (Bali is one of the smaller islands of Indonesia and possesses a legendary charm and culture that is entirely its own.)

While there, she lived in Ubud with an artisan family, and by the time Rachel, Rowan and I had joined her there, she had a conversant command of the language and was able to put it to daily use. Our host family was warm and friendly and went out of their way to make us feel comfortable.

Ubud itself is known as a historical home of Balinese Royals. A few of the Balinese traditions and cultural norms stood out to me. It is rare to hear a Balinese adult shout at a child. In Bali, the principal religion is Balinese Hinduism—a version of Hinduism based on respect and observance of strict religious ritual. When a baby is born in a Balinese Hindu family, for example, they are not allowed to touch the ground until 105 to 210 days after their birth. Before that they are considered too close to the sacred realm. The island is also famous for its dance, drama and sculpture, and devotion to intricate and prolific ceremonies and offerings.

As Hinduism is a pantheistic religion (meaning one with many deities), every morning someone would lay fruit and flowers at a small temple area of the compound near our cottage, as well as on the well, in the kitchen, at the feet of a home security statue and elsewhere—all this just to honor and placate various high and low spirits. As we walked through this beautiful little town, we observed the work of local artists and passed women headed to temple carrying bowls on their heads stacked high with fruit and flower offerings, all while dressed in colorful batik sarongs and lace kabaya tops.

From our cottage patio, I admired the complex irrigation system, called Subak, developed to cultivate rice in wet-field terraces sculpted into the hillsides. The humidity in Bali was uncomfortably high. At night the chorus of frogs was cacophonous, and the constant hum of gargantuan mosquitos was downright intimidating. (We definitely had to sleep under mosquito nets at night.)

One afternoon, we had gone on a long walk through the rice paddies. When we crossed over a field, we passed a woman who was doing her laundry in a stream. She asked us if we had had a Mandi yet? This was her polite invitation to us to bathe and find some temporary relief from the intense heat and humidity.

After climbing Mt. Merapi for a sunrise barely visible through the clouds, we left Ella and returned back to the dry weather of California.

On graduating from Vassar, Ella returned to Indonesia, to the main central part of Java this time, spending two more years teaching at a college in Yogyakarta. She lived on the edge of a small village out of town.

Ella fondly recalled that in the mornings she would chat with the local women who would greet her on their way to the fields. In the distance the live volcano, Mt. Merapi, smoldered away, looming high over the landscape.

For her commute, Ella would be one of the thousands of helmeted riders mounting their mopeds and headed off to work. And when we visited, she took us to eat at a place that she had indicated would be, "The best food in town." (It was.) Soon enough, we found ourselves sitting on mats on the sidewalk, being served bowls of *gudeg* from a gargantuan pot.

Our friend Gavin Hodge had mentioned that a friend of his, François, was managing and operating the new, high-end Amanjiwo Hotel not far from Yogyakarta.

*World's largest Buddhist temple at Borobudur, Yogyakarta, Java.*

In a matter of pure synchronicity, Ella, without our knowing it, had already made friends with François and his wife, Olivia, which underscored both our ability and our desire to spend a few days at this exquisite hotel. The Amanjiwo rests at the foot of the Menoreh Hills in central Java, looking out onto the breathtaking Borobudur, the largest Buddhist monument in Indonesia.

When the Asian financial crisis hit and triggered a people-power revolution in Indonesia, things became a little scratchy, especially for foreigners. Back home in California we obviously were very concerned for Ella. But she quickly informed us that she had been invited to take refuge at the hotel. That made us feel better but found out later that she had declined the sanctuary there, choosing instead to stay on at her university. Quite concerned for our daughter, we asked her to come back home, but Ella remained intent on finishing her two-year commitment. There were daily protests, riot police and tanks in the streets. It was a formative time and truly, "A Year Of Living Dangerously." When she asked the English Embassy for some advice they told her to stay safe and have a cup of tea! But Ella stuck it out and came out stronger and more centered for the experience.

In defiance of the political instability of the time, we enjoyed our time with her there in Indonesia; and it shaped her future. After returning to the US, Ella found her way to Washington, DC where she did her Master's Degree in International Economics and Southeast Asia Studies at Johns Hopkins University. While there, she was able to do temp work at the Council on Foreign Relations and after graduating moved and worked at the Council in New York and became the head of Foreign Government and Board Relations with the Population Council, before joining Americares, a disaster relief and global health organization that does phenomenal humanitarian work.

At Americares, Ella served in numerous roles, working her way up to become Vice President of Emergency Response and then Senior Vice President of Strategy and Program Development. She is now CEO of the social enterprise, VisionSpring, which creates access to eyeglasses for millions of people in low-income countries so they can see clearly to work, succeed in school and care for their families.

Although he had spent many days and those long hours with me on stage and on location during some of the feature films while he was growing up, Rowan made it clear early-on that he did not want to be in my field of work. Instead he went to the University of California Berkeley to major in Conservation, Resources Studies and Physical Geography. He spent the first semester of his third year as an exchange student at the University of Otago in Dunedin, New Zealand—a stint "Down Under" that included surfing with the penguins—and later went to French Polynesia where Cal Berkeley had a research facility on the small French Polynesian island of Moorea. There he studied seagrass and swam with the mother whales and their young.

Rowan later returned to Berkeley for a master's degree in Civil and Environmental Engineering and went on to work in the world of water conservation and management. He is now with The Nature Conservancy as a Director of Global Urban Water where he is bringing nature into cities to help solve urban water management issues like water quality, water supply and flooding.

Earlier in his career, Rowan had worked on planning and designing integrated water infrastructure for the international design firms Arup and AECOM, an assignment that took him on many extraordinary journeys to work on projects in Asia, the Middle East and Latin America. He spent six years living in Shanghai and Hong Kong.

Aside from his university degrees, Rowan is also a Professional Engineer (PE) in California and Chartered Scientist (CSci) through the Chartered Institute of Water and Environmental Management in the UK. (Like his sister's, an outstanding resumé by any system of measure.)

Rowan is a remarkable young man who has seized all the opportunities that came his way with tenacity, focus and dedication. And though he has chosen to express his art in very broad environmental strokes, he has far more talent with his paintbrush than I ever had.

Both our children would agree to this, that Confucius was right after all: "Comparisons are odious." Impact ultimately uses entirely different metrics, and they have successfully carved their own paths in life.

*Yes, it's true, penguins do surf. And they're pretty good at it!*

# Forty-Two

# The Last Hurrah!

I had met Bernie Williams back in 1964 at Shepperton studios. Bernie was an associate producer on Stanley Kubrick's *A Clockwork Orange* and *Barry Lyndon*. He produced or associate produced six films with director Frank Oz., beginning with *Dirty Rotten Scoundrels*. He also produced a remake of the 1946 film, *The Big Sleep*, *Flash Gordon*, *Ragtime,* and *The Bounty* (a *Mutiny on the Bounty* remake) starring Mel Gibson and Anthony Hopkins—just a few of his amazing works in film. So, to say the least, he had a full portfolio.

I had been approached by Malcolm Hitchcock who used to work with me as a prop master on a plethora of commercials. Malcolm had recently moved to Mexico and had shortly after approached me to direct, restructure and rewrite a script titled *The Advent* written by Albert Hagger. We signed contracts and I began to work on yet another project that looked as if it was going to go.

My research began on *Our Lady of Guadalupe*. The script, although set in present day dealt with the image that was on the cloak of Juan Diego that hangs in the Basilica in Mexico City. Les Dilly, a Production

Designer friend with whom I had worked on *Star Wars*, now lived in California.

I asked Les if he would come down to Mexico and work with me on the film. He mentioned Bernie Williams as a possibility to come on as our line producer. Malcolm came to the house with Alberto and the contract was signed—Bernie was onboard. At this time, despite his deep resume and exceptional body of work, Bernie was unable to find any work. Surprise though: Two days later he was offered a job to work with Taylor Hackford and turned it down, thinking that we were all going to get paid.

This project suddenly became yet another hurdle of a time spent, and promise after promise of money flowing. We were both so into this story of the image that was on the tunic we continued to write, not receiving any monies. Working with Bernie gave me a perfect tutor who had such an insight as to how to breakdown and to give each scene a rhyme and reason.

After almost four years of dissection, we were finished and really exultant that we had received confirmation from the Vatican that we could film within their premises. The finished script went to CAA and Liam Neeson (Bernie having given Liam his breakthrough role on *The Bounty*). Showing an interest and liking the script, Liam returned a call within three days to Bernie.

The Vatican may have approved it, but it apparently couldn't get by Albert Hagger, who vigorously disapproved of us having taken out much of the Catholic dogma and conceptual beliefs and he could get his own permission to film in the Vatican. So that was that!

Bernie sadly died only two months after we had completed this work. And I certainly miss this man for whom I had such high regard, and who had become a close friend.

During those four years of writing with Bernie, I had also been approached by a dear friend, John Slowsky, who was now working as an art director for Universal Vivendi, a computer game subsidiary of Universal Studios. John asked me if I would like to work with him and sketch the environments for *Lord of the Rings.* He mentioned that I could not see the Peter Jackson film until I had finished all the drawings, as Universal had a separate contract with the Tolkien estate.

I signed a contract that would allow me to own my original drawings. And John was to receive the brown line prints. Without fail, I would clear my desk every morning then, surrounded by my books, went ahead and completed more than 90 sketches. I did all this while being assisted by a Tolkien historian who would send me a weekly breakdown of the nature and history of every environment from the Tolkien trilogy, *The Lord of the Rings.*

*Top, my sketch of the interior of the Prancing Pony Inn Parlour. Bottom, John's computer rendering of the above sketch for* The Game.

On completion, I then went ahead with the environments for *Van Helsing, The Hulk,* and *Dirty Harry,* enjoying every minute of just allowing the pencil to flow to the 24" x 36" white sheets of paper and always permitting myself to be surprised as to what appeared at the end of the day.

My last commercial was under the aegis of Dark Light Productions with Sheila Flaherty producing. I had worked with Sheila many times with Caleb and Vincent, and she was an absolute delight to work with. Gil Cope was directing the four commercials for Boeing. Creating a state-of-the-art control board and design was paramount. So, Gil and I spent a considerable time going through the agency boards. I then drew for Gil our own storyboards. At the same time, Gil created his production book, as did I with the help of an Art Director and friend, Timothy Beach.

A meeting was set up at the offices of Boeing's new agency in Century City. Vincent, Sheila, Gil and I went through the books describing every detail of the locations, the studio builds and various special props that would be made before we went on location to the Boeing headquarters for the final days of the shoot.

It was a very complicated job on all levels, requiring finding the right locations and creating a futuristic look while fitting it all inside a very tight budget. I worked with two construction companies in order to meet the schedule, both on location and onstage. They created phenomenally elaborate props, while I used designed walls and set elements in such a way that they could be repainted and re-attached to each other to make various modern environments—ones that the agency had obviously approved.

Knowing how thorough Gil, Sheila and I had been with the presentation books and in the meeting with the agency's Creative Director, I could not believe what they put Gil through when he was ready to set up for the next shot.

"What is this? What are you doing now?!" Their attitude was abrasive, paranoid and confrontational. They were constantly in Sheila's face about the budget and how she was ripping them off, not knowing how she struggled and strived with me to get the numbers so they would fit the allocated funds. The supervisor continued to badger us in the middle of shooting.

One morning at the old David Selznick Studios in Culver City, I found Sheila on the stage at her desk, crying. I asked her what the problem was, only to hear that the agency head of the project had again verbally abused her. That was it! I went over to the First AD and asked him if he could have quiet on the stage. Once silent, I looked directly at the couches where the agency and the client sat, walked towards them and directed my words at one man: "I am no doubt the oldest one on this stage and have been in our world of film for over fifty years. I have never experienced such rudeness and lack of productive understanding as I have with the team of this agency's Creative Director." There was a long silence that followed, and I walked over to Gil, not quite knowing what to expect.

"Thank you," he said, quietly…and we discussed the next shot.

They moved north to Seattle and Boeing for the final shots. By then, I had finished the stage work along with my final budget and finally called Sheila. I could tell from her voice that she was again very upset. She also needed to confide her feelings…to someone she could trust.

"Alan please keep this to yourself but…last night, as I was sitting in the lounge, I was confronted by (no name) who continued to verbally abuse me. The security said that if he did not stop, they would remove him. He not only pressed on but also pumped up the volume. So, they literally had to walk him out of the hotel. Then, despite being booted out of the hotel, he barged back in and smashed me across the face. This time they took him out."

I could not believe what I was hearing and asked if Vince had been told? She said he had been and was flying up. Gil had not heard about it until that morning and pulled the man outside of the hotel and verbally reamed him "a new one."

As a point of reference, this man was one of the heads of the agency, and the Account Supervisor for the Boeing package. Although encouraged to do so, Vince decided not to sue him.

After that experience, I realized that I truly had gotten a stomach full of it all—the lack of respect, the know-it-all arrogance and the constant sense of entitlement ("We want it now!")—the full panoply of sordid politics that had now become the new face of modern advertising. It was then that I made the decision that I would retire. No longer were we given time to truly prep most of the jobs, and I usually ended up backing into a budget.

No regrets, I had an amazingly long run and marked success, working with so many wonderful mentors, directors, producers and crews, without whom I could never have accomplished the work. As the Irish would say: "It is what it is."

*Top, futuristic designs for the set of the Boeing commercials. (Every dollar spent showed up on-screen.)*

*Right, design for Boeing computer desk.*

# Forty-Three

## Let the Infinite Be Your Guide

**Life is a banquet of surprises.** Neither good nor bad, they present themselves as a challenge to our discernment. *Martyrs,* as of now the last film that I worked on, was based on the most successful French horror film with the same title made for $10 million. The Goetz brothers only had a budget of $600K and politely wondered out loud if I would work with them.

When I sat to view the French version, I had to turn it off; it was that horrifically frightening! As both Kevin and Michael had been very loyal to me in the past, I agreed to work on the project with them for a fee that was deeply discounted from the rates I would usually charge since it would only be a 19-day shoot.

We agreed on a farmhouse set in several avocado groves north of the Simi Valley, and an empty prison complex east of the 605 Freeway in the area of Whittier. We were able to use areas within the complex for many different sets that were required in the script. Like the French film though, there were frighteningly twisted, brutal and horrific scenes. For that reason (and since my presence was not required) I did not hang around while they were being shot and took off to prep the next location.

They were ready to direct another amazing script that was financed, and I was delighted by the quality of the writing. "This could be a classic," I told them. And Sir Ben Kingsley, upon having read the screenplay, described it in exactly the same terms and immediately agreed to sign on.

We had time to build the interior of an elaborate Victorian House on stage. Sir Ben had been signed, yet the producers and directors found it surprisingly difficult to fill out the rest of the cast. This could have been due to a number of factors. First, the actors had to remember a lot of dialogue in most every scene, which frightens many an actor in today's films, as they seem to only be able to hold a two to three-line dialogue scene. Second, the fees offered didn't allow enough money for an "A List" cast… or even a high "B List," thus costing us some leverage with distribution.

Day by day, week by week, the time drifted away. Then it was decided that we would film on location in Canada. I did a complete art department breakdown of the script. After that it became obvious that we could not meet the time that was required to get everything ready in order to meet the tight schedule for the actors currently on contract. All that hard-focused work was now placed on the back burner…and despite the setbacks the producers still continue to see its potential for a future production.

I taught at Otis College of Art and Design as well setting up various exhibitions for artists as a board member and ad hoc director for the Malibu Art Commission. One was for the Kites of Tyrus Wong, a great artist and film designer, responsible for the look of *Bambi*. A high life-force human being, Tyrus lived to the age of 106 and was, until the time of his death, still flying his kites on Santa Monica Beach.

We set up another for Dan Eldon, a young photographer who was killed in Mogadishu after an American military drone meant for Al Shabaab went off target and killed many innocent people, including women and children. He was there as a photojournalist for Reuters news agency. They called the photographers to come and take photographic evidence of the horror—and a mob so angered by the family deaths stoned three of the men to death. Dan being the youngest.

Dan's sketchbooks were brilliant and his mother had enlarged them. We mounted them in the Malibu Convention Center for a one-man show, along with his unique photographs of various war episodes.

* * *

Time often sweetens the sauce of remembrance. As I again let my mind expand to embrace so many vibrant memories, I see so many faces of friends now passed, cherishing moments spent with them both indelible and special. For me, and my wonderful family now replete with grandchildren, there is the hope of the next generation—Reed, Jasper Alice, and Morgan (Rowan's lovely wife).

Memory is a storage vault. Its contents are dense yet forgiving. There is no limit to my time inside it. As I journey into my past, it unfolds volumes of experiences that I otherwise might have missed. Music plays a very important role for my inspirational moment-to-moment daily sequences that have the ability to unlock hidden chambers of recollection. Ancient ethnic, classical, blues, jazz, folk, rock, soundtracks, international, rap, Latino rhythms, salsa, reggae—if you name it, I will listen to it, for within the depths of their mystical rhythms these composers have been the conduit for creation to inspire and nurture our souls.

As I approached the ancient imposing weathered doors, chiseled faces from times gone by beckoned to me to join them. My hand hesitatingly turned the rusted iron key. The heavy doors creaked open on their two-thousand-year-old bronze hinges.

A silent voice had invited me to open these doors to a historical architectural wonder, whose walls were lined with endless stone shelves filled to the brim with rolls of parchments and leather bound volumes of all sizes. A wood-beamed ceiling with crisscrossed arches recreated a cavernous vault stacked from floor to ceiling with volumes of what I felt were maybe my eternal memories. My eyes scanned from volume to volume, noting titles, Greek, Latin, and Roman history of wars. Chinese silk trade, poets, Ethiopian campaigns of past kings, many penned by the Russian masters—a dust covered leather-bound first-edition of *Crime and Punishment* by Dostoevsky, novels dating from the 17th century to modern day mavens.

Who had compiled this amazing collection of priceless works? I did not have the faintest idea. I felt there within these walls and upon one of the shelves was a book awaiting my hand to reach out for it.

I closed my eyes, stood silent and approached a shelf. I reached out and took hold and opened my eyes to see a very old, well-worn parchment with a gold engraved title: *The Meditations of Marcus Aurelius*. I blew away the dust and slowly unrolled it. Although penned in Latin, the words came clearly. I read a random line, a pearl... "If a man is mistaken, instruct him kindly and show him his error. But if thou art not able, blame thyself, or blame not even thyself." Then another, "Attend to the matter which is before thee, whether it is an opinion or an act or a word." I thought that there it had been waiting for me, Marcus Aurelius who inspired me when I was a student, reading Greek and Roman history.

Thoughts of the noblest of Emperors who ruled a Roman Empire were made manifest with a single eye to the welfare of its subjects. Although his reputation is stained by his persecution of Christians, his reign still expresses the best of what has come to be known as secular humanism. Now if there was a book waiting there for you and you turned the key, quietly entered, what book would your hand take from the endless shelves of your life's eternal journey? I wonder.

When recently asked about my passions, they become ones of legacy—mainly those that involve leaving our planet Earth in the trusted hands of our children and those generations to follow—to heal and bring an awareness that life unfolds with grace within each breath we take...

that all living creatures are one and that humanity will realize what it is to be human.

It is time for The Awakening, for all of humanity to rise up to Mother Earth's magnificent perfection without whose loving care we would not be able to exist.

As I began to conclude the final pages, we had the devastating news that our family home had been completely destroyed in the horrendous fires of November 2018 in Malibu. Statistically, we were one of more than 7,500 homes and business, involving more than 100,000 acres in Malibu alone (more than 2 million in all of California) that had been leveled, burnt to the ground—those were the naked statistics.

When I write the word, "completely!" I truly mean everything: The house, the two studios and all their contents had been razed to the ground, melted into a pile of rubble, cinders and dust. Off visiting our son and daughter-in-law in Mill Valley, we were not there to save any of the precious mementos, works of art or treasured furnishings from our world travels, or the photographic albums that had formed the fabric of our family's memories for the 34 years of living in this home.

Prior to the fire I was going through the contents of a drawer in the upper studio and I came across one letter that was from Henry Fonda in a response to one that I sent him when he was in England in 1975. Wondering if he would be interested in playing the fabled Winged One the Master in my screenplay "Karas". He had replied almost immediately stating that he would be more than interested to read the script. The other was a card from Ursula Le Quin ( Earthsea saga ) responding to a letter I had sent her wondering if she would be interested in reading the same script and maybe writing the book. She had kindly thanked me for my letter but was unable at that moment to take on anyone else's work. I had completely forgotten about those two amazing talents who kindly responded to my letters, those I now no longer have.

As our son Rowan wrote:

> *We are shocked by the loss that has occurred but trying to remain forward thinking toward the opportunities this event has opened up—both karmically and physically. Blank canvases are not unfamiliar to my amazing, creative and irrepressible parents—this one is shockingly large, but they continue to press on with courage, optimism and amazing resilience.*

Well…what is left to do but to redesign and rebuild? What faces us now comes in the form of both a challenge and a promise. After each death there is a rebirth. And so, I bring out my blueprints, sketch new plans, meet with architects and other designers to draw up a new book of life. Each day is a new canvas after all, and an opportunity to create a new reality even better than the last.

When recently asked what are my passions, I had to give it some thought, but came up with a run of things that mean a great deal to me: mainly those that involve leaving our Earth in the care of our children, who seem more aware of their legacy for the generations to come; another is bringing in an awareness that life always unfolds with grace, that each breath of life carries a message inside it—that all living creatures are one and that humanity will finally come to realize what it is to be human. For me, and for us all, I think this is the time for Earth's Call, for we as human beings to awaken to Nature's perfection: that it gives so much, and we must give back if we're to survive at all.

How rapidly the river of life has flowed. How much I have cherished every year, month, week, day and moment—of those 683,260 hours 78 years later—for they never do truly return.

Ultimately, if I've learned anything it is this: Life is an Empty Stage—dark for a few hours waiting for yet another play and a new group of players…and a reminder that what comes next is also only a passage. I know it's been said before by countless masters and teachers. So it steps beyond subjectivity and into an indelible truth: "Be in this world but not of it."

That way, by not being of it, you can love it for what it is. ☺

*There is a rhythm of Life—unfolding within the eternal unspoken silence of Creation—Yet within the silence throughout the vast universe there is a sound—The sound we can hear within when all thoughts cease—cease—A stillness—a silent heartbeat—there Creation reveals her Divinity to us—She and we are One.*

One Life. One Source.

*Cities and Thrones and Powers,*
*Stand in Time's eye,*
*Almost as long as flowers,*
*Which daily die. Unconsidered*
*But, as new buds put forth*
*To glad new men,*
*Out of the spent Earth,*
*The Cities rise again.*
*This Season's Daffodil*
*She never hears,*
*What change, what chance, what chill,*
*Cut down last year's:*
*But with bold countenance,*
*And knowledge small,*
*Esteems her seven days' continuance*

*To be perpetual.*
*So time that it o'er-kind*
*To all that be.*
*Ordains us e'en as blind,*
*As bold as she:*
*That in our very death.*
*And buried sure,*
*Shadow to shadow, well persuaded, saith,*
*"See how our works endure!"*

## ~ Rudyard Kipling

# Epilogue

## Pieces of a "Paradise Regained"

**Aldous Huxley once famously said:** "Experience isn't what happens to a man. It's what he does with what happens to him." Feeling blessed from our life's experiences—all of them—Rachel and I have come to realize that our latest loss is an opportunity to rebuild, restore and rise again. Like the Phoenix from its own ashes, we shed the molting feathers of our past and embrace the newness of creating yet another beautiful new chapter in a life still fraught with so much promise.

The poet Carl Sandburg once observed, "The past is a box of ashes." In our case that is literally the truth. And yet it is so much more than that. It is also a treasure trove of rich experience, of loves shared, of worlds explored, of milestones achieved and of friendships cherished.

So, this is not an end but a beginning. And like that Empty Stage on the cover of this book, life becomes a palette for new creation. We rebuild. We plan. We design. We create schematics and work with architects and builders. We do so, knowing that the one gift Creation and the Universe have granted us is that endless urge to create, to make something beautiful out of what has been lost and to use it as a tabula rasa for a new level of awareness.

With that, I close with our grand new plans, with no mourning for what has fallen away and with a bright new face to the future.

*Avanti!* It's a Latin word that the Italians have kept alive for a very good reason. It means "forward." And that is where we'll go…

# Acknowledgements

*To those who have been buddies,
cohorts, mentors, inspirations and friends,
who have motivated, inspired and guided me
in this my life's journey.*

*My greatest gratitude goes to my wife, Rachel, my daughter, Ella, and my son, Rowan—so supportive and with whom so much love has been experienced.*

Prem Rawat the young boy who in 1972 turned my consciousness within and dropped me into the middle of Creation's Ocean.

Grandmother Ingram. My mother Irene. My aunts Esther, Kit, Lilly, Doris and Ned. Uncles Chris, Frank. Grandmother Jones, My father, Frank, his brother, Fred, & his wife, Rene. Rachel's parents Peter and Diana Gillingham. Bruce, Rick, Mary Gillingham. Teachers, Cecil Peacock, Father Peter, Fred Brill, Elizabeth Frink, Henry Moore.

Friends, Pamela Smith, Tonja Blackmore, Gary Warren, David Smith, Dicky Dobson, Zulika Dobson, Gabriella Licudi, Lucy Bartlett, Fabian Peake, John Daneshvesky, Robert and Sally Montgomery, Peter

Mines, Robert Richards, Sebastian Sed, Gavin Hodge, Jane Lumb, John Gilbert, Mim Scala, Ian Quarrie, Jose Fonseca, Adrianne Hunter and Annie Hanson.

Mentors—Geof Drake, Carl Foreman, Ted Clements, Wally Smith, John Bodimeade, Reg Bream, Maurice Carter, Jack Maxsted, Robert Cartwright, Brian Eatwell, Alan and Leslie Tompkins. Brian and Terry Ackland-Snow, Michael Lamont, Peter Lamont, Peter James, Peter Young, Tony Woolard, Peter Murton, Ted Haworth, Donald Ashton, Vincent Korda, Ray Simm, Michael Seymoore, John Graysmark, John Barry, Gus Walker, Ernest Archer. Director of Photography—Freddie Young, Ernest Day.

Producer—Bernard Williams, Sam Spiegel, Peter Beale. Friend and director—Peter Medac, Friends Lorraine and Meralyn Ashton. Friends—Anne King, Mortima Schuman. Actress Ava Gardner, Director—Franklin Schaffner, George Lucas, Friends David Coyne, Stephen Sedoti, Pierce, Keely & family Brosnan.

Elizabeth & Michael Dalling, Russel & Pamela Lyster, John and Bo Derek, and Thom Kessler. Producer— Sandy Howard, Donald Borchers. Actor Richard Harris. Producer— Donna Woodruf, Christina Stephens and Vincent Arcero.

Sheila Flaherty, Lance O'Connor, Antonia Holt. Commercial Directors (Director of Photography) Caleb Deschanel, Rick Levine, Fred Peterman, Lee Lacy, Melvin Sokolsky. Rupert Wainwright, Brian Gibson, Brian Cummins, Gil Cope and Ernest Dickerson.

Doug Taub, Ken Arlidge, Klaus Obermeyer. Director of Photography—Conrad Hall, Allen Daviau, John Toll. Joseph Grasso. Construction—Christopher Hyde, Douglas Morris, Tony Soja, Danny & Michael Needham ( Greensets ).

Friends—The Rawat family Maralyn Rawat, Premlata Rawat Hudson, Hans Rawat, Dayalata Rawat, Amar Rawat. Teddy & Danise Tannenbaum, Michael Nouri, Vicky Light, Gregory Allen, Kymberly Chase, John Slowsky, Michael Wood, Celia de Flers, Carol Wilson, Christopher Medac, Allan

Thomas, Andi Campbell, George Ghoen and Stewart Lennox. Producer Taku Hikida and Actor Toshiro Mifune.

Director Neil Tardio and Producer David Schermerhorn. Directors Kevin and Michael Goetz. Property Assistants Alan Bracket, John Vonk, David Cory, Tom Ford, Craig Rose, Art Directors Timothy Beach, Carol Clements, Julia Lockland, and Craig Weeding. Scenic Artist—Bill McGuire.

Friends—Jonathan Rinzler, Michael Fitzpatrick, Mark Leisure.

*My editor, Robert Joseph Aloha, had known my work in the world of film design and, upon reading my first rough draft saw the potential of* The Empty Stage, *offered to help with the edit, some rewriting and was becoming a close friend. Robert has written over 50 published books and plays, including* The Return of the Hummingbird Wizard, Judas Agonistes, The Silent Healer, NARCISSUS/The Last Days of Lord Byron *and* I, Dragon. *So, he was eminently qualified to help get this to press.*

*Katie Haber whom I first met in 1968 then reconnected with her when I started to work in America and became a member of BAFTA. She was my initial reader of the first draft and became my grammar gestapo. (Hemmingway had someone similar to read and work on his writings.) She founded the Compton cricket club in Los Angeles, received a MBE, Member of the most excellent order of the British Empire for her charitable services to the community of Los Angeles, as well as co-producing Ridley Scott's* Blade Runner.

# About the Author

Alan Roderick-Jones is an artist, painter, art director, production designer, screenwriter and director who has worked in film and television since 1961 and has lived in Malibu, California with his wife Rachel for the last 41 years. As he has so successfully done in the past, Alan is joyfully redesigning the rest of his golden years.

*AVANTI!*

www.ingramcontent.com/pod-product-compliance
Lightning Source LLC
Chambersburg PA
CBHW071259110526
44591CB00010B/719